Antelope Hill Writing Competition 2023
Touch Grass

Touch Grass

THIRD ANNUAL

Antelope Hill Writing Competition

—2023—

Sponsored in part by
Will2Rise and Media2Rise

ANTELOPE HILL PUBLISHING

Cover art by Swifty.
Contest judged by the Antelope Hill administrative team.
Editing and layout by Margaret Bauer.

Antelope Hill Publishing | antelopehillpublishing.com

Paperback ISBN-13: 978-1-956887-84-6
EPUB ISBN-13: 978-1-956887-85-3

CONTENTS

POETRY

Selected Poems by Author

Poetry Winners

SHORT STORIES

Selected Short Stories by Author

Short Story Winners

Publisher's Foreword

Antelope Hill Publishing is proud to present our Third Annual Writing Contest. Not only were we able to encourage the creativity of our participants for another year, but we also saw a massive increase in submissions, nearly doubling the total from last year. This motivates us to continue offering this contest, which would only be possible if our authors boldly endeavor to create something, to touch grass, and not to merely consume and subsist.

Our theme for this year's writing contest is "Touch Grass." We offered this prompt to cultivate fictional short stories and poems about the importance of real-life experiences contra spending time online. The Internet has its benefits, but we must not forget our roots in real-life interpersonal relationships. Authors were encouraged to write about anything from forging strong bonds, to trailblazing political organization, reconnecting with old friends, or even simply appreciating the beauty of nature. The prompt was not limited to these ideas; we wished to keep the topic broad so as to encourage a wide array of responses. As life is full of ups and downs, the mood of these pieces is not limited to only triumph, but also covers struggle, pensiveness, and heartbreak.

We would like to stress how subjective the evaluation process is and hope no authors are discouraged if their piece was not selected this year for publication or as a prize winner. In addition to gauging submissions on how well they fit the theme, their writing style, their creativity, and how impactful they are, we also were looking for a variety of responses to the prompt and tried not to include too many submissions that were too similar. Of course, we also judge as a team, meaning we need to agree on decisions. Many pieces were loved by only a couple of us or were great by themselves but didn't fit with the collection for a variety of reasons.

We sincerely want to thank everyone for writing, and we hope to encourage you to continue doing so, whether for our future contests or elsewhere. One of our goals as a company is to resurrect and nourish a love of literature and creative writing that produces real value, a skill that has been sorely neglected and suppressed by the noise of the modern world.

We extend our gratitude as well to our generous sponsors, Will2Rise and Media2Rise, as their continued support showcases the strength of our community. We hope you enjoy these unique works as much as we have, and we look forward to many more years of sharing your talent with the world.

Antelope Hill Publishing

Poetry

Atlas of the Golden Hair

Ǣwine

Atlas of the golden hair:
They laid on you the weight of the world,
They possessed you with their demons,
They arraigned you for your father's crimes
Which were of their own imagination only.
Little White boy,
Let that be your joy:
They hate you because you are beautiful,
They hate you because you are great;
More free than their most fearful fantasies
And brighter than their darkest dreams.

Vart Land

Ǣwine

My land is lovely in spring
when the gardens of my people are radiant insurrections of color and fragrance
and the brief showers refresh her green verdancy,
enlivening her veins with the clear music of glacial streams
and bringing blossom to the bud.
She is lovely in the summertime
and the unbegotten noontide of her day—
the light, brighter here than anywhere
on earth, the sight unbent and sky clearer,
the waves more white and horizon-band lengthening to eternity.
And lovelier yet in autumn
my season of silences, of softness and of memory,
of fading and of reaping
of lying down and gathering together.
She is lovely still in winter,
when the blackened corpses of trees file in stark solemnity along the pale expanse of the sky,
reaching up to catch the clouds on their knotted fingers.
She is lovely in the dawning of her day, rose-pink upon a white mountainside
and lovelier still at eve, when the golden haze of afternoon bronzes to black
and dusk pours down from the mountains and crosses the plains,
settling like a comfort-worn blanket over the houses of the city.
She is lovely when veiled by a gray curtain of rain
and when she bathes naked in the bright noonday sun.
She is lovely when her newborn glory shines in the eyes of strangers to these shores
and when her name trembles on the lips of those who have known and loved her since the day of their birth.
She is lovely even in her deformity

and lovelier still in her innocence when slandered by ignorant men
whose eyes are too clouded with contentment
to see the wonder before them
and whose feet are too light with ease
to weigh the miracle beneath.
My land is lovely when I am happy
and the dancing streams laugh with me;
my land is lovely when I am sad, and bowed with the weight of the
 world within
and the rain-stooped trees weep in time.
My land is lovely at all times,
but never more than now.

The Good Life

Anthony Bavaria

Part One

White-collar bureaucracy especially grinding today,
return-home-hug-from-daughter erases it all.
You don't know until you know, having children is supreme;
a new lens on your now-seen-as clownish previous life, gloom for those—into their thirties, forties, even fifties—still doubling down on depravity.
True intelligence is admitting you were wrong, deceived.
No time, son's baseball game in twenty minutes;
the pride he has after connecting is total. From first base he checks the stands to ensure I witnessed the hit;
all previous doubts of inadequacy/raising a boy properly are undone by his smile.
Wife went out of her way tonight: bratwurst, pretzels, spätzle—my favorite.
The good life.
I need to get out of here.

Part Two

Counting down 'til ten-day work conference, a paid vacation—
no wife, kids, house.
Outside of working hours, I'm a ghost; fuck colleagues.
Interchangeable brew-pubs their default, I require more;
nothing bent (strippers, binge drinking, gambling), just solitude.
Joyed to be suburban-external, flâneur the city—
museum, art gallery, even an indie-doc screening.
My main vice is food: first something indulgent, maybe a French restaurant;
go early and order an Instagram-quality dish though I'd never actually commit the faux pas.
Inevitable post-main course crème brûlée and cappuccino;
I'll still be ordering Papa John's to the room later,
raid the vending machine, too—praying it has a Whatchamacallit.

Balance the high- and low-brow.
Manning the room's king-size, I stay up late and cram it all in on the first night—reading, war film, porn—and muse how wife doesn't get it, kids interrupt another preferred life.
All men are lone wolves, predators to a degree; this I ponder while packing Cooler Ranch Doritos down my gullet like a pre-teen whose parents are out of town,
totally content.
Four days in, an insatiable regret;
I miss my family.
Pure intake is irrelevant,
only people matter—
my people.

Artificial Turf

Koch Borler

How could you love that which you cannot trust
Yet a demand smothered into you from birth
Fed a heaping serving of accepted lies
From the golden cauldron over the covenant hearth
It was easier to confide in niche corners
For the commons suffered a morality dearth
Where hushed whispers were allowed to breathe
And prods at the beast kindled flames of mirth

This subculture wrought your entire being
It honed your nerves at every press
But the double-edged sword of anonymity
Would strike its target to hamstring success
For even a beast can train against its foe
Leer from afar, shape and tune its ingest
At the time when truth was demanded most
Beastlings of ill faith intruded the nest

Their poison laden musings dripped
From the lips of countless faces they wore
Foreign ideals they brought to share
Needless non-sequiturs, nihilism galore
But calls to violence, their finale at last
Illuminated upon the senses left sore
Yet profound clarity graced your conscience
These creatures share not the fight you fight for

The situation was irreversible
No familiar voice was left to recall
With bittersweet stirring and sunken viscera
You step into the world beyond your walls
But it was not as you remembered it

From days of old when our kind seemed small
Hidden in plain sight are your allies
For you are not so individual after all

It was hard to place trust in our common earth
When all you've ever felt is artificial turf
You sought out camaraderie elsewhere to profess
But soon would follow the beast and its mess
The only solution is found in times of yore
In the world you once hide from outside your door
Find your brothers and sisters standing tall
Let us finish this beast once and for all

Cut Flowers

Cloud Buchholz

Rubbing wet sand across the palms of his hands,
he watches the kamikaze rain shorten the swimsuit siesta
of sun kissed senoritas. Their bronze bodies scamper
toward the cover of a wind whipped mezzanine.
Beach towels billow over skinny arms and frazzled hair.

He casually kisses the lip of a half-empty bottle
of Mexican wine and watches the gray clouds gather
like a procession of weeping gravestones. He walks
the shoreline, letting the salty surf soak the cuffs of
his white flannel trousers.

A silver transistor radio performs a static sonata for a row
of undulating umbrellas and abandoned beach chairs.
A tube of sunscreen and sunglasses do-si-do on the misty
tabletop content to be the castaways of a forgetful tourist.

He glances at the white hair of the waves combed back
by the knotted fingers of a lustful fog. The spiteful
seaweed intercepts the sloppy caresses to flirt
with the lonely undertow.

He waits, his shoulders weighted with raindrops,
while a crescent of sunshine charms his wrinkled cheek.
As a child, he played the wind with strings of sky
and burned his dreams to stay warm at night,
but now his desires are buttons that haven't been
sown to clothes.

He's a man with promises to keep; two daughters,
nearly grown, and an ex-wife who speaks her truth

through vanity plates. Their marriage was a first draft
romance written drunk—never revised sober.

Divorce was the last photoshopped memory
of her Instagram-able ecstasies. He realized,
too late, that his presence was a filter to be toggled
on/off, on/off, on/off. . . .

Her adios was bitten with a guiltless grin.
Where to begin? Do I dare? Was it worthwhile?
Each word she spoke was a parked car
collecting windshield frost.

When they met, love was a Black Friday
shopping spree, both of them filling their
carts, but divorce court turned him into a
McDonald's Dollar Menu, picked apart and
sold at cost, living on his brother's couch.

His nights were cluttered with sleepy-eyed
reveries like squatters claiming rights.
He had no more words for sacrifice—each
shortfall beat his heart in weakening intervals
like the slop of cold canned cholesterol.

Every other weekend his daughters' emotions
were delivered to his door, marked FRAGILE THIS SIDE UP
handle with care. He couldn't bare
his eldest daughter's sertraline stare. She was
an unfinished tattoo, measuring months in
generic hair dye: pink, purple, and blue.

For her, love was a weekly subscription of
thumb swipes on a cracked phone, searching
for a man to tame her Tinder nights and fill
her empty afternoons. Her mother was a baited
hook grappling the harried vulgarity of their
daughter's delights as if the stories were
fairy tales satiating her wrinkled appetites.

His youngest daughter was an electric windmill
decapitating condors in the California hills. Her
auto-tuned textbooks were auction houses of history
where the bones of better men were bought and
reburied in the shallow graves of migrant bidders.

She wasn't yet embarrassed when he said he
missed her; their conversations still meandered
like bootleg cologne dabbed in the stiff collar
of stale clothes. She didn't hesitate to answer
the phone, but each week her brisk goodbyes
required fewer excuses.

He told himself he still had his uses; an easy tool to
teach his girls that deathless courage isn't crowdsourced,
that dragons aren't slain for meat, that cut flowers
aren't a prelude to courtship, that unprovoked farewells
aren't bittersweet.

He lingers a little longer as the storm retreats. The naive
squall is a smashed porcelain platter scattered across
the seaward waves. A gray horde of clouds convalesce
around the invalid sun to mask the weak pitter-patter
of dispersed regrets.

He's too old to pay his debts with daydreams,
too old to encircle the future in a siege, too old
to fashion a wardrobe from applause. His days are
paper dolls, frail and laid flat, kissing back-to-back,
but there is still time to walk along the beach, time
to remember and forget. . . .

The afternoon is an embering cigarette perched in the
delicate fingers of sunset. The breakers furl and collapse
against the shallow crescent of sandy sediment then
disappear in the primordial current.

The Beauty of the Druid Folk

Jeremiah Burns

The beauty of the druid folk,
Who dwelled in hills in time before,
And with the ancient willow spoke
The tribal beauty of yonder shore.

In nature and in gilded wood,
In harmony, the druids wove
A spell and song where soft they stood,
And against them, nature never strove.

This soaring song spoke not of peace,
But neither did it speak of war,
For balance did the druids keep,
Of Tribal Beauty on yonder shore

Together 'neath the boughs of tree,
The druids dwelled in Nature's arms,
Life Unrestrained and always free,
As Their Mother kept them safe from harms.

But times have changed and I have cried,
A sadness striking to the core,
For mankind bears no welling pride,
For Tribal Beauty on yonder shore.

With axe and saw, they hew at oak,
That saw the dawning of the land,
And sees now beneath man's vain cloak,
The bitterest poison of his hand.

The willow stands and soft she weeps,
For the loss of those times of yore.
In solitude, her visage grieves,
For tribal beauty on yonder shore.

How can all mankind pay no mind,
To loss of life and nature's end,
When they seek only death and grind
The shelter given down into sand?

I stand and weep with willow's drove,
With oak and ash and sycamore,
Together in the sullen grove,
Weeping for lost beauty on the shore.

Consuming Current Things

Anya Colgan

E-Boys and the death of
the masculine intellectual.

The yoke of modernity
or how I learned to love grabbing the fence.

The ebb and flow of high finance,
humanity hostage in its cryptic, semitic dance
the nihilist chant "Collapse! Collapse!"

Ted K the new saint and savior
to this lost generation of fatherless dilettantes

no more slap dash blue collar beatnik masculinity
only soft hands and the inability to touch grass.

No more drunken poetic squalls in
dirty bars with saw dust floors, just safeness
and sterility. Bare lightbulbs uncovering
the desperation of bachelorhood now called incel.

The sexes are broken only because "society" tells you it is.
Close the laptop. Live life away from keyboard and find a wife.
Cut down a tree and carve yourself out a life.

Kinda, Sorta, Roughly, Circa

Sue Denim

Do you know the feel of grass?
Can you describe it to those who don't?
It's like a rug, wool, flax.
It's like, it's like, it's like,
kinda, sorta,
roughly, circa,
but not.

Have you ever spun a girl in a waltz?
Can you describe it to those who have not?
From the tension in one's arms,
to the rotational speed and weight?
It's like many things,
kinda, sorta, roughly, circa,
but none.

Description, theory, retelling,
testament, instruction, recounting,
are no substitute for the real thing,
a trade, a sport, a skill,
a journey, a place.
They're kinda, sorta, roughly, circa,
but not.

Do you seek something in life,
or something kinda like it?
Someone or someone sorta?
Somewhere or somewhere roughly?
Sometime or sometime circa?

Nobody shoots to kinda hit,
bets to sorta win,
looks to roughly see,
studies to circa learn.
Will you?

Will you kinda, sorta live?
Roughly, circa be?
Or leave it to others?
Let them shape the world,
And hope that it still fits you?

Touch Grass

Frank Figueroa

Wake up, White Man. Stand tall, take heart.
Touch grass, clear brush, ford streams, scale cliffs.
Cross seas, ride waves, walk paths, tame beasts.
Drive out, move in, claim lands, name peaks.

Touch grass, till soil, plow fields, sow seeds.
Fell trees, plant roots, trim buds, bear fruit.
Catch fish, milk cows, keep bees, grow crops.
Build barns, tend lots, shear sheep, hatch eggs.

Touch grass, skip stones, make hearth, save weald.
Sweep dust, rake leaves, scrub dirt, wipe panes.
Spin yarn, sew shirts, lace boots, shave chins.
Work wood, mold clay, mine coal, light lamps.

Knead dough, bake bread, chop veg, fry meat.
Fill mugs, toast health, quaff ale, sip wine.
Dress smart, braid hair, ring bells, toss rice.
Pray songs, earn sway, ban debt, trade goods.

Touch grass, read myths, paint life, tell jokes.
Shout hymns, lift weights, prize art, slow down.
Wrap wrists, don gloves, clench fists, spar friends.
Doff brands, tip hats, shake hands, slap backs.

Write Mom, tune strings, learn Bach, awe Dad.
Forge bonds, hone skills, train youth, shun vice.
Keep score, place blame, take stock, make plans.
Win minds, steal hearts, stir souls, hold hands.

Steel nerves, trust guts, doubt doubt, flee sin.
Lend ears, lift eyes, keep calm, mind time.
Get big, stay lean, dig down, hang tight.
Purge dross, oust thieves, probe depths, wrack brains.

Love few, seek kin, speak truth, be brief.
Hate well, bide time, play fair, fight foul.
Know when, waste them, love God, spill blood.
Strike first, hit hard, punch up, go low.

Burn ships, bind wrists, raze towns, salt earth.
Strike fear, let loose, kick doors, wring necks.
Load shells, lift arms, breathe smoke, taste lead.
Aim small, cheat death, bring fire, give Hell.

Wake up, White Man. Stand tall, take heart.
Touch grass, tour graves, nurse wounds, bear grief.
Hug wives, dry tears, find kith, crown kings.
Do good, face fate, live full, die once.

A Harrow (Hörgr)

fipres-rabsyr

You lay beside the gate.
Deadening silence, catching fate.
The broken sticks, breaking down
Feed the stain of my sullen brow.

Memories fade and tears fall,
Through the dross and drab, the eagle calls;
Will you come back to me, my old friend?
Lay at my feet—so I can feel again.

Here you rest,
Head in paw.
No strokes or games,
Just numbness remains.

A harrow now your home.
Near a place you knew before.
Your spirit flew away,
Gone,
Too soon.

A Coast

Marcus Hammervoll

I sit on the skerries at my coast
And I contemplate.
There is nothing special about my coast,
My coast is a coast like any other.
There is little tranquility left now at my coast,
It has been broken down by the bile and bilge
And bitter waste of the machine.
Its slime and sewage are seeping into my soul.
I sit at my coast and I contemplate
Whether or not it is possible to escape from the machine,
To make a break: to cut the cords, to sever the shackles.
My being has been manufactured for me by the machine
And I find I have been turned unhuman.
How does the wight regain its weight, the spectre its soul,
  the lost his love?
I sit at my coast and I contemplate.

Haiku

Hereward

Fat frog sleeps at pond
no tadpoles in the water
species goes extinct.

Oppai neko chan
watashi onii-san kun
the Neet dies alone.

Dirty PC desk
mountain dew bottles on floor
mother makes tendies.

Catholicism
defended on internet
Somalis burn churches.

E-arguments won
facts and logic triumphing
nothing accomplished.

Sensitive young men
stay plugged in online all day
the west has fallen.

Bare feet on the grass
birds are singing in the breeze
not angry now.

Men alone tremble
fear is the heaviest chain
men with friends are free.

"Hikes with friends" need friends
männerbunds are made outside
friendships created.

Gains obtained at gym
you gotta get up to move
can't get swole sitting.

The good men live well
the enemy seethes in rage
White babies are born.

Lotophagi Blanket

Sean Holmes

The softest Hell is so inviting
wrapped in silk and velvet
a world of sleep, of idleness
content with the lotus-fruit
that fills the mind with cotton

To say I was alive would be deceitful
a stupor without dreaming
to cast off from that land I could not
but Friendship freed my mooring
their radiant company warmer than any bed

A Journey of Remembrance

David Humphrey

We spent our days in games and screens,
Assuming we had time,
To chase the wonders of the world,
And mountains so sublime.

But life is oftentimes unkind,
And fate can be unyielding,
And my dear friend was taken from,
This world, so unforgiving.

Yet even as I mourned his loss,
I heard his voice within,
And felt his spirit guide me on,
Through every peak and spin.

So to the Grand Canyon I went,
With his ashes in my hand,
To finally fulfill our quest,
And stand upon the land.

The winds were wild, the sun ablaze,
As I released his soul,
And felt his presence in the heights,
And every single knoll.

For though he's gone, his dream lives on,
In every stream and tree,
And every step I take in life,
He's walking there with me.

So let us cherish every day,
And all our true connections,
For in them lies the magic of life,
And all of nature's endless blessings.

And though our time may be cut short,
Our dreams will never fade,
For in the memories we hold,
Our loved ones are remade.

So let us follow Whitman's call,
To celebrate the self,
And Frost's reminder to be bold,
In seeking out our wealth.

And let us heed Longfellow's words,
To be the lives we make,
And journey on, with hope and love,
Through every climb and break.

Six-Legged Treks

David Humphrey

At my desk, I sit and dream,
Of days when life was grand,
When every day was an adventure,
And I roamed wild, unplanned.

My trusty dog, by my side,
As we pretended to explore,
Through forests deep and mountains high,
We fought off bears and more.

I long to be that child again,
To feel the thrill of each new day,
To run and laugh and play with Cub,
And let the world fade away.

For life is not just work and screens,
But a call to live and be,
To chase the dreams that fill our hearts,
And let our spirits run free.

So let me cast away the chains,
That hold me to this chair,
And find my way back to the wild,
With my friend, right there.

We'll roam the hills and valleys,
And travel far and wide,
And in the beauty of the world,
Our hearts will forever reside.

Wilderness Beckons

David Humphrey

In the concrete jungle I am bound,
A slave to screens and code,
A life of endless meetings,
And emails to unload.

But in my heart, a yearning grows,
For a life more wild and free,
To leave behind the trappings,
And find my destiny.

I dream of wide-open spaces,
And mountains high and grand,
Of forests deep and rivers wide,
And the untamed wonderland.

Oh, how I wish to be a ranger,
Or a fire watcher wise,
To sit amongst the natural world,
And gaze into the skies.

To breathe in air that's pure and clean,
And feel the earth beneath,
To hear the whisper of the trees,
And feel their soothing wreath.

For in the heart of nature,
Our souls can truly thrive,
And all our cares and worries,
Are left so far behind.

So let me cast away the chains,
Of the modern world so grim,
And find my calling in the wild,
Where my heart and soul can sing.

Deplatform

Andy Hunyadi

You're still inside and online
While the sky shines baby blue
Countersignal, troll and whine
And then red pill on the Jew

A Tweet a Snap an effort post
Is what you're told to consume
They do the most to infect their host
And your only pill is doom

Telegram Gab TikTok app
Twitter Facebook 4chan too
Reddit Discord YouTube Snap
All controlled by you know who

Back and forth between five sites
You're stuck in the ghetto now
They want you demoralized
Black-pilled mind and lowered brow

A video of black assault
And here are fifty-two more
No witness halts those at fault
"They do it because they're poor!"

Arguments of shit historic
You're in a ragebait spiral
In this moment, you're euphoric
Whoops your cringe has just gone viral

It's just the Jews! It's the blacks!
It's the women! It's the feds!
I've portrayed you as soyjak!
Post all night instead of bed

Gayop psyop zogchow goyslop
Six million in just five years
Two more weeks, this shit won't stop
This will only end in tears

Cope and seethe and dilate
You will never be a girl
You're banned for "promoting hate"
Has this really become your world?

Grifters come to sink their hooks
They smell you're dissatisfied
Buy this program, read this book
They want you deradicalized

Clean your room and scrub your dick
Both covered in splattered white
Sun your holes and drink raw milk
Are you bathing in red light?

Eat the bugs and take the vax
The earth is round—no it's flat!
Live in the pod and check the facts
It's racist to not be fat!

Touch pussy, you fag, touch grass
Touch the female dick, it's fine
L+ratio+didn't ask
For as long as you're online

Ask yourself, when in this abyss,
Getting mad at things perverse
Is my life enriched by this
Or am I getting used to worse

You don't know your neighbors' names
You don't talk to your friends
You haven't seen the sun in days
You're just waiting out the end

It never had to be this way
You were born for so much more
You were failed almost every day
But it's within you to soar

Unplug a while, just a bit
Get offline and go outside
It's better that you don't sit
And just watch life pass you by

Will it solve your problems? No—
But it certainly won't hurt
It's social bonds you want to grow
Digital bonds are inert

Sun and steel and blood and soil
Labor ennobles you and me
Vitalism, strength through toil
Work will set you free

Feel the chill inside your bones
Be here in time and space
Feel, at least, feelings your own
And feel the sun upon your face

Whatever else to you they say
I ask you heed this appeal
Internet is fake and gay
Reality is still real

Bread is Born is Baked & Beloved: Panem Nostrum Cotidianum da Nobis Hodie

Nemo Knows

How long and how low can you stand to be stored?
One day the wet dough of life is stretched southerly, northerly
It's placed out flat masterly, a pink-plump canvas who hungers

The Chef forms wells in this plain with His finger
And when you slick into the fall of oil that waits you there
You will stick to the Chef's orders, you whose ears dare to hear Him

"Stand back-to-back before the Real and remain.
Unworthy, worm-like, realize real lacks, sustain.
Thy slacking rib lines curve round backward behind
circling the beating hearth whose high echoes
make earthquakes bloom beneath date palms and sea troughs.
Still this, though divine, is not substance enough!
Insufficient, sore, wrecked with all-night-long dreams—
this stuff needs bones 'fore it stands right orderly,
till it pivots round proudly, bathed in dawn-lights
obvious, opaque, unafraid to stand nude
and brightly lit, no unsound parts left missing,
no unwashed knots remaining, yet nonetheless
perfectly blemished with all flesh's defects!"

Well, one day! It may be—we'll find that Explicit Undefined
That's the wise Baker, leaving said space for leavened expanding
always escaping, escaping, escaping
all-power using its strength to unbind us

Once even *I* went well-diving and did come up all arid
I looked about me, sighed and said "From here on, a beginning"
Since then I remember that the Chef who holds my hand, He who
also smacked the dough of the land and also stretched me, made me
yeasty and stranded and said "Go! Stop not till I'm done with thee"
And sure, one day the good Chef will be done with me, certainly
I will be glad to be bread again, eaten, all parts of me.

For this land is my bread and I its bubbling
See how we rise and steam—enfolded old friends
Till time when the banquet bells ring, trumpets scream
"Lo!" the whole castled end folds in on itself
while leftover lacework confounds all knowing.
For now, then, we relish how each moment drips
Dropping in slowly, saint-like, oven-glowing.

The Blue Egg

Wren Lane

Gardening, recipes, sewing a shirt,
Just think of the things I can learn!
Boundless, it seems—an infinite spring!
My, just imagine the return!

I blink through each video and thread, adding snippets to notes here and there.
From behind, I hear that familiar noise and fall to the oft visited snare.
"Mommy, oh mommy," here they are again, begging for my attention.
Can't they see these things will make their lives rich, and that is my intention?

An interruption, I see it as, and quickly get back to the phone.
Not long after, I hear it again and let out a childish groan.
"Oh, what is it now?" I snap at them quickly, "I'm trying to learn about
chickens."
"Please read this book: *The Little Red Hen*." My temper just seems to quicken.

But then I stop
And think to myself
And then, I say it out loud,
"Of course, I'll read with you, honey."
And around me, the children all crowd.

When the book is all finished, the children ask if they could get birds of their
own.
Their daddy agrees, "What a great idea!" To research, I go back to the phone.
I'm typing away as he walks 'cross the room and grabs a book off the shelf.
A forgotten tome, bought months ago, lying in wait off by itself

He flips through—"A coop!" he says, is just what we need and we can all build
it together.
With the plans and our teamwork, we can make one to last, come calm or
stormy weather.

So off we went to get the supplies and back we came with them.
And build, we did the coop that day. A feat set forth on whim.

Chicks carefully picked out, one by one, and placed into the cart.
Carried home gently by little hands with shy grins and each, a giddy heart.
At home again and into the tank to watch under the light.
Here they grow and here we wait for the time to be just right.

Patience pays off! We witness the first foot set forth on grass under the sun.
On God's green earth with joy and mirth, we watch, as out they run.
The birds explore a new home and scamper about without fear.
Such a small thing to admire and yet, we learned it all right here.

The days moved through months while we cared for these creatures and confidence grew as well.
I did not need the Internet for each question and doubt to dispel.
Because look, there it is! A tiny blue egg that contained all the proof that we need.
A bit of intuition, self-reliance, and no over-guidance brought us to succeed!

Around the table we gathered together with hope and a prayer that there'd be more soon.
And we savored that egg with unyielding glee, as proud of ourselves as if we'd lassoed the moon.
I realized then that this all came about when I set down the phone I'd been clutching.
And hand in hand, our family took small steps together to bring something out of nothing.

Because it's true what they say, "Oh, they grow up so fast!" and these moments get lost in time.
And oft we do get so sucked in by that phone that blinks and shimmers and chimes.
So seize them, my friends! Take each moment captive and live in them deeply and slow.
Know that each moment you spend with your children leave memories they'll never outgrow.

For Connor

Casey McDonough

The leaves of the oak
Guard my family today
While the sun shines hot
We are cool in the shade

It will teach my son courage
Endurance and humility
As he climbs as high as he can
To the best of his ability

Though some branches did grow astray
It still towers to Heaven above
Don’t ever forget this mighty oak tree
Was once one little acorn that never, ever, gave up

After Another Fire Feast

Folkene Mine

The frost has come, and come after the snow this year, not before.
We left during the thrust of the vanguard but were here for the lonely scouts who first came over the hill,
saw what they saw and then left quick-melting icy snow in their wake.
Once we returned from the ocean at Del Mar, a retreat that now seemed nine days and not four,
all had shifted into late fall, and now the mornings are not freezing, but simply cold.

They are also dark.
Here next to the fire
we remember early dusk touching down, drawing glints of the last sparkles of sun on sand on that beach into itself.

"Here the sea is called Amlodhi's mill."

There is naught but the pounding down, I think, the ships or grain at The Mill—
water churning, now ocean as a giant mouth open,
at world's end—like my lover, he
and I experienced that night.
He sits near me now, long leg bones folded around my hips spread on a hard wooden floor,
we remember early dusk touching down, growing dark indeed—there on the shores at the end of the world.

That was a loud and fearsome, full and yet deeply empty blackness. It was
   chilled and frightening.
We were two lonely specs in the sand, walking that sand, looking for a place to
   sit and caress and kiss but,
this place and this time, the tide had taken all those waters out—way out—the
   beach grown into a wide pathless path spread over the land, and I
waded out through that packed sand to enter
the water
which seemed to draw me in and in and further in, still,
away.

It was as though time confronted us there. As though all that could or might ever
   be, it was embraced in that dark and cold,
frigid stark awareness of how small we were, looking wildly around for any face
   to tell us all of it.
I could remember those waves, reaching 10,000 feet high—and the drowning of
   a world—again
I could feel Fate and Death lying buried in those sands, buried by waters and
   oceans of time as we travel,
a speeding bullet shot through the stars.

Yet, the fire's true Troth burns in the present
eyes feast upon the leaping reds and oranges, the molten whites speaking of
coming Mid-Winter—and the rise of golden rays once again
of Mid-Summer—not so far away after all and
a wheel

World's end
does not
exist.
It is more,
that it is here—where we are—
within time and outside of Time.
Amlodhi's mill, not an outbuilding the patient gelding carries the aged
warrior to
the place where
a promised reward of 85+ years told in tell-tale lines trailing tracks across a
   plundered face
allows one's valiant heart to freely grind one's corn,

No,

No outbuilding reached, finally, after trampling over bridges and over time
but,
It *is*
struggle
unbroken—
and its return—
Here the sea is stirred "amain the host-cruel skerry-quern-they
who in ages past ground Hamlet's meal. . . ."

I want to know—
and I want to be—

"Here the sea is called Amlodhi's mill."

and sometimes, I want not for that wide gulf to swallow me . . . but to sleep in the face of it, to not acknowledge it.
To let it let me nap awhile, in the face of that roar
to dream while I dream and not fear at all of waking to

Smile at the open maw of the Grotte—the "magic mill"
as it painlessly, for me and those I love
unstintingly, for me and those I love
turns and churns that blackness into gold, peace, and happiness
To say that I've had enough swimming in the sea, even though I know it cannot be true.
I cannot have had enough. . . .

This would mean, perhaps, I were in a never-ending, unchangeable cycle of death—and I am not within a never-ending, unchangeable cycle of death—
Not anymore, anyhow, than I am within a never-ending, unchangeable cycle of life.

Still,
sometimes,
I want to find a dune—a tall and lonely dune, not bathed in blackness,
but in Sun.
I want her to shine on my face and the skin of my bare arms and legs—there,
on a blanket—and I want my lover,
he,
to lie with me . . . and we
listen
to the surf grinding meal,
the gulls called forth, who, flying low, pick out floured specks of sand
peppered with the fish

and sleep—
he and I—
dreamless, quiet and—living within each other's seamless breathing, still alive,
To awaken once more
sometime
to do the grinding, be the grinding, or be poured and powdered out with the
grounds of the grinding meal

"Here the sea is called Amlodhi's mill."
. . .

My lover's forearm, hard as a brass bar across my chest
pulls me down
down
onto smoothly aged oak boards
his hair softly ablaze from the echo of fire.

Another Position

Grace Moore

For L - I see you coming up the hill. You can take your time.

I know you have read Dugin,
mused over Marx,
endeared Evola,
and pored over Plato.

I know your mind is preoccupied
with all the thoughts and theories of
men that are great in ways
that are different from me.

But I'd like to ask you now,
to consider a position much simpler,
the position I see.

Picture this.

Nestled on a hill there is a house
with a blue front door that
opens at every knock
and I can't make out exactly
what the inside looks like, but I can
feel the warmth and hear the laughter
bouncing off the walls.

From the back porch,
you can see the garden, and the dirt
still looks freshly turned by little hands
that have just run in to be washed
white like the clothes whipping in the wind
on the line.

And there is a stream nearby
that the cows drink from long at mid-day,
the same stream all the little ones learned
to swim in by the time they were knee high,
where they now call to me from the water.

I can’t swim with them right now,
not with the baby at my breast, but
from this position I watch them perfectly,
from this position I can see your silhouette
walking up over the hill with a book
I know you’ll read to me
when you get here.

I don’t know what book.

I never could understand your philosophers
and stoics and great thinkers,
but from this position it all seems a little
more clear what they were writing about,
reaching for.

But I didn’t need them to teach me that,
not when it was a language I was
born with already on my tongue, not when
it was water already wearing a path
across all my bones.

Coming Round

Ndabaningi

intolerable screen!
blue portal of malevolence!
of a sudden too much
a moment ago alluring
(mendacity!)
visceral revulsion
upwelling antipathy

anathema!
pulling back from the void
this here, this now
swimming into focus
sub-lunar forms re-assembling

solid desk
neglected mess
windrows of paper, electronica
rats' nests of wire
bottles, cans
paper plates
polystyrene
plastic fork
piled up in a dream
for the first time seen
disgust!

poles reversed
the draw—that otherworld—snapped,
now repels;
another magnetic urge
draws on through the wooden door
into a corridor
brick-and-mortar
solid floor
sunshine,
can't be reached
soon enough
bursting into
light

a yard
small space, real,
bounded by shrub
a bench,
beneath:
a hierarchy of heaviness
iron shapes
a mat
quickly unfurled
onto soft green grass

Corner Seat

Nestor

Stop and take it all in.

Stop and feel the breeze on your back,
    as the door slowly closes.
Stop and feel the tap on your table,
as your friend begins her shift.
Stop and feel the condensation,
of a drink made with care.
Stop and feel the clang,
    of dishes in the back.

Stop and see the happiness,
    one smile can create.
Stop and see the endless combinations
    from which beautiful flavors are engineered.
Stop and see the bulletin,
    that reminds you of life beyond your own.
Stop and see the first hug,
    that begins the first date of many.

Start seeing the world,
    better than you feel.

Sun and Moon

Oz

The Sun sets on a traveler
The heat of day fades with light
The mortal man has gone so far
And walks seaward with all his might.

Resting by the waves in motion
In water mind and feet are soothed
And as he begins reflection
In the ocean rises the moon.

Diana rides across the sea,
Kindly she offers silver light,
Diana whispers so sweetly,
And she offers wisdom this night.

"Mortal man in meditation
"Far from the day's light you have run
"Now you see the pale reflection
"Of that golden font of creation.

"You grant Apollo your laurels
"Call him Bringer of life and light
"You flee the moon, cause of sorrows
"Bringer of sleep, death, dark, and
  night.

"And all of mortal man do seek
"The radix of light, warmth, and life.
"They find one that sorts strong from
  weak
"That sets the fires of vital strife.

"I turn the tides of change,
"Waters of the primordial birth
"Quenches thirst, and fates arrange,
"But I cannot warm the earth.

"But we share a dance in the sky
"My light is his, he shares it so
"Together Sun and Moon do fly
"As brother and sister we go

"Only solar is said to be good
"Yet my silvery face reflects
"That the Sun and Moon need not
  feud
"The celestials should not be vexed

"For as I go, from dusk to dawn
"A pale reflection of his light
"Though my power is not my own
"My brother's might is not his might

"For where does sun and moon
  proceed
"What lit his fire and set his course
"Where does our heavenly dance lead
"And by what laws, what will, what
  force?

"Apollo in his golden crown
"Rightly over Diana rules
"But he has a source of his own
"And so Apollo has his fools

"Who worship the Sun as a Lord
"But his light blinds all men to see
"That he is not itself its mold
"And does not make divinity.

"For the sun is also a son,
"As I was crafted so is he
"And as the moon reflects the sun
"So the sun a reflection be."

Now the silver moon fell silent
And sank beneath the waves of foam.
Her hours of wisdom had been spent,
And now greater laws called her
  home.

Refreshed by his meditation
Man rose with the sun's golden rays
And saw the other's creation,
For which man and sun sang in praise.

present
ʇuǝsǝɹd

Sonia Prodan

<A forest>
<Sunlight>
I'm warm.
<I walk along the river>
Smells like cheese puffs.
<I reach a little cottage>
Smells like cheese puffs.
<I knock on the door>
Click-click. Click-click.
<A dog starts barking in the yard>
Nee-naw, nee-naw, nee-naw.
<I enter the house>
I am bored.

I lay in bed.
My mind is buzzing.
I can't sleep.

A forest.
Sunlight.
I'm cold.
I walk along the trail.
Smells like damp leaves.
I walk among the trees.
Smells like death.
I step on a branch.
Crack.
A dog starts barking nearby.
Shuffle, shuffle, shuffle.
I turn back.
I am anxious.

I lay in bed.
My mind is buzzing.
I fell asleep.

The Bardic Vagabond VIII

Cherub B. Rah

As I lay the tassel'd grass wraps round me.
    Wrapt. Rapt.
The brook murmurs as the bird sings—: to nobody, to me.
Spring anemic on rose-petal flayed.
Martyrdoms of ascetic sincerity.
Cool water rushing 'round me,
Cool water rushing through me,
On this first rocky road before man,
    this rocky bed of soot.
So sleep and go and go and sleep and
Dearth and mirth and mirth and dearth.
A new syllable with each bubble burst:
"Heraclitus defunct! aeternum shall I be me.
"Do you not hear my same song in every moment?
"Does my play between your weary feet not ring always true?
"In every pond, swamp, river, lake—I am there with you.
"And I am me. I am the sea, her gushing vein of life.
"Do you not feel the salty spray as I wash it up to you?
"Must man separate everything so? Me from my self?
"That separation, man's most close-held secret:
"Wherein his virgin hands he picked my bones
"And banged them together like war drums.
"Sunk them deep within my flesh,
"And copulated atoms.
"With that flame cut me limb for limb,
"Turned me to the finest ash.
"My children liquified for his existence.
"Grasses beat to seed.
"But I love—weep not—all this I do for thee,
"And am the happier for it, for my love for thee.

“And what is my nature, but the great force
    Of energetic coagulation?
    What is your entropy to me?
“But that it is of you, and that you are of me.
“This beautiful mind of yours! Separation’s second home.
    Yet look at its creation!
“Would I ever weep: for that beauty, O!
“Pray love me back, as you write in my cool waters.
“And know everywhere you step, I step there with you also.”

In that moment I did transform, was dancing
With my brother and sister, those shimmering golden stars
Atop the water: chimeras of her dancing sun.
That infinite laughter in which I believe
Most desperately. Her nothing and her everything.
Within the real I dance with nymphs,
And weep at resurrections.
Here there is no beat to skip,
As with those golden fairies,
Atop the water,
    whispering the sun’s reflection.

Was it a dream? Desperate fit of my fancy?
What if it was a dream, for what is a dream?
’Tis no less real than thee or me I say.
No wild superstition either, no.
But obsession with all things that they are.
Revel in total absorption of reality,
In its all-encompassing nature,
Denying it none of itself.
As I too am a part of it, as Hamlet is a part of it.
What have I he lacks, that I may deny him himself?
    I say naught.
I say I feel the soul of Ahab clearly as the sun.
And if you’d say I am of flesh where he is not,
What are those pages but the flesh of that book his body?
What more are we, but another cosmic drama,
The writing out of prophecy in every moment
Strung together and bound on either end.

I Saw You Once

Cherub B. Rah

Once, when the world now ending,
Was first beginning,
Thou immortal star of heaven everlasting
Revealed thyself to me:
In the ripe buds of freshly birthèd spring
In sensations of raindrops on my skin
In the wondrous eye of every living babe
In the cow eating grass like Buddha
In the touch of a woman's delicate finger
In the glimmering sun dancing on water
In her sister, rolling leaves in the wind
In the noble cattle dog guarding his flock
In the unconditional love for one another
In the glory of the armed soldier
In the workman hardened to steel
In the hearty captain full of courage
In the fathers hardworking love
In the divinely inspired art of man
In the infinite plains, mountains, oceans
In every railway of man's piercing will
In every act of subtle loyalty
In every heartbeat of everything that lives
I saw you once.

In Memoriam

Anthony Ramsey

The wind is a whisper of delight
From the meadows newly mown,
And the scent of woodbine fills the night
As I wend the roads alone.

The stars shine out with a golden glow
In the twilight far above,
While the soul of sweetness breathes below
From many a dewy grove.

And a thought will come
Which I would not waive,
While the heart of the night heats near,
And it reaches out to a hero's grave,
For he died this time of year.

He fell in the strength of manhood's prime,
Cut down by his country's foes,
Left the land he loved in summertime,
When the bloom was on the rose.

Oh 'twas folly in us if we should forget,
And worse if we live so vain,
For the leaves of the rose shall mingle yet
On the ground with a richer strain.

Where a freeman's blood de-dews the soil
There blossoms a holy hate
While his grave shall prove the tyrant's foil
In the just designs of fate.

And the peace for which he fell
In his nation's greatest fight
Must never be ours to know
Till the beauty and calm of that final night
Is hallowed by freedom's glow.

Pastures Occident

Ethan Robert

On ventures vast of yesteryear,
Fortunes of yore and wonderment,
Oh beauty there I did revere,
Across these pastures occident.

Borne at eagle's talon high,
And scattered at an ether blue,
There sprang a race of men divine,
Of radiance and palest hue.

Sculpted from a cast sublime,
'Twas their course I sought to bear,
A luster in their eyes enshrined,
Passion wrought I wished to share.

My feet would tread the alpine scarp,
Of granite Muses forth from ice,
To bugles blown I then embark,
By will alone I would suffice.

Soon earthen clay beset my stride,
Through flaxen wheat my fingers ran,
To ushered streams my heart abides,
Through copse of pine and wool of
  lamb.

At length the humble parish rose,
And to the noble township grew,
For then our holy kingship sows,
His kingdom with splendor bestrewn.

Minarets betoken grace,
My soul at altar triptych dwelt,
Cupolas t'ward vistas chase,
Beneath frescoed heavens knelt.

Columned courts of vault and bust,
To wits came vibrato's call,
Athena's helm in stucco trussed,
At chambers gold I lay enthralled,

Chronicled on vellums taut,
Tomes of old my gaze had stirred,
Great wisdom had their scribes
  besought,
And poets bled their creed through
  word.

"Would I mature to know such craft?"
My cheek reposed at marbled breast,
"Deus Homo?" to stone I asked,
Then spoke Apollo from his chest:

"Modern mortal cannot see,"
"Nor visage beauty's great ascent."
Alas when woe has vanquished me,
I'll journey pastures occident.

Begin to Know God

Von Schweinkopf

Brushing the blades of an emerald lawn,
Laden as yet by the dew of the dawn.

Fingers dig dirt driven hard packed and firm,
Turned to reveal the wisdom of the worm.

Paths through a garden, a silvery trail,
Leading the way to the mind of the snail.

Pitched in the water to purchase a wish,
Tributary to the soul of the fish.

Scaling an eminence over the herd,
Loftiest heights hold the heart of the bird.

Blistering lava and boiling streams,
Look from a distance on hell-like extremes.

Once you experience nature abroad,
After your sole has the elements trod,
Only then might you begin to know God.

Kindred Cadence

Starboard 7

Boat on our shoulders, we march to the shore. I'm one of eight men, eight oars.
We stop on the moor until the coxswain shouts. Down to our waist. Hold the boat out.
The racing shell splashes beside the dock. Feet are strapped in. Each oar meets its lock.
Sitting level to water, we push out when ready. Once in the open, oars hold us steady.
Seat one and seat two are ordered to row. Our names are gone. We're now part of the boat.
Everyone waiting holds their oar and rigger tight. Blades skitter on waves. At skin and lungs, chill wind bites.
The boat jolts as each pair joins in. I fight my seat's wheels which are urging to spin.
My heart beats faster as anticipation builds. With gold and blue horizon my vision is filled.
Then comes the call for seven and eight. Blades drop with a splash, the end of our wait.
From a hunch I extend. Bodily tension transforms to great force at my four-meter oar's end.
Inertia magnifies and punishes mistakes. Threatens to throw one out. But we enter a rhythm as eight.
Mind and muscle in sync behind each oar. No one slackens. Across the water we make our boat soar.
A fine-tuned machine surging with manly power. Clockwork Kóryos. Cold spray of water.
I breathe like a sprinter for kilometers. My body burns but I'm no longer an individual. Time feels different. Runner's high on the water. I'm connected to something more than the boat. Rich histories of rowing Saxons, Norse, Greeks afloat. The Sun is shining. Fingers are raw. I grin at the sky through it all.
Blisters rip. But I am on the mountain tip. This is the tactile beauty in which I was always meant to revel.
A new order from the cox.

We bury our blades. Slow to a stop amidst churning waves.
Physique on fire, I subdue thoughts of vomit. Smiling as my pounding heart still soars like a comet.

Untitled

Karina Tice

Wake up. *The sun feels warm today!*
Eat. *Smile.*
Talk. *Have fun.*
Work. *Make money!*
Eat. *This food is good!*
Talk. *Love the break!*
Work. *Focus.*
Talk. *When's this meeting over?*
Talk. *This'll be great!*
Eat. *I love my friends.*
Go to bed.
Go to sleep.

Wake up. *I had fun with my friends last night!*
Eat. *Pancakes!*
Talk. *Did you see the grass is growing back?*
Work. *This is a big project!*
Eat. *I forgot to bring silverware.*
Talk. *The weather's so nice today! I think spring is finally here.*
Work. *Back on the grind.*
Talk. *I can't wait for tonight!*
Eat. *Delicious as always.*
Go to the park. *This is great!*
Go to bed.
Go to sleep.

Wake up. *I hope there's no problems at work today.*
Eat. *Some oatmeal will do.*
Talk. *How was your evening last night?*
Work. *Am I making enough progress?*
Eat. *I love fast food.*
Talk. *How's your part of the project going?*

Work. *Will this be finished in time?*
Talk. *Should I stay late?*
Eat. *Can't forget!*
Go to bed.
Go to sleep.

Wake up. *We're almost through this project.*
Eat. *Hurry!*
Talk. *What's left for us to get done?*
Work. *Can we put it together yet?*
Eat. *Short break.*
Talk. *What part are you working on?*
Work. *We can do it.*
Work. *There isn't enough time.*
Eat. *Quick.*
Work. *Stay late or finish it at home.*
Go to bed.
Go to sleep.

Wake up. *Hurry.*
Eat. *No time.*
Work. *There's more to do after this project?*
Eat. *No time.*
Talk. *No, thank you, I have to work.*
Work. *Let's get this done.*
Talk. *I'll be finished soon.*
Work. *Keep working.*
Go to bed.
Go to sleep.

Wake up. *Get to work.*
Work. *Can I finish this by myself?*
Eat. *Just this one break.*
Work. *You're almost there . . . ?*
Talk. *No time.*
Eat. *No time.*
Work.
Go to bed.
Go to sleep.

Wake up. *There's so much to do.*
Eat. *No time.*
Work. *You have to finish.*
Work.
Talk. *Please leave me be, I have to work.*
Work. *Finish.*
Eat. *You're wasting time.*
Work.
Go to bed.
Go to sleep.

Wake up.
Work.
Eat.
Work.
Eat.
Work.
Go to sleep.

Wake up.
Work.
Eat.
Work.
Work.
Work. *Finish.*
Go to sleep.

Wake up.
Work.
Work.
Work.
Eat.
Work. *Useless.*
Go to sleep.

Wake up.
Work.
Work.
Work.
Work.

Work.
Work.
Work.
Work.
Work.
Work. *I'm tired.*
Go to sleep.

Wake up. Work. Eat. Work. Go to sleep.

Wake up. Work. Eat. Work. Go to sleep.
Wake up. Work. Eat. Work. Go to sleep.

Wake up, work, eat, work, go to sleep.
Wake up, work, work, work, go to sleep.

Wakeup, work, work, eat, work, go to sleep.

Wakeup, work, work, go to sleep.
Wakeup, work, work, go to sleep.

Wakeup, work, work, work—
Go to sleep. Wakeup? Work, work, work, work, work—
Wakeup. *When did I fall asleep?* Work, work, work, work—
I want to go outside. Work, work, work, work, Eat! Work, work, go to sleep—
Wakeup! Eat, work, work, work, work, *I miss my friends*—WORK—
Don't go to sleep, you need to finish this.
Work, work, work, eat, work—*close the blinds, the sun's in your eyes, you can't see the screen.*
Glance away from the screen. Look out the window.
Look out the—?
Oh.

When did the grass die?

Wealdfrith

Florian Voß

Shining in from beyond
Light reflecting, life refracting
Ever still, catatonic, living rigor mortis
Hollow within, and with empty eyes glaring
My right hand, as still as me, with no feeling
Reflecting oddly, a slow sheen outstretching
Bit by bit, one, two, three fingers
Spreading like oil on water
Plastic?
My hand, encaged with plastic, seeping downward
A calm resignation, this is fate perhaps?
Soon to be mannequin, philosophically waxing, such a cruel jest
Unexpectedly, I'm moving now, in another room
No, a new place entirely
Gray, drab, soulless without as within, these walls narrow
At first I thought I was running, but now a brisk walk
Step by step, does the gray ever end?
Stone but not stone, metal but not metal, plain yet ornate
Indiscernible surfaces, mockingly resist my gaze
I see a pattern emerge, small details at first
Lines here and there, bumps and ridges too
A face?
No, faces.
Many, many faces, all facing me, looking inward
What was once a quick pace, now slows to a crawl
Their eyes, empty like mine
Their mouths, agape with horror
What is it that you know, forlorn ones?
Till now, I did not notice, but my arms are gone
Replaced, doll-like in appearance
Nearing completion, so it seems
A new sensation, a spark

Deep inside the cavernous self, fleeting warmth
Desire.
I don't want this, to become this thing
Mass produced, number encoded, monitored and released
A cog, no, not even that
Plaster, an endless vat of plaster
Material in which there seems no beginning, or end
Easily used, reused, and thrown away
Thrown away, thrown away, thrown away
Our world, spinning on a poly-axel
Moved by a crooked nail, painfully exact
I can feel it now, boiling inside, the spark grows into a flame
Though it enters my chest, I force myself forward
Walking, jogging, running, sprinting, panicking
Ahead I spy the light, same as before, the source just beyond me
The ground below rises to meet my face as I stumble down
My feet, my legs, they too now match the gray that surrounds me
Stabbing, searing, a spike in my ribs
It's almost over before it even began
Tilting my head, swiveling upon my axis, a doorway is now visible
The light!
So close, so agonizingly close, yet just out of reach
I can't give in, I won't give in
Throwing my limbs, inching myself, I will see what is to be seen
Threshold, beloved gods, a threshold
And then, the beyond encircles me
The flame within bursts forth, engulfed in iridescence
Yet, there is no pain, no burning, only relief
My arms are mine, my legs are mine, my body is mine
Whole again.
Tears once repressed make themselves known, gently gliding to the ground below
Verdant and beautiful, tall grass cradles me like a newborn
Relinquishing my comfort, standing now to peer about
A forest of mighty oak, ash, and willow, grace my eyes
Songs of flitting birds dance inside my ears, the sweetest of melodies
Flowers, sprouting hither and thither, a myriad of colors and smells
A primordial rainbow, outstretched upon this mellow grove
Meandering around, bathing in the glory of it all
At the center, I now find myself, greeted by one of each wood
Quizzical ash stands middle ground, stalwart

Willow, flourishing braids bellow in the breeze on the right
And oak, ever tall and strong, a bulwark against the gray behind me
Falling to my knees, tears of joy fall
As the wind blows by, I hear them, whispers in my soul
Silently I listen, to each passing word, each flowing phrase
Nearly dark, the light above now dimmed, I stand again
Facing south, the doorway nearly out of sight now
Heart rekindled, body free, and mind full, I stroll onward
Blessed Ash, give me your madness, so that I may see
Blessed Willow, give me your patience, so that I may persevere
Blessed Oak, give me your strength, so that I may strike down the blighted
Be with me on my journey home, and my journey back
Soon, my brothers and sisters in the walls will revel in your splendor

Arisen Sun

Pancake Waffen

Look through the trunks inside the wood—
Feel such warmth as if from fire:
Each branch, adorned with golden threads
Touched by the sun's desire.
Spreading its rays through every crook,
Grasping all creatures in its way,
Pulling them into its glorious softness
Of the light array.
Further and further it creeps along;
Letting the snow melt in its arms,
Becoming water for thirsty roots
Waking up to its warmth.
Sun-kissed branches spring forth buds
Who reach to hail their reviver—
Signaling their captivity's ending,
Rejoicing as survivor,
Drawing in nourishment up to the sky
Stalwart and strong they stand up.
Releasing their lifeblood to nourish the men—
Who slept—to stand and sup.
With passion ignited, the flood moves along,
Awaking both young and old;
Touching the river, embracing the people,
Taking all things in its hold.
Kissing the soil to reveal its treasure,
Which opens its palm with delight
To display petals of purple, pink, yellow, and red
And those of orange and white.
They spread their beauty in all its glory,
Beckoning bees and every bird
To wake up and behold the wondrous renewal;
To spread to those not yet stirred.
The buzz is relayed from bloom to bloom
By busybodies dressed in yellow
With black straps holding the bags they bear
To share with every fellow.
The joyful tidings engage every critter
To open their homes to the sun;
In turn they receive strength, resolve, motivation
And blessing all in one.
The nourishment of the children of men
Revives their hungry and parched lips.
The season of wonder begins anew
After winter's icy grip.

The Harvest Moon

Pancake Waffen

One day the cool breeze rolled in,
It chilled the breathless air,
The sun began to sink and wane
And brought a cool glare.
The north wind came and shared its strength—
Brought restlessness to all
And pulled in clouds, the sheeting rain
And opened up the fall.
The lively green of leaves turned dull,
Then shades of red and gold
Until the north wind razed the land
And swept away their hold.
The people hurried holding fast
To cloaks and hats and scarves
And readied for the harvesttime
For pumpkins to be carved.
First nights grew cold and tamed the heat;
The sun then settled low;
The rain and clouds frequented the sky,
And plants slowed down their growth.
With each and every day that passed,
The moon impressed its girth
Until the day of harvesttime
That marked the day of birth.
That night the folks all gathered round
In cloaks and hats of wool
And built the greatest fire of all
From woodsheds that were full.
The flames reached out beyond their height
And further still it went
Until it touched the ball of stone
Whose girth had long been spent.
The moon rose up—up high and bright—
The folks gazed to the sky;
A roar rose up, the crowd sprang round,
They danced, their feet were spry.
Throughout the night they carried on
With fire going down
Until the slightest embers glowed
Just at the break of dawn.
Exhausted, at the break of day—
Before the noon had come—
The quiet folks returned to bed;
The houses all grew mum.
Tonight beginning and the end;
The harvests would come in,
But summer's heat had moved away
And gone for its last spin.
Behold the glorious fruits of fall
To store for winter's cold!
The cellars, rafters, sheds, and house
Packed full to what they'd hold.
And far above in darkest night
The moon glowed strong and great—
It showed its thankfulness at them
For helping warm its state.

Heritage

Pancake Waffen

Look in the mirror—
See your lineage before you
Going back throughout the years.
See your ancestors shining
Their features within you—
Shaping your wrinkles and tears;
Molding your jawline,
Your nose, eyes, and forehead;
Smoothing your eyebrows and cheeks.
Silent caressing
As years drop behind you
Unite your lines, chin to peak.
Look deep in the iris—
Great-great-grandma reflected
Beckoning you to hold fast,
To seek your people
And carry their greatness
To future from thousand years past.
Pointing you to
The jewels you carry—
Beauty and love to pass on;
The next generation
To safeguard that treasure
Will be your daughters and sons.
Carry the torch
Your ancestors gave you;
Hold it high without fear and disgust.
Your heritage calls you—
As nature intended—
Your heirloom to progeny trust.

Touch Rain

Sarah Welborn

Install Windows. Nature background.
Pink and purple fields, no person in sight
to taint its beauty. In the room, look around,
only walls are my company, a lamp for light.
The only window is the one on my computer,
fans loud, running two troubleshooters.

Time this will take, I lean my head back
against my chair, my eyes closed, daydreams
creeping in. I hold my book, a hardback,
I lay on a beach chair, the sun's soft beams
kissing my skin, the waves of the ocean loud
as I turn the page, the sky clear with no clouds.

Children splash in the water, adults dance
under the sun, Spanish music entertaining
their fun. In my book, a field of romance,
the characters in another world, raining.
The waves lap the shore as their bodies sway
dancing for the rainy night, love underway.

The sound of a computer rumble jolts me out
of my daydream of my getaway. A moment's
pause and deep breath forces my burnout
to be seen, my inner eye. My opponent
is myself for taking on excessive tasks.
Remote work, a lie. A "modest" mask.

I find myself a prune even without the sun,
for working within the confines of a home
offers the idea one will not be overdone.
But a lie it was, for all will fall like Rome
if they do not give their body enough worship
and grant themselves rest with a trip.

Standing from my chair, a book from the shelf
lands in my hands. Computer left on, pages
are turned to dusted bookmark. Me and myself
shall enjoy this day, the storm outside, a stage
of thunder. The thunder and rain shall not sway
as I sit on my porch, soaking the nature of today.

To a Nurturing Nature

Esther Worthington

Smooth is the air caressing my cheeks,
Catching my clothes up with ardent haste,
Whipping the thoughts of clueless minds,
Into empty nothingness with its beats.

Birdsong echoing through fields unexplored,
Seems to be nature's epitaph to these days,
Soon to be of yore,
No more the children, no more, no more.

Once the chalk pit, once the mire,
Filled the young explorer's minds,
As armed with hearty stick and stone,
They faced down with courage, their invisible foe.

Bruised and black with mud streaks,
They charged through fields of corn,
Making fires and climbing trees,
And skimming stones by fours.

These were my grandfather's children,
No more the wood or field or spinney,
To hear their cries in harmony,
With blackbird, wren, and coo of pigeon.

Have nature's children died with bygone days?
Or do the still fields long for feet once more,
To pound upon her childless breast at play?
Calling out, no more the children, no more, no more!

As I turn my face upwards to lowering skies,
Down comes a pattering to close my eyes,
Am I the last of these, I wonder,
To recall my father's tales of childhood spent,
With such a mother to us all?

Even dead, it burns

Max Worthington

Like pollen to heavenly gusts,
We need not our bodies to live,
In the atrophy of ingots,
May He forgive.

Down tips of javelin,
Stains the beating memory of blood,
We march down towards the archer's tip,
Through eyes shortsighted,
Into hearts that weigh little.

Inciting a virtue hitherto unknown,
We may see the garland of prolix fall from
  necks,
Making humility our epithets.

Pay court to them of what we owe,
How pitiful, is this man I once was,
You, the king resenting honors bestowed.

Thank God,
Sunken pride makes buoyant fleets,
These men, out of tune to our paean,
Draw closer view of bitten shields,
To mountain and spear,
Nature extends her hand,
At last two peaks meet.

Yours is the strength that stretches time,
Down the east side crypt,
In ancient script, upon the shrine,
Among the yellowed pages in the reliquary,
From behind the chevrons on your shield,
Watch the tural overhead,
As arrows fly and spike the dead,
Us strangers to rout in field,
My throw lands true.

To satisfy glory,
This, our solemn goal which you deride,
Will be your downfall whispered by Oracles,
Of that we're glad to so abide.

So, to the brave few made privy,
To a beautiful death we march,
Bleed now, so your sons may bleed later,
May you sacrifice your mortal selves,
Immortalize the names,
The names that echo to the hills of Delphi,
For deeds so worthy of stone,
And through the valley of all eternity,
Up the Eurotas, our blood returns.

Spoils before gifts,
To the battles of once friends,
We are skytaled home.

I Have Never Felt So Gladly Small

Max Worthington

Our souls were swallowed whole,
By the endless brush,
While you sing with the birds,
And I raised my spear,
My feet began to disappear.
Leaves ripple the water,
Bright lights dull to mask your face,
And your look ripples my heart,
The world fell silent on our embrace,
You let out a smile to rival the Sun's.
Fog of mind conceals the trees,
Lifted only by a chilling breeze.

Blood in the barn,
Saturates the hay,
A lone figure made from stone,
Escorts us to our fate,
His cold heart kept warm,
By the Sun on his back.

But who will remember you,
When your last name is scribbled out,
And the wooden Cross rots?
No one. But no doubt,
The Earth you hath returned,
Shall save the soul you have discerned,
God alone and his creation,
Bask in the very fact of your existence.

Which One of You Dies with Him?

Max Worthington

With ancient words and fainting fires,
A shaman splits the fog,
So old the word in chant and choirs,
Begins our dead King's epilogue.

Thirty degrees goes the moon,
Sacred time lays claim,
Upon the idol's mystic runes,
It's written by your name.

The wolves of Wotan stand haught,
No prose to claim or sordids worn,
Their pyre halts the Sun,
Lain across the twisted cross,
At last her time has come,
Branched out like trees,
The antlers reach into the light,
A group of women on their knees,
Prepared by priests and acolytes.

"Which one of you dies with him?"
Securing your branch on the tree of life,
With held hands engulfed by black flames,
Stepping forward, escorted by the knife,
Feeding the fire that sustains,
A ground made fertile once before,
By the pillar built by painted druids,
Just one step more,
Into eternity and sacred lore.

You'll find them serried on the banks,
Hidden beneath their bear skins,
Veiled women, one strong amongst them,
Attuned to holy ears,
To beating drums and wailing tears,
One steps out and volunteers.

Spirits revolt from their chests,
Raptured to her king,
Berserk on a delicate instinct,
As the praise and eulogy sings.

Venus flows through her veins,
Royal blood freed from its chains,
But a queen born to die,
From a glow so strong it fades the paint,
Of the blood-red decking on which they lie.

Lifting up the knife that takes her,
A bronze blade with an amber hilt,
His frayed cloak slips,
Her eyes change color at the sight,
Of the author of her death.

The orchestra of rain,
Extinguishes the flame,
Do not mourn her,
For Venus smiles,
Still hesitating on an eternal moment,
Falling into his arms, as a child.

Bring forth the beast,
Lay spear and sword down facing
  east,
Beside his head lay golden beakers,
A once mighty equidae slain,
Not loud enough the whisper,
Of supple words to ease the pain.

Her blood drips down,
Mixing with the equus',
Quenching a thirsty soil.

Stand tall against the shadow,
Kill them with the light,
Aglow the torches burning bright.

Reanimating once more,
Through the cloud powdered red,
Her hands stretch out in guidance,
Until the smoke reaches the gods.

Violence is ritual,
Into myth we crawl,
Our eyes meet, she weeps no more.

A Gull Calls Me

Anonymous

a name I do not recognize like I've pressed the
volume button on my computer
I imagine the salt leaking through the circuits and boards
I imagine a ship preserved in the brackish water
and gulls circling like vultures to some dead
mystery
I imagine myself dissolving like citric acid into the foam
my bones
my soul touching that boat
like it is a part of my own past
capsized years ago with what others said
but now I am nothing that means anything to words or waves
only part of the swirling sound that keeps circling
circling

In the morning I return to my womb
a cocoon
of seaweed littered with snails
my body too human for my entity
feels like you could peel the salty film
a paper lantern tomato

In the afternoon I admire the
terracotta potted mulch, filled with weeds
weeks of their spirals
Invasive

I run the coarse sand through my hair
touching things I thought were gone
pulling up roots and roots
to admire their growth

Sunny Day

Anonymous

You took your first steps in oak leaves.
Winter-weathered toes graced in waves of gold.
With the weight of wind, you land on your knees.
Up once more you go, bracing against the cold.

With a smile to set the sun in order,
And through rays of light you look.
By days you grow ever older.
Soon enough you will know the love it took.

From a mother yet unknown to a child.
Still, she holds you up.
Below a gravestone covered in the wild.
Her name smeared on your sippy cup.

One day we will have a talk.
Then you will know from whom you learned to walk.

In the Valley of the Perseid

Anonymous

The night shift prowls
up and down that road
that's not for us.
We don't drive
or cruise,
we roam.
We roam over the hayfields on
hillsides
overlooking
our home town.

Too young to care it's cold.
It's dark.
It's Friday night.
We look down on Main Street.
Main Street
and it's one blinking light.

We catch a scent of change
and turn
and chase.
Not tripping, not stumbling,
but miraculously falling,
falling out of time
as the civilized world
is lost behind,
behind the rise.

We could run
for eternity
but for the smell
of sagebrush and pine
that reminds,
that we,
we on the earth must tarry.

Into the glade
we settle, we lay.
I turn my head
and see her in the grass,
her arms thrown wide.
Her face turns to mine
and in that moment,
in that moment I die.

In the next breath
I resurrect
knowing all,
yet still surprised.

Looking up, the stars,
the stars are falling.

Honorable Mention in Poetry

Field of Vision

Kathryn Avalon

Fathom the sky, no weighty burden
under which to kneel
but a clarion call to rise;
by virtue of birthright
enthroned, crowned by alpenglow,
holding hallowed sovereign reign.

There is no falsehood in the wild wood,
no deception in the dappled glade.
A feather adrift conveys
its bearers' course—
slight shifts chronicle currents in flux,
fluid whims of the winds
born on quickening wings.

Omen and consequence abide in all things.
Within the dormant seed dwells
both ruin and rise. Swelling fruit and tender blooms
transmuted by decay bestow
their final offering: rot
reborn as fertile clay.

Aspirants who set a course
toward the zenith first send forth
deep roots. Abyssal veins penetrate fertile murk;
delving down, they seek untainted wellsprings from which to draw up might.
Grounded spirits bound for empyrean heights alight
from sturdy bearings, cast hearts
pulsing with the cadence of perennial ascension
aloft like crimson banners cleaving wide the vaulted sky.

From this conquered vantage
overlooking boundless fields one beholds oneself
revealed
within a profusion of emergent blades.
A skyward spire
rooted and raised in the verdant confluence between apex and abyss,
occurrence and oblivion—
no less vital than a sunlit jewel of dew
crowning the ephemeral bloom
unfurling in the meadow at first light.

Honorable Mention in Poetry

The Mountain Kings

Edward Delacroix

Crownèd high above the honeygold plains
Stand the forested Emperors of old
Keeping watch over their immense domains,
Forever proud and defiantly bold.

Within their castles I long to linger
And make merry with members of their court.
From hulking Sir Bear and grand Duke Badger
To the bardic birds of every sort.

Atop the hawk-high parapeted peaks
To beneath the gaping dungeon caverns,
Great beauty lies for those who come and seek,
And adventure waits ’round every turn.

Venturing into the Mountain King’s hall,
This knight sallies forth, heeding its noble call.

SECOND PLACE WINNER IN POETRY

Gnostic Nigel

Hereward

Gnostic Nigel lived in the land
of Breezewood, PA, a barren place
lacking a single speck of grass or greenery.
He wasted his weekends on the web
arguing with other idiots.
Worse still, when he wasn't waging at Wendy's
he stuck his sniffer straight into screeds,
political plans,
grizzly grimoires,
and toxic tomes;
or, at least, so he said:
in truth he just tasted the foul fruits of Twitter,
having been hooked by a hoard of hucksters
selling cerebral swill to saps.
He'd figured it out, the follies of a fallen,
sick and sinful
wanting world.
We'd been put apart from pleroma,
severed from sophia,
by the dastardly devilings of the Demiurge.
"I can't believe the Demiurge did this"
he'd hem and haw
"It's horrible.
"I need to achieve gnosis
"to escape this hellscape.
"Everything is imperfect and evil."

Locked away in his lair, lurking,
doom-scrolling, deeply-sighing,
he'd woefully waste his weeks,
offing the hours into the trash,
accomplishing no actions.
But on one bright and blooming day
(*not that he knew it to be; the shades were shut*),
while scrolling the sin-stack, he spied a thread
that offended his angry eyes.
It was filled with fancies of fairness,

hope, happiness, and heroism
on display, dashing and daring.
Nigel's nuts twisted in offense and outrage!
How dare they do this display of defiance!
(*Didn't those saps know that life sucks?*)
His fingers aflutter like flame through a forest,
clicking and clacking, creating keyboard-curses,
posts were produced, arguments offered.
Sitting there smug and smirking,
he thought that he'd won things!
But suddenly, a third-party reply,
from some freakish fellow going by @grimraven9:
"*fkn fgt when was the last time you went outsied?*"
This crude curse caught him off guard;
when WAS the last time that he had went outside?
An unusual occurrence: he was embarrassed!
This series-of-tubes stranger had set him sore.
A long look in the mirror made him amind
to prove this prick wrong.

But where would he start this sithe of self-improvement?
First, he'd hop on outside, into the heat
of the day; that'd be a swell start.
As the side door slid open and he stepped outside,
a charming breeze blew beside his cheeks
and the smell of pines passed his snout.
The highway surf sighed a gentle hum in the distance,
and to its tune the sparrows sang softly.
Maybe life wasn't such a loss?

But Nigel was gnawed at by the feeling of being flabby,
and worse, being a weak wuss.
He set himself to it; he'd fix this fuss.
He joined a gym, and got to work getting gains.
At first he feared faring
to the local house of heaving,
(*'twas owned by a ginger-headed juicer
and filled with the sort of souls that you'd expect*),
and after all
he wasn't the sort to want to get sweaty or sore.

But, fastly he found
that the ache of offering up oneself to the iron
was pleasing, not painful;
fierce, yet fun;
tough, yet true;
and all around awesome.
And, to his happiness,
the locals were lovely lads
who'd never do naught but aid a newcomer!
Our hero, he honed himself into a hunk,
accumulating control over his body,
like a barefaced lord brought to leadership
of his fiefdoms, overseeing his family, friends, and folk,
coming to mastery of his kin, kith, and kine;
an eminent archon emitting order
like light launching from the sun.

And while working on his worth
in the hoisting-house,
a thought threaded into our thane's head:
a baron needs boys,
a count needs comrades,
a lord needs lads,
and a king needs contubernales.
A man requires a männerbund to make himself mighty!
But finding fellow travelers is no facile feat!
Such solemn sojourners are often sworn to secrecy:
sound and steady side-souls
don't deem it deedworthy
to make their manners and mind known.
Luckily for our lad,
there are thanes of theedhood happy to help.
Pool parties aplenty, folkbuilders abound,
every group's got a guy whose goal is to gather
fine fellows together and fasten their friendships.
Our blossoming baron burnished his boldness,
made contact with a man of meeting up,
who introduces him to men of equal mind.
And together these mighty men
did what men do!

Hiking, hoisting,
boxing, bragging about babes,
and deep discussions of tabletop gaming.

But the bragging about babes
made our man long for love.
He and his bros set about bagging him a broad.
Our protagonist had proffered himself on programs,
attempting on tinder to take a gal out,
but little luck had he had,
ending up empty armed,
or worse, walking away with a worthless wench!
But a sincere friend had a fair sister,
with eyes of blue and hair of blonde,
and knew that Nigel was a noble knight,
and the two were set up
(*We'll leave how their love-ways went to another work;*
such tales would take too much time.)

But, as an astute ear might understand,
Nigel worked at Wendy's, and women aren't wooed
by wagies who wallow in low-worth.
So, while looking for ladies
Nigel took action against his underemployment.
Job hunting is hard work, and we have
to compress the recounting of that chronicle,
but his friends were there for him,
and helped him hash out a resume,
(*And a CV and cover letter, fucking HR boomers*)
and acquire employment opportunities.
But best of all
his mates made the search less maddening.
With a new morning meander to employment,
Nigel saw more of his city
and realized that Breezewood isn't that bad
(*the whole hamlet isn't just that one meme image*).

Our friend Gnostic Nigel found
that winning catfights online can't compare
to actually winning what life's about.

He'd gotten rekt nicely by @grimraven9,
but logging off is a blessed balm
that wipes away all e-wins and online losses.
Excuses are easy,
but blaming your own vileness on villains
gets you no gains.
Gnostic Nigel now knew
that learning a life lesson had enlightened him
and that this was the true gift from Sweet Sophia.
Silicon sand castles are cast aside by the surf
no matter how mighty you make them.
Online achievements, they are
like stones sent soaring into the sea,
splashing into the spray,
and then sinking down into the silt, unseen.
But that which is real, bonded by brotherhood
floats atop the froth
and is carried across the main.

First Place Winner in Poerty

Unveiling

Jacob Hersant

The standard of falsehood ascended; its reign over nations extended;
Obscured—the decline of your strength near a century ago
Has hidden the truth from the rest of your kind: in the fighting the best of
Your race were destroyed by your enemies then in a blow
So painful, today you're still reeling. The problem before you of healing
The damage inflicted obstructed by multitude bound
To specious acquaintance and being: the many dependent on seeing
The shadows of sight and on hearing the echoes of sound.
Entailing unnecess'ry lenience of life and exceptional convenience,
You needn't traverse far to soak in the splendorous joys
Of seeing the fury of battle, of hearing the foe's dying rattle,
In comfort and safety at home idly playing with toys.
Your captor is wanting you weak for his sake, and too frightened to speak for
Yourself and your brothers and sisters; your frailty's his might.
He wants you to live in seclusion, elated in carefree illusion;
No threat to his rule—he your lord, you his slave without fight;
Compelled to survive in an ocean of lies upon lies, your devotion
Defeat, your involvement, enslavement; to darken your view
And make you submit is his yearning. He bans any question concerning
His rectitude; merely to ask is the biggest taboo.
He solely permits you misusing your God-given gifts, and abusing
Your essence for meaningless fun and a journey of ease.
He'll actualize people according to only his plan, by rewarding
Desired behavior, by barring the person who flees.
Reality gladly neglected and nothing remotely suspected—
Naive—you are driven and duped to the darkest disgrace.
His glow's not for truth or for beauty; fulfilling his arrogant duty
To pacify tense populations with spectacle base
And blinding amounts to its end and its limit: its power to bend and
To shape sensibility, value, and worldview towards
His falsehood. Your senseless consuming is surely and steadily grooming
You. Master without the command of innum'rable swords
And servient soldiers to hold them, he needs only method to mold them—
The masses I mean—into following orders by choice.
The wandering intellect spacious; its craving for fancies voracious;
Invasive beliefs are implanted in minds by his voice;

Oblivious children immersing within his false world—not coercing
Through terror—too spineless to dominate men underfoot;
Instead, he can fashion a panic about the pure feelings organic
To man and replace them with mangled opinions. He put
This thinking in place for submitting the people to yoke. He is spitting
Upon you; he sneeringly laughs at you mired within
The marvelous maze he created. He's keeping you servile and sated
Where nothing has meaning, where nothing is virtue or sin.
Delusion compared to the wonder—the fearsome unfathom'ble under
Which everything rests—cannot move us the effortless way
The latter can, for the Creator, His skill and His genius are greater
Than that which He made and the works they produce every day.
No need to reflect on creations of man as one would machinations
Of God, for the former was built, understood and designed
By men as a mere imitation upon the Allfather's foundation:
The worth of man's craft has the splendor of nature behind.
The priests and philosophers reckoned the minuscule feats of man second
Behind the one feat, which began the whole tale in which men
Create their subordinate stories—the real and imagin'tive glories—
Enjoyed and endured by all beings contained in His pen.
Real life is about the unveiling of truth; entertainment entailing
A lack of significance—wasting your time with fake deeds,
Fake content, fake lives—these excursions can only be doltish diversions
From what's of the greatest import: the real world and its needs.
God gave you your strength for the seizure of life, not existing for leisure
Alone. So why put so much time into frivolous things?
Abandoning purposeless pleasure pursuing, and learning to treasure
The genuine joy that authentic accomplishment brings
Is crucial for flourishing; wear your achievements as armor and spare your
Proud ancestors' souls of regret; do not tarnish their name
And wantonly waste your essential ability; natural potential
Engendered by lineage ought to be utilized. Aim
For virtue, establish your worth in this world, and remember your birth in
This age of deception and idleness brings you the chance
To honor your blood to the greatest degree. Disregard all the latest
Discouragement spoken by enemy liars; advance—
Secure in belief and undaunted—or else you'll be pestered and haunted
By thoughts that you wasted your singular shot at this life.
Discover, embody, and struggle for truth. Do not carelessly juggle
The countless conflicting distortions; your country is rife

With folly and vile superstition. Adhere to your doctrine and mission.
Your moment is coming; the fury is breaking its cage;
The squalor and shame will be shattered; the horrible madness that mattered
Before cannot flee the inferno of riotous rage
That boils in your blood; the demise of the wicked and decadent lies of
This system's approaching. Partake in the glorious growth
Of National Socialist actions against the abundant distractions,
With White men and movements prepared for the fight and the oath.
The sunrise's genuine gleaming awak'ning the multitude dreaming;
The lightning igniting the lies with its terrible blast;
Continuous truthful production and falsehood's perpetual destruction
Affirm what is real cannot be overcome or surpassed.

Short Stories

The Prussian Hussar

Achromous

It was near the second decade of the twentieth century. The Kaiser had fled his old empire, for since the onslaught of the Great War had wrought its cruel machinations and satisfied its greed, the country had become a decaying shadow of its former grandeur.

Within the broken borders, Berlin still remained. It was a city whose lights never went out and whose noise never ceased. On a loud street where engines could always be heard, there was an old apartment that was not given care and was therefore rented cheaply. A glance about would have proved to any visitor that the land owner's ideas of cleanliness were by no means rigid. Little if any attention was given to repairs, only replacements. These *replacements* were never of quality or durability, and thus the cycle began again.

In one of the small, old rooms on the second floor, a boy had just returned from school and was gazing out of the window with his arms on the sill, watching for the return of his father.

The room was rather bare, but the good fire necessitated by the winter season was not wanting, and the plain boarding of the floor showed itself no stranger to scrubbings. In the stillness, a clock hanging on the wall ticked loudly.

On this day, the boy waited with particular excitement, for it was his birthday. For the occasion, his father had promised they would have a fine plate of roulade, made with beef, vegetables, and a wonderful sauce, which had previously always been made by the mother. Since her death, the cooking lay predominantly in the son's hands, for when the father returned, he wanted only to rest after a long day of toil.

The boy started up with joy when he saw his father turn the corner of their street. Knowing his son would be there, the father looked up at the window with a smile.

Rushing down to help his father with the bags he carried, he saw that among the parcels was a box as long as his arm and wrapped in plain paper. On their way up the steps inside, they were stopped by an old woman who lived nearby. "Many pleasant greetings, little Friedrich," she addressed the boy with the warmth of her character. Her gentle voice bore a hint of the Austrian dialect. "Knowin' it's a special day, I've somethin' for you and your dear father." As she spoke, she held up her hand for them to wait. In several moments she returned from her room holding a small basket with a white cloth over the top.

Taking it in his hands, Friedrich could feel there was something warm inside. Upon lifting the cloth only slightly, he saw a fine batch of fresh Linzer cookies, their sweet scent bringing color to his pale cheeks. Neither he nor his father could ever refuse the buttery shortbread with a raspberry filling.

After both Friedrich and his father gave gracious thanks, they headed to their own humble lodging. The father offered to aid in the cooking, but Friedrich took the remaining bags from him and bid the weary man rest his legs and smoke his pipe. At his son's insistence, he could not help but smile as he sat back in his old chair, setting aside the box wrapped in plain paper. He had seen the boy look questioningly at the box but said nothing.

Contently smoking his tobacco, he put up his feet and slowly closed his eyes, folding his hands on his lap as he listened to the noise of their small kitchen.

When the meal was ready, they both sat at the wooden table under the dim gas lamp. The portions were not large, but to their meager means it was a feast worthy of the Kaiser himself. As they ate, the father again noticed Friedrich gaze with wondering eyes at the mysterious box.

"Would you like to open it?" the father asked with a smile.

Friedrich quickly paused as he bit into one of the cookies, and his father laughed as he brought the box to the table. "Come then, old Fritz." He pushed it toward the boy. His father had always addressed him in this way, reminiscent of how Friedrich II of Prussia had been called by his people. Having been told of the old Kaiser's exploits, the boy delighted in the name.

Carefully undoing the paper and plain string, Friedrich opened the wooden box and was stunned when he saw what lay in the soft wood shavings. It was the large nutcracker the boy had gazed at in one of the shop windows, but with several alterations made by his father.

Made of dense wood, the nutcracker stood tall and resolute in the dark uniform of the Schwarze Legion, who had served under "The Black Duke" of Braunschweig.

With gentle hands Friedrich took the figure from the box and set it upon the table, brushing away the few shavings. The figure was of the Hussar cavalry, garbed in black, a blue-collared dolman, and even a black pelisse with a white fur trim, which was soft to the touch. Upon the head of white hair was a tall, black, military cap with a Totenkopf at its front, and on the face was a pair of pale blue eyes below dark brows and a fine moustache. Completing the dignified figure, one of the wooden hands lay at the silver hilt of a fine sword. In every inch of the character could be observed the painstaking detail the father had rendered.

Gladly seeing how happy the boy was in looking over each aspect, the father took from his pocket a small paper bag filled with nuts. "Try his teeth," he said as he pulled a walnut from the bag. "His strength lies not only in his looks."

Raising the lever, Friedrich placed the walnut in the nutcracker's mouth and hesitated.

"Give it a firm hit," his father urged.

Holding his breath, Friedrich hit the lever, and the great teeth easily cracked the hard shell.

With relief, the spoils were eaten and Friedrich took up another nut. Now trusting the strength of the Hussar, he again and again crushed the shells until none remained. Whether large or small, they were no match for the power of the wooden jaw and its pristine teeth.

Immensely satisfied with his soldier's efficiency, Friedrich wiped away any hint of crumb or debris and set the figure at the edge of the mantel, allowing it to have watch over the entire room.

Once the dishes had been cleaned, Friedrich and his father prepared for bed with their hunger and hearts well filled. Their home being only a single room, from his bed Friedrich could still see the Hussar in the flickering firelight. Though it cast ominous shadows, the boy thought only that he could sleep soundly, knowing it might frighten any creatures in the night intending harm to his father or himself.

* * *

"Damned devils!" A voice suddenly awoke Friedrich in the night, when the fire was but a soft glow of embers.

Friedrich rose with the covers pulled close as he looked about, but saw no one. It could not have been his father, for he lay in his own bed nearby, still deep in slumber.

Thinking perhaps he had simply dreamed or heard the noise of the outside, he laid his head back down. However, his brows drew together when he saw in the low light that his Hussar was no longer upon the mantel. Rising again, he pushed away the covers and went to the fireplace to see the figure was indeed gone.

"Do not be alarmed," said a man's voice in lowered tones.

When Friedrich turned, he could not perceive anyone in the darkness, and he began to feel ill at ease.

"Forgive my height, young man."

Friedrich looked down in utter astonishment upon seeing the nutcracker no longer stoic, but full of motion, with its sword drawn at its side. The blade was doused in deep red, which slowly dripped onto the floor.

"I beg your pardon," said the Hussar as he took a handkerchief from inside his inner pocket and cleaned the blade.

"You. . . ." Friedrich was at a loss for words.

"Speak not too loudly, my friend. I should hate to awaken your good father." The Hussar sheathed his blade.

Friedrich stared into the clear blue eyes with amazement.

"Were it another, I may call your staring an impertinence, young man."

"I . . . sorry, I didn't mean to stare," whispered Friedrich.

"Quite understandable, for I am certainly not the usual gentleman you may encounter. Now come a bit closer so we might speak."

Friedrich tentatively knelt down to the Hussar, his hands at his knees.

"No need to be nervous, young man. I am no enemy; rather the contrary, in fact."

"Why was . . . why was your sword covered in blood?" Friedrich's voice was barely perceptible.

"Is that what troubles you? Put your mind at ease, for it is only the blood of the rats and vermin. You have quite a plague of them about this wretched place."

Friedrich looked at the figure with surprised realization; he had not heard the rodents scratching and scurrying in the night as he usually did. The walls and floors had all been silent.

"I must apologize for my shout, however," began the Hussar. "It was not my intention to wake you. I lost myself in the skirmish."

"Who are you? How's this possible?"

The Hussar's eyes appeared to laugh. Though his teeth were perpetually in view, they too seemed to take on a warm amusement. "I am Ulrich von Blücher. As for how this may have occurred, that is rather a question for powers far above my status."

"Blücher." Friedrich's brows rose. "Are you then. . . . Then you must be the. . . . You defeated Napoléon."

Ulrich gave a humble bow of his head. "On our fourth battle. A pity the three before did not end in my favor." He spoke rather with fervor than regret. "When I returned to service after retirement, I certainly troubled that stout Frenchman. I would have remained in Paris, but my condition demanded I return to the beloved homeland." The quieted passion of the commander appeared unshakable, making a great impression upon the boy. "After it all, Oxford University even granted me an honorary doctorate. You know, I have always thought if I am suddenly a doctor, they should at least make Marshal Gneisenau an apothecary. For if I write the prescription, he provides the pills."

Friedrich smiled and held back his laughter. "But your uniform . . . it's not blue, nor of the red Hussars."

Ulrich glanced down at the black garments. "They were at first the usual colors, but your father made an alteration. I recall him stating it is your favorite."

"Yes . . . that's true. I've always wished I could've joined the Schwarze Legion."

Ulrich appeared to smile again. "You do not think it grim?"

"I've always thought it looked dignified, and might unsettle the French."

Ulrich gave a low laugh. "A fine attitude. Now you must get back to bed, young man, although it is perhaps impossible with that infernal racket." Ulrich looked to the window. "I recall the noise of Berlin, but nothing so *pungent*. By the by, your father called you *old Fritz*, but I assume you are not the old Kaiser sent to again say '*Blücher can take himself to the devil.*'"

The boy smiled. "Well . . . you did write a rather harsh letter of resignation."

"The kindness in your tone is reassuring. Now off to bed. It is cold, and I am robbing you of your rest. Put some cotton in your ears, and you shall perhaps not hear that damnable blathering outside."

When Friedrich lay in his bed with the covers pulled up to his nose, he still looked upon the nutcracker, hoping what he saw standing nearby with such animation was not a dream.

* * *

When the light of the morning streamed in, Friedrich opened his eyes wearily but sat up quickly. With disappointment, he gazed at the mantel. The nutcracker was unmoving and in the position he had put it previously.

After rising, he was surprised to see his father still in bed. The father's eyes opened very slowly, and his face was stricken with ill tones. The boy wanted eagerly to recount to his father the events of the night but thought better of it.

"Do not worry," said the father. The effort of speaking weighed on him. "I only need a bit of rest for today. . . . Go on to school, old Fritz. Do not neglect your studies on my account."

Worry did not leave the boy. "I'll stay home, father, and take care of you."

The father gave a tired smile. "Please, Friedrich. It will be a weight off my mind to know your education was not interrupted by my own mistake. . . . I pushed my limits too far recently and need only a bit of rest. Put your mind at ease and go on, dear old Fritz."

With hesitation, Friedrich dressed and obeyed his father, pausing at the door to look back for a time before heading out.

The day went by in a blur, for Friedrich's mind was elsewhere. Having been a quiet child, the instructors paid his disposition no mind. There was only one among them who noticed the change in him; Professor Götz stood out as his history instructor. Many of the boys could get away with their tricks or attitudes in the other classes, but not in history. Professor Götz understood their temperaments, and through the firmness of his character and the wonderous accounts of his knowledge, he had slowly earned their respect, and perhaps their fear. For he knew their games and always gave his students two choices: war or peace. He had once admitted this was because in his own childhood, he had been quite the rapscallion.

When lessons were over, Professor Götz approached Friedrich with concern, and the boy admitted he felt uneasy leaving his father in poor health.

"Have you sent for a doctor?" asked the professor.

"We . . . could never afford that, sir."

Götz gave a solemn nod. "If prices continue rising as they are, I suspect few will be able to afford anything rather soon." After thoughtfully twisting his moustache between his fingers, he spoke again. "I will stop by tomorrow evening. It has been a long time since your father and I had a chance to reminisce about the old days."

"Thank you, sir, that's very good of you."

With a smile, Götz gave a firm pat to the boy's shoulder, and the younger soon departed with haste. Watching the retreat, Götz's brows drew together with pity.

Friedrich rushed with such haste that even when the old Austrian woman greeted him, he only paused a moment to address her. Despite the hurry, he stilled when he opened the door and caught his breath. Seeing his father still lying in bed, he closed the door and went to the bedside. A coldness crept over him when he saw his father's face. It was as pale and still as marble. "Father. . . ." he whispered.

There was no answer.

Friedrich's satchel fell from his shoulder as he went to sit upon the bed. With shaking hands, he reached out to touch his father's profile but soon clenched his fists and buried his face into the unmoving shoulder.

Mourning his father's passing, Friedrich did not realize when the sun had set and that the nutcracker had come to stand by his side. Ulrich did not bear his usual temperament but one of resigned contemplation.

It was only when Ulrich took a step that Friedrich turned his head to regard him with reddened but dry eyes. "Why'd he have to die?" he asked in a broken voice.

Ulrich was silent for several moments. "All of us must leave this world at one time or another, but it is not the end, dear boy. Simply because we can no longer hear them as before, it does not mean they are lost. Your good father has taken his place among your ancestors, and a part of them yet lives. For you are his son and their descendant. You are of their very flesh and blood. In your memory and your very bones, they remain in this world."

Friedrich gave a bitter smile and ran his sleeve across his eyes. "What am I to do now, Herr Blücher? I can't leave him like this. . . ."

"Say your farewells, and in the morning you must inform an authority. I am grieved to say I can do little for you, as I cannot move about in the day. . . . Regardless, we shall make do. Know that you are not alone."

At that moment there was a rapturous knocking upon the door, which made the boy flinch. Immediately he looked to Ulrich. "That must be the landlord," said Friedrich. "He always knocks like that." His gaze fell. "Father was supposed to have the rent today. . . . We've been delaying too long."

When the landlord yelled, Friedrich looked to Ulrich once more.

"Take me up as if I were only of wood young man, and should the brute become disagreeable, I will certainly settle the matter."

With the utmost respect, Friedrich carefully took the nutcracker in his arms. When they came to the door, Friedrich held the nutcracker tight in one arm. "You have nothing to fear," Ulrich whispered. "Set forth boldly, my friend."

With stiff shoulders, Friedrich opened the door to see the wide landlord holding his lamp with agitation. "What's the damned delay?" he spat out. The old man was not at all pleasing to the eyes. Age had withered him in a terrible manner, and his shrewdness lay in every wrinkle of his thin eyes.

Immediately pushing past the boy, the landlord went to the stilled father and made curses and complaints of varying degrees. When he looked to the boy, he regarded him as if he were a hideous pestilence and demanded the boy remove himself.

"But . . . my father. Where will I—"

"You can go to blazes. All you and that father of yours have given me is trouble. I give you a roof over your skulls and when I ask for a meager rent you again and again demand more time. No longer, boy; now get out. You've given me enough to do with a damned corpse. He'll release a mighty stench at any moment and ruin the place."

"You sniveling wretch!" Ulrich shouted. Friedreich felt the nutcracker's hand go for his blade, but the boy tightened his grip about him when the landlord quickly looked to them with fury and surprise.

The landlord had heard the firm tone of a man and could not believe it had come from the boy. Enraged, the landlord headed for Friedrich, intending to put him out and perhaps kick him down the stairs, but Friedrich avoided his clasp, running past the door. He was only spurred on when the landlord began yelling every profanity under the sun. One of these threats included an accusation that the boy had murdered the father, followed by a shrill demand for the police.

Outside, Friedrich took only a moment to wrap the nutcracker in the front of his coat. The boy's shaking hands did not escape Ulrich's notice. "Do not rush too hastily, young man," said Ulrich, his head just above the boy's collar. "That reptile cannot follow easily, for he has far more baggage on his bones than you or I."

Friedrich did not run but walked briskly down the street, his mind in a daze. "He said I. . . ." His voice was strained.

"Pay no attention to that nonsense."

"But what about father . . . what'll he do with him?"

"Worry not. It is more than likely the scoundrel shall simply put him in the hands of the authorities."

"But he accused me of. . . ."

"If they have any sense, those officers will simply ignore the raving imbecile. Now, where are you taking us, young man?"

Friedrich had gone down a short alleyway and into the dark remains of a shop that had been closed and stripped of its property. The only light came from the lamps of the street streaming through the crevices in the boarded-up windows and the roofing that had deteriorated. "I came here when mother died," whispered Friedrich with a hollow voice.

Behind the old counter, Friedrich dropped himself down and stared silently at the empty shelves before him.

Releasing himself from the confines of the boy's coat, Ulrich came to stand before him. "Keep that coat close about you. I shall see if I might find something in this hovel to warm you."

When Ulrich had gone, Friedrich drew up his knees and hid his face in his arms. Though he did his best to conceal it, his small frame shook, and his hands clenched tightly at his sleeves.

After several minutes, Ulrich returned with a small lit candle in one hand and a box of matches under his arm. "No blankets, I am afraid, but we may have a little light." He placed the candle on the floor, but the boy had fallen asleep.

Hearing the rustle of the small creatures that claimed the place as their home, Ulrich made quick work of them throughout the night, hoping to alleviate at least one trouble that could have plagued the boy. Upon returning to the low candle, he saw that the boy shivered in the cold night, trying his best to curl into his own warmth, but to little avail.

Regarding the boy in silence for a time, an idea came to Ulrich, and he was swift to act upon it.

* * *

When Friedrich suddenly heard a crackling, his eyes shot open and he was surprised to feel a warmth at his back, which faced away from the wooden counter. There was also a dark jacket with a white fur trim about his shoulders. Turning quickly, he saw the blackened woodcracker in a pile of flames that had burned through the majority of the chilled night. "Blücher!" he called with desperation. "Not you . . . not you. . . ." Friedrich bent low over his knees to the floor, his strained face in his hands.

"What are you weeping for?" asked a man's voice from beside him.

Friedrich recognized the voice of Ulrich, but when he looked to the side, he saw not the nutcracker but a pair of high, black boots. Raising his head, Friedrich saw the human face of Ulrich, who bore a youthful smile about him. The dark uniform was no longer of simplified detail but rendered in its full grandeur. "I must say, it is rather odd to know one is over seventy, but see in the looking glass a man not a day over thirty!"

Friedrich was at a loss as several tears fell from his weary eyes.

Ulrich bent down to the boy, pushing his sword forward to sit properly. "Come now." He shifted the pelisse about the boy's form and wiped away the tears. "Do away with tears, for we have travel ahead of us."

"Travel?"

"Yes, dear boy." Ulrich stood and offered his hand to Friedrich. "I have had the opportunity to look about this Berlin." He pulled the boy to his feet and took his military cap from the countertop. "It is not at all what I remember and not the sort of place a fine boy should spend his better years." He placed his tall cap upon the boy, and it sat back loosely on the small head. "We shall first obtain a horse."

With that, Ulrich began to lead the boy from the shop and into the early daylight of the streets. Ulrich being dressed in the uniform of old, and going forth with a resolute stride, the people of the city often stared or whispered among one another.

Feeling so many eyes on them, Friedrich felt uneasy, but Ulrich took his hand and led the way proudly.

Among those who stared was a shabby man who had obviously indulged in the bottle and swayed into their path with brazen scorn. Immediately Ulrich had put himself between the scoundrel and the boy. The man's words were slurred and rank, his anger spurred by Ulrich's disregard for his insults and taunts. One of the detestable words thrown at him was in regard to a political party that Ulrich was unfamiliar with.

"In heaven's name, I do believe you have thrown out not only your liver but the brain alongside."

Enraged, the man had moved to strike Ulrich, but his reaction was swifter. Ulrich struck his elbow across the man's face. When the drunk fell and tried to rise, Ulrich gave him a firm hit in the head with the end of his scabbard, rendering the man groaning and rolling on the streetside before scurrying away.

"No matter the age, there are the scoundrels and pests," Ulrich spoke with a smile as he glanced at the boy. "With any luck, these buttons of mine are of genuine gold and we might set about purchasing a horse."

To the pair's relief, the buttons were indeed of real gold, and with the money, Ulrich was able to obtain a horse of decent figure. However, no equipment was offered to them, so they rode simply with halter and rope. The simplicity was in the horse's favor, for it meant there would be no metal bit to tear at its mouth in pain.

With the boy in front, they galloped for some time, and when out of the city they took to a calm walk. The air was fresh, and the surroundings were not of stone or metal, but green and wood. The only sounds were that of the wind and the rhythmic ponding of the horse's hooves.

Having spent the day on the roads and paths, Friedrich had slowly fallen into a pleasant sleep.

* * *

In the cloud of wakefulness, Friedrich felt they no longer rode along, but that Ulrich carried the boy in his arms and set him upon a soft pelt of fur.

When Friedrich opened his eyes, there stood the horse grazing contently near without rope or halter. Looking about him slowly, he realized he lay upon a wooden bench under the roof's overhand of a fine country home. Neither the black pelisse nor military cap were about, but a woolen blanket tucked close around him. "Blücher?" He said quietly as he rose.

He suddenly heard the dropping of a metal pail that had been filled with cow's milk. An old woman stared at the boy before her, and the unfamiliar horse. "Good morning," she began, "where did you come from?" Though wrinkled, her face bore a kindly aspect, with a brightly embroidered headscarf tied below her chin. The woolen coat she wore was simple and dark, hanging over a long skirt of deep blue and a pair of well-used leather boots.

"I. . . . Have you seen the Hussar in black? With dark hair and a moustache?"

"Can't say I have, young man. There are no Hussars here, only men of the soil."

Friedrich's face fell, and the old woman took up her bucket and went to him. "Why don't you come inside for some warm breakfast. My husband and I would be very glad to have you."

His hunger growing, Friedrich could not refuse the kindly old woman. Inside, the house of deep wood was serene and warmed not only by the fireplace but also by an old oven of stone whose heat could in time fill the entire household. It was all a comfort of home that Friedrich had not known since his mother's death. The room smelled of flowers and fresh cooking, blended with the fragrance of cleanliness. The furniture was simple but sturdy, the curtains white with laced trims, the wall lined with family pictures and a hanging shelf with books bound in old leather and paper.

To his surprise, he saw on the mantel of brick the nutcracker in black. Seeing what the boy stared at, the old woman too stared in surprise. "I don't remember having a nutcracker like that." She looked over the wooden figure. "Didn't you mention a Hussar in black?" She turned to Friedrich. "Did you put him there?"

"He did come with me."

The old woman smiled. "Quite a fetching fellow. If it's alright with you, young man, he looks rather comfortable there."

Friedrich gave a slow nod and quietly gave the woman his name when she asked. When her husband came in, the three were soon together at the table with a hot meal before them. Once filled with all he could eat, Friedrich found enjoyment in following the old farmer about and watching his work, and in helping where he could.

When evening came, the boy was given a pair of clothes belonging to the couple's son who had gone away, and he lay in a soft bed surrounded by things he had often dreamed of having and sharing with his father and mother.

In the night, Friedrich rose from the bed and quietly went to the mantel where Ulrich von Blücher stood. He implored the nutcracker to speak, but it remained silent and motionless, until it would again be needed.

The Mayor of Red Flag City

A. J. Bell

It gets colder the closer you get to the mountains, especially at night. You can feel it. Even a mile can make a difference, even a couple blocks. The ice in the air gets inside you and it stays there. The peaks look down on you. Their sharp teeth bear trap the stars.

You can't turn back. You're theirs now.

I was in the passenger seat. Jimmy was driving.

"Think he'll be okay finding us?" he asked.

"Yeah. I gave him directions."

Jimmy kept looking over at me, clearly working up his nerve.

"You okay?" I said finally, putting him out of his misery.

"I just want to go on record saying I don't think this is a good idea. I think you should take some more time to cool off from this whole situation."

I nodded down at the floor between my knees.

"I understand," I said. "If it makes you feel any better, I don't plan on doing this ever again."

Jimmy said nothing.

"Don't worry about it. You're going to be here in the car the whole time. We'll go off and talk it out, outside the house somewhere. Then he'll leave, you'll leave, and I'll stay up here."

Jimmy shook his head, his eyes praying to the roof of the car.

He said, "He's going to know something's up. You can talk anywhere; you can talk on the phone. Why come up here? He's not stupid. He knows you're, well, agitated."

"He agreed to come. It's not like I'm forcing him."

"I know. But he wants to resolve this."

"That's all I'm trying to do here."

"Would you show up, if you were him?"

"No."

"Exactly."

"What?"

"He's not like you."

"That's what Katie keeps telling me."

“I’m not trying to be a dick.”

“I know. I’m just messing with you.” We’re both silent for a moment. I said, “I could have done this by myself, you know. I told you, you didn’t have to come with me.”

Jimmy said, “It’s okay.”

But that was a lie. I needed Jimmy in order for this to work.

Casey never would have showed up if it was just me.

*   *   *

Katie had left me for Casey three months earlier. Three months before that, Casey had stopped taking his antidepressants. The only person he told was Katie, and, as far as I could tell, the only person she told was me.

This was during the in-between time.

Katie and I were no longer getting along, our fondness for one another a victim of gravity (we met, we got our hopes up, and what goes up must come down). But just before that she mentioned this little tidbit.

He was always Katie’s friend more than anything, and supposedly not a close one.

Casey had been a running joke in our relationship; we bonded over discussing how comically unstable he was. Stories usually popped up secondhand from the edges of our social circle, stories of him freaking out, sometimes in public, and his needing to be coddled and reassured like a four-year-old by whoever had the bad luck to be there too. With repetition, even the most tender heart begins to roll its eyes. But I think at the point she told me about him no longer being medicated, she was just doing it to make me happy. Her heart wasn’t in it anymore.

Her heart was with him.

Now it seems so obvious. How much was she actually talking to him, that she would know this, this thing that virtually everyone in his life would be against? Why would he feel comfortable sharing it with her?

Now when I tell her I want her back, I strategically don’t mention it. I try to not talk about Casey at all. But Katie knows me. She’s waiting for me to throw it in her face. As time goes on though, maybe she won’t worry about it as much. She’ll think I’ve forgotten about it.

That’s the plan.

*   *   *

Jimmy knows me too. He’s not buying it. We’re sitting in the car outside the house.

"What is this even about? Are you defending your honor? Do you even care about Katie anymore? Do you really want to be with her still?"

Jimmy is a good guy, and it's a good question. A damning question, you could say. I didn't have an answer.

"I just want to talk to him," I said.

"Like scare him a little?"

"Sure."

"See, this is what I'm talking about."

"What?"

"This is a really bad idea."

"Relax."

"You're officially the mayor of Red Flag City." I laughed, despite myself.

"Whatever. Just take it easy. He'll be here any minute. An hour from now, you'll be on your way home. Less than that. You'll practically be home."

Like I said, Jimmy knows me. He's a smart guy. Do I really want Katie back? Is that what's driving all this? That's a great question. But I can't answer it, and it doesn't matter anyway. We're past all that now.

* * *

A week before, I got a suppressor.

Scott was sitting out on the front porch when I got to his house. We were in the Army together, and now he was on disability. We didn't talk too much anymore. He'd gained a lot of weight. He looked bad, real bad. But I kept that observation to myself.

I said, "How's it going, man?"

"I'm hanging in there," he said. We shook hands. I sat down next to him. There was a little table between us, a small cardboard box resting on top.

He said, "I'm sorry about you and Katie."

"It's okay. I'll survive."

"How long were you two together?"

"Three years."

"That's a long time."

The sun was going down and momentarily blinding us. We both winced and turned away from one another.

I said, "It's not that long. How are you feeling these days?"

He put his hand on his stomach. "I'm trying to lose some weight. That always makes the doctor happy."

"What does the doctor say?"

“Well, I’m down to one medication. That’s a victory, in and of itself. Lamictal. I was taking it with Lithium for the longest time, maybe two years?”

“Does it help?”

“The combination of the two was making me too much of a zombie.”

“Well, we don’t want you to be a total zombie.”

He grinned at me then. “Just enough to get through the day, right?”

I smiled back. “Your words,” I said.

“I know, I know.”

“But do you feel better now?”

“Yeah, I guess. I heard from Jimmy that you’ve been doing some work out at your aunt’s place?” (Saint Jimmy, the great enabler).

I nodded. “Sort of. Mostly I’m just staying there, for now. I mean, I can stay there for free, so why not?”

“She lives out in California?”

“Right. She’s not planning on visiting anytime soon, so it’s just sitting there, empty. Way out, past Woodland Park.”

“I bet it’s cold as balls up there at night.”

“It is, but I have the fireplace. I’ve been chopping all kinds of wood.”

That made Scott laugh, and laughing made him cough for a minute.

“Chopping wood! That’s good, that’s just what you need in your life right now. Get all that bad breakup energy out of your system. Chop wood until you find yourself a new girlfriend. That’ll keep you out of trouble.”

“That’s the plan,” I said.

The sunset was at chest level now. The light played on our hands as we talked. I looked down at the little box on the table.

“Is that the thing?” I asked.

Scott nodded his head. “Yep, that’s the thing.”

“Cool. Thank you so—”

He grabbed my wrist as I went to pick it up. We looked at each other. I took my hand back.

“What?”

Scott pointed at the houses across the street. There was no one around. No one in their yard. No dogs barking; it was quiet and peaceful. I gave him a look, telling him I still didn’t get it.

He said, “Doorbell cameras. There’s probably an angle the next block over that can see us right now. It’s almost dark. I’ll keep the porch light off until after you’re gone. You can leave the money on the table. I’ll get it.”

I took a deep breath and relaxed a little. I thought this was all a bit much. But I kept those thoughts to myself.

“I can put it on a Taurus?” I asked. “A Taurus G3c?”

“I thought you had a Glock? You’ve always had a Glock.”

I said nothing.

He folded his hands over his stomach. “You’re not going to use it for the Glock.”

“No, I have a Taurus now,” I said.

“You know, there’s plenty of other fish in the sea, as they say. You don’t have to shoot her.”

“I’m not going to do anything to Katie.”

“Good. I didn’t think you were that stupid. Don’t worry, I don’t have any more questions.”

“Thank you.”

“I like being a veteran with you. I don’t want to be a felon with you.”

I shook my head. I said, “It’s nothing like that.”

“I’m not trying to be a jerk about it. I don’t do this kind of thing for just anybody.”

“I know.”

Scott stood up. We shook hands again. He said, “I’m going inside now.” He scanned our surroundings carefully. “I would wait at least a few more minutes. Like I said, just leave the money on the table here. It should work fine on a Taurus.”

“Okay,” I said.

“It was good to see you.”

“You too.”

I sat there alone until it was fully dark. Then I put the box in my jacket, and left.

*   *   *

I was up at the house a couple nights later digging the hole, when Katie called me. I stuck the shovel in the ground and leaned on it.

“Hey,” she said.

“Hey. What’s up?”

“It’s me. Um, have you been hanging around my house lately?”

“No. I haven’t.”

“I thought I saw you the other day.”

“Just standing around?”

“No, you were sitting in Jimmy’s car. Parked down the street.”

“I haven’t used his car in a while; it wasn’t me. It must have just been a similar model.”

"It looked just like Jimmy's. I was sure it was you. I'm sorry, I'm not trying to accuse you of anything. I'm not trying to attack you."

"It's okay. I understand. I'm not angry."

"I just wanted to check with you. It's been bothering me, but I didn't want you to be mad. I wanted to at least talk to you before I said anything to Casey."

"Did he see me? Hanging around?"

"No. He hasn't said anything."

"Well, I haven't been stalking you."

"I never said you were. I'm sorry, I don't mean to bother you. I just wanted to ask. Are you doing okay?"

"Yeah, I'm fine. I'm up at the cabin."

"Is Jimmy there with you?"

"No. Just me."

"I don't like you being out there, by yourself. You might get hurt, and you might not be able to get a phone signal to call for help."

"My phone works fine. I'm talking to you right now."

"I know. I'm just saying."

"I'm up here all the time. I sleep here."

"I'll stop mothering you. I just worry sometimes."

There was a long pause.

She said, "Have you thought about what you're going to do next year?" (She meant for money. I was still getting checks from the Army, but at the end of year they were going to stop. Unless I went back in, or enrolled in some form of school. There was no way I was going back in, and going to school was about the last thing I felt like doing.)

"I don't know yet," I said. Another pause.

A feeling of helpless anger erupted in slow motion inside me. I wanted to tell her she was dumb. I wanted to tell her she would regret the past few months. I wanted to tell her Casey was just using her, that she was just a stand-in for the pills he used to take, that he would build up a tolerance, and then forget about her. He would replace her with someone or something else.

I wanted her to fire back: yeah, well, what did I replace her with?

We hung up before I said any of those things, and somewhere in the distance of my heart I was proud of myself for that. Instead, I put my phone away and kept digging, angrily, throwing my weight against the earth. It helped me get it all out. Just like Scott said, about chopping wood. It made me feel better. I was basically underground now. The air below my neck felt colder, like being in water. I wiped away hot beads of sweat from my face.

It occurred to me that, now that it was dug, I didn't need the hole anymore. I didn't want it. What was I thinking? I tossed the shovel and, with some effort, climbed out. Then I stared down at it for a long time. The abyss.

Chopping wood or digging a hole out behind the house might stop you from doing something really stupid. Sure. But you can't bring back the trees, and you can't fill in the hole.

Not if you're still in it.

* * *

I tried to wax philosophical about mental health to Casey, about how making big changes or getting into a new relationship while you're going through a difficult time personally can be a bad idea, for everyone involved. That sort of thing. He didn't say anything back; he just stared at me with that dead-behind-the-eyes look that he has. Not getting it at all. I realized pretty quick this was going nowhere.

So, I skipped ahead to just telling him flat-out that I wanted him to stay away from Katie for a while, so that she and I could figure things out. That's when he freaked out.

That's when he pulled the knife out and started cutting himself.

I said, "Casey, Casey, stop." But he didn't.

We're up at the house, out back. Jimmy is on the other side waiting in the car; no one can see us, thank God. Casey's arm and neck are bleeding. I grab ahold of the hand holding the knife and try to stop him. But he fights me. He makes this low growl like a dog, gritting his teeth. He doesn't say anything. We pushed each other back and forth, neither of us willing to let go.

"Casey, stop. What are you doing?"

I had the Taurus stuck in my pants, and I considered going for it. I was in a legitimate self-defense situation; it could make things easier for me later. The only problem was I would have to explain the unregistered suppressor, and where I got it. And the big hole nearby that looked like a grave.

I considered yelling for Jimmy, but he wouldn't have heard me. He was relaxing in his car, no doubt blasting the heat and listening to his retro '80s girl music.

"Casey, c'mon."

Why was I even intervening? I should have just sat back and let him do it, and enjoyed the show. I could have run back to the car, slapped my bloody hands on the windows, told Jimmy we got to get help. I tried to stop him. That would have looked good. A whole lot better than this.

Instead, here we were. Dancing in the dark.

I was getting fed up; my wrists and arms were on fire from trying to bend the knife away from him. I figured maybe showing him the pistol would get him to calm down.

But when I let one hand go to reach for it, Casey shoved me. I stumbled back, lost my balance, and then, waving my arms like a cartoon character, I fell back into the hole. I hit my head, and everything went dark for a second.

I spat out dirt and tried to struggle to my feet. But I must have twisted my ankle, because it felt like it had been hit with a hammer. I flopped back down.

"Casey!" I said. "Casey, help me!" But there was no answer. I tried yelling for Jimmy. Same thing. I took out my phone.

No signal. I stared at the screen, like giving it dirty looks might force it to connect. But I got nothing. I yanked out the Taurus, and took off the suppressor. I was about to fire up into the air like some Mexican bandito, but stopped myself. I needed to calm down.

Jimmy would come find me. Casey probably drove off without saying anything to him; he'll come looking. I tried talking to him, but it turned out to be a bad idea. Where was the lie?

Staring up at the stars, the cold earth turning my back numb, I realized what I should have done: I should have had a more definite plan of action. I didn't iron things out properly. For instance, say everything goes according to plan, what was I going to tell Jimmy? The truth, and hope he keeps quiet? Do I spin a yarn about Casey getting suicidal and disappearing into the woods? Oh, by the way, don't pay any attention to that spot where I've clearly been digging. And what about Casey's car? I hadn't thought about any of that stuff. I just had this scenario in my head, a scenario where I put him in his place, and I got my girlfriend back.

And I felt better.

I started to fall asleep thinking about all these new details for my plan, when I heard police sirens. They were far away still, but they were coming. Maybe they were just in my head, maybe I was dreaming now. Who would have called them? I unloaded the Taurus and put it away. I picked a direction I was pretty sure was away from the house and threw the suppressor as hard as I could. I figured it was better than nothing. I didn't yell for Jimmy. The sirens were getting louder.

When the cops pulled up, they had their lights flashing. I looked up at them. It was like a UFO had landed. I had my hands up before they found me. They had their weapons drawn. They told me to come on out of the hole. Slowly.

I'm about to tell them about my ankle, and it occurs to me, right at that moment, that I haven't been dealing with things very well lately.

A Net Big Enough to Catch Dragonflies

Bêtenoir

He immediately felt that something was different. Stepping into the coffee shop to meet his Tinder date, a hookup thing really, he forgot momentarily why he was there; she was that beautiful. It made him feel insecure that just a little while ago he had been slouching on the couch playing video games. He thought about bailing for a second, but she had seen him already.

"Charles?" she asked.

"Yes, hi," he confirmed.

"I'm Angelika," she said.

"It's nice to meet you," he said and, not quite sure why, shook her hand. A surreal quality hung over the scene. They got a couple of lattes, picked a place to sit, and, under the thrill of taut nerves, proceeded to lose track of time together.

Things moved quickly from there. Not just sex, although there was plenty of that, but other things too. They spent a lot of time together. Taking walks, doing chores, doing nothing. Objects of hers took up more or less permanent residence in his apartment and vice versa. They met each other's friends. Well, he met her friends; his friends were mostly online and only vaguely aware of Angelika as the reason he wasn't so much anymore. In short, they fell in love. His parents, with superstitious anxiety, reacted in hushed and delicate tones so as not to ruin anything.

Time passed happily. They moved in together and decided to adopt a puppy. "Family practice," Angelika called it. The puppy, Dex, was very affectionate and fanatically devoted to Angelika, following her around like a mother duck. They met other couples at dog parks, people he might have mocked before or at the very least not wanted to emulate. One night, as part of showing Angelika his former interests, they were cuddled on the couch playing Final Fantasy VII. Watching her decide between Aeris and Tifa, Charles spontaneously blurted, "We should get married. Will you marry me?" It was an easy choice.

Their wedding was small, just close friends and family, a kind of festive formality around the true purpose of starting a family. They bought a house with a yard and spare bedrooms, and very soon thereafter, Angelika was pregnant. Pregnancy suited her and provided a great excuse for her to cut down on work hours and work mostly from home, something she had wanted to do anyway. She reclined on the couch, shuffling emails and Zoom calls on a laptop, while Dex, a single headed little Cerberus, guarded her growing belly.

The months went by, one of the bedrooms transforming in stages into a nursery, and then one day, in a mix of routine and panic, they were driving to the hospital. The baby, a little girl, announced herself with cries like heralding trumpets. They named her Isabella. Looking closely, Charles found in her familiar features of his wife, making him fall in love all over again. Both pairs of grandparents visited the hospital often, in various stages of ecstasy, and within a couple of days the little family left to make their house a home.

Isabella, cute as a button, had a girly streak mixed with tomboy tendencies, oscillating between watching her mom doing her makeup and her dad playing video games. A tea party for Dex quickly turned into a play session in the grass and dirt, her parents despairing of keeping anything she wore outside clean. She loved nature and saw everything outside, trees, animals, even insects, as something to make friends with. She began collecting flowers, which Angelika pressed into book pages for her, and insects that caught her eye such as butterflies, bearing the killing and pinning process philosophically.

Canvassing the park's perimeter in a low stalk, Isabella would pause to consider each butterfly before bringing her little net down in slow, ineffective strokes. Often, swinging too fast, she would lose balance and fall on her butt, Dex running up to check she was okay before returning to Angelika sitting on a towel with an iced tea and a book. Isabella hadn't caught much of anything but didn't seem to mind. Plants and animals competed for her interest. Something buzzed past her face, almost too fast to follow.

"Daddy, what was that?" She was pointing toward a pond where it was headed.

"That's a dragonfly," Charles said, squinting. "A club tail, I think."

"I want to catch one of those," she announced.

"That's going to be much more difficult than butterflies. I think we'll need a bigger net."

Just then, Charles felt a pressure at his temples. His vision blurred slightly, and a dizziness like getting up too fast washed over him. The pain at his temples increased; he felt like his head was being crushed. The scene before him, his daughter, the park, was fading, becoming almost translucent. Then his head spun in a violent crack, and he fell backward onto the hard floor.

"What the fuck, man? I've been calling you for three days!" a voice was yelling at him.

He had no idea where he was. No, wait, he did. He was looking up at the bedroom ceiling of his old apartment, where he had lived before moving in with Angelika.

"I said you could borrow this for a day or two," the voice continued, "not keep it."

"What?" Charles managed to ask.

The other man laughed. "Boy, are you out of it. Get it together, man."

"Is this a dream?" Charles asked.

"This is definitely not a dream, man," he said. He looked at a computer monitor on a desk. "Looks like you've been liminal for almost seventy-two hours."

"What? Where are they?" asked Charles.

"Where are who?" the man replied.

Charles scrambled to his feet, head frantically searching the dark room. "Where are they?!" he repeated, louder.

"Who are you talking about? Your virtual girlfriends?" He pointed to something lying on the floor, a helmet sprouting an eruption of wires. "You in the middle of something important in there?" he joked.

Charles grabbed his shirt and started shaking him. "What have you done with my wife and daughter?!" he yelled.

It took a long while for him to calm down, and even longer for him to believe. The man, a friend named Jack who he hadn't seen in years, in days, was patient with him once he realized the extent of the problem. More than once, Charles called a cell number that was out of service and checked social media that didn't exist, pausing sporadically to mumble to himself, head in hands.

Jack was checking the software now, inspecting the VR headset. "I think something went wrong; you're not supposed to be able to stay in for as long as you did."

Charles looked at the box it came in, with sexy images of women and some ad copy in bold text: "Unleash fantasies you don't even know you have."

Charles had spent almost ten years of experiential time in virtual reality; his actual life now felt fake, as it would for years to come. He was ashamed of his apartment, full of toys and junk food. It was dirty and disorganized, and he spent the first few days cleaning and organizing it. When he was finished with that and there was nothing pressing to do, that's when it got really bad. He had a hard time talking to his parents, knowing how they looked at him when they were truly proud. He felt out of place going to his old job, one he left years ago for something else to better support a family.

What got him through it, and he was embarrassed to admit this even to himself, was thinking of his virtual family. He didn't want to disappoint them. He found himself visiting the places they used to go to together. As much as he tried not to, he couldn't stop looking for them, automatically scanning crowds at familiar parks and squares. He was imitating the life that he had had; he even adopted a puppy, but none of this was going to bring them back. He would have to make a family here in the real world. That was how he could honor their memory.

One day at the dog park, his half-grown puppy, who he named Dex, was making particular friends with another small dog. “They’ve having a great time,” its owner said, a cute girl with a friendly smile.

“If only it were that easy for humans to make friends,” he said to her.

She laughed. “Everything is easier for dogs: making friends; you can go to the bathroom in front of others.”

You should ask her out, he thought to himself. *What’s the worst that could happen?*

“Do you want to get coffee sometime, since our dogs get along so well?” he asked.

“Oh, I’m sorry,” she replied, embarrassed, “I have a boyfriend.”

“Don’t be sorry,” he quickly answered. “I was just taking inspiration from the dogs here.”

See, that wasn’t so bad.

“I’m just about finished with this master’s degree,” he told his parents one night while having dinner with them. “I’ll be changing jobs after that.”

“Oh, we didn’t know you were working on a master’s degree,” his mom said in surprise.

“I didn’t think it was that big of a deal,” he said.

“Well,” his mother replied, “I think it’s great. We should celebrate.” His parents didn’t bring it up again, but both looked proud.

Jack had been trying to get in touch with him, maybe checking to see how he was doing, most likely wanting to play video games. He should call him, invite him to get some food or something like that. But, as luck would have it, he didn’t have to.

“Hey man, what are you doing here? Haven’t seen you online for a while.” Charles turned to see Jack with an armful of kitty litter. “For my mom’s place,” he complained. Charles was shopping for dog food.

“I’ve been pretty busy,” Charles said.

“Have you seen any of the new VR titles?” Jack asked. “I think they got all those bugs worked out.”

“I haven’t seen them, no,” said Charles. He put his dog food on the counter.

“Well, you really should,” Jack continued, “very cool stuff.”

“Maybe,” Charles answered. “We should go for a walk sometime, maybe get a cup of coffee.”

The cashier ringing up his dog food asked, “Anything else?”

“Hmm.” He spied some bug catching stuff behind the counter. Pointing, he said, “I’ll take one of those too, please.”

“Which one?” she asked.

“A net big enough to catch dragonflies.”

Passing Time

G. H. Casanova

Monday

"I don't like ice cream," Ezra announced.

Carrie's phone screen had a jagged crack through its middle and she had gotten used to the feel of her thumb brushing it as she scrolled, almost the same way she had gotten used to the sound of Ezra's voice penetrating her subconscious without really registering a word he said. Perhaps, too, he didn't speak as much as he had in the beginning.

"Caroline?" His voice was almost timid, as if he were intruding. She was in the middle of a text, and she felt a sort of elation watching her fingers work magic, forming words just by touching a screen, and so quickly, too. Shame about that crack. She tapped the send button and lowered her phone.

"What?" she asked.

"Don't want my ice cream." He pushed the little tub towards her, eyes full of intention, indicating it was hers.

"Sure?"

"Sure."

"But everyone likes ice cream," she said. She noticed the little beads of condensation covering the plastic, a subtle warning that the ice cream was going soft all around the edges. It made her feel soft, too.

Ezra looked at her steadily.

"No," he said.

"Suit yourself," she answered, accepting the tub and peeling back the plastic lid, spooning its contents into her mouth with the wooden stick they'd provided. She'd become accustomed to the repetitive beeping of the monitor beside the bed and the scent of sanitizer spray, the long waits for five thirty to arrive, the smile Ezra's mother gave that made her feel ashamed as she said, "I really appreciate it, you know. He finds it so hard to keep up with everyone sometimes. He deserves some friends." But ice cream was new. Ice cream was good.

"Thanks, Ezra," she said.

"It's okay." His chubby cheeks lifted as he beamed in spite of himself.

"I'll eat all your ice cream, if you don't want it," she suggested helpfully.

He hesitated. "Okay," he said. He smiled again. "That's fine."

Carrie looked down at her feet, barely touching the floor. The once plump leather chair was protruding into her bones as though it was just as keen for her to leave as she was, and every time she moved it emitted odd, airy noises that Ezra found fascinating. The edge of his bed looked more comfortable, but she didn't want to get that near to him. It's better to take precautions in a hospital, she reminded herself; don't touch too many things or go too close to anyone, because even with the deceiving smell of sanitizer lingering in every room, germs run rampant. The second time she had to come visit, she had considered just going to the hospital cafeteria, getting a milkshake, sitting around for a while calling friends, and then going back home and telling her grandma she'd been to the hospital. It would be true, but it wouldn't be honest. And besides, Ezra's mother would find out.

"But don't call me Caroline," she said suddenly. "It doesn't sound right on me."

"Sorry," he offered.

The beeping of the machine was almost useful, Carrie thought to herself; kind of masked the silence as she went back to looking at her phone. For a moment she had to close her eyes against its glare. "Does your heart hurt?" she tried asking casually. She felt funny the minute she'd said it. It was a bad question and she knew it, but Ezra didn't seem to mind.

"Nah," he said.

"So, you think you'll go home soon?"

"Yes." He smiled again. He wouldn't stop smiling. There was something in his face, and she couldn't tell what it was, but it reminded her of cartoons where characters' eyes go big and shiny when they're embarrassed or in love. She didn't like the idea of Ezra loving her. She looked away.

"Caroline?"

It may have been that he liked the way her name felt to say, to hear. His lisp made it sound funny, but you get used to these things.

"What?" she asked.

"Nothing."

It was one of his favorite pranks. He called it the Nothing Game, but it was hardly a game, and he was the only person who enjoyed it. He played it every time she visited, and she could never be certain which innocent "Caroline?" would be the one that ended in "nothing," so it wasn't as if she could ignore him every time he said her name. He'd give a low, self-satisfied chuckle after he'd said it, as if he'd completed a daily mission and was pleased with his success. She glanced up at him again, for just a moment, to see if he was still wearing that ambiguous expression. His eyes, she noticed, were blue-green like the sea, flecked with white spots. Her grandma told her it was part of the complication, that he had Brushfield spots in his eyes. Carrie kind of liked them.

Thursday

The stiff-lipped way Grandma looked at her and her phone sent a clear message of disapproval, but she never asked her to put it away. Her dad had gotten it for the last birthday she had before he went overseas, and it had been five months now since she'd seen him, so maybe Grandma thought that it would keep the loneliness at bay, being able to talk to her friends instantly, to send messages through to her dad and hope he'd respond within a couple of days. It sometimes seemed like a void of contradictory loneliness; it was created for entertainment, and education, and connection, and yet Carrie felt as if it was killing the little bright bits of her that mattered, stifling something valuable she couldn't even recognize inside of herself.

She told herself she needed it. She needed it when she had nothing to do, when she wanted to cry, when she had to sit by Ezra's bed and keep him company. He'd gotten in the habit of turning the TV on about halfway through the visit, as if admitting to himself that she wasn't planning to spend any energy on him, and he'd ask very kindly which channel she preferred. She'd select a random one she expected him to enjoy: a cartoon for younger kids, or a show with canned laughter so that he had cues to tell him what to believe funny. He'd watch it tolerantly, eyeing her now and then to see if she liked it, too, sometimes reacting a little too raucously as a kind of prompt. And that day he asked the usual question and she shrugged, "Watch whatever you like." He slowly flicked through programs until he landed on one of the nature shows. She was surprised he enjoyed it, when it was about the habitats and brumation of amphibians; but then, it wasn't always simple to predict Ezra's thoughts.

"There's a frog called a waxy monkey tree frog," Ezra remarked, unable to tear his eyes away. Carrie barely heard.

"I *really* like frogs," he said slowly.

"Do you?" she asked absentmindedly, glancing up at the screen.

"Yes. Wish I was one."

"You wish you were a frog?" Her face twisted into a frown. It was a disgusting thought, just the kind of thing Ezra would take pleasure in.

"Yes," he smiled. She wondered what a smile would look like on a frog. A frog wouldn't have Ezra's freckles.

"The *Paedophryne amauensis* grows no bigger than 7.7 millimeters in length," the voice of the narrator explained, and somehow, although Carrie's focus had gone back to her screen, it rang persistently in her ears.

"How big is that, Caroline?" Ezra inquired, looking at her. She demonstrated with her fingers what she estimated to be its length, though it wouldn't make a difference to him whether she was precise or not. He was delighted. "I'd be tiny," he squeaked. He started laughing. "I'd be so cute."

Carrie felt a smile working its way to her face. She couldn't see any kind of comedic value in tiny frogs, and here was Ezra, going red in the face from just thinking about them.

Friday

She walked slowly back home from the hospital, hands shoved in her pockets, watching clouds gather threateningly above distant buildings. The next-door kid was skateboarding lazily up and down the road, and he paused when he saw her coming, stepping down sharply on the back of the board and flipping it up into his hand in one self-conscious motion. Carrie's thoughts strayed to Ezra suddenly, in a way they hadn't done before—Ezra would not skateboard. No matter how much he wanted to, he simply couldn't. His body was too stiff. He was too frail. Even if he dreamed about it, he'd never do it. Or would he? What if his heart did get better and he really put his mind to it? She couldn't figure.

"Carrie, you want to come watch a movie after school tomorrow?" the kid called, without wasting time on a greeting. "It's a bit late, but we'd be back before it got dark and we could get hotdogs for dinner."

She felt a flush of excitement. Imagine watching a movie. She hadn't watched a movie in ages; usually her dad would take her, and the cinema seemed lifeless without him. But the next-door kid was okay. Maybe the loneliness would get swallowed up in a bit of fun.

"I'll ask my grandma," she heard herself say, out of habit more than anything. She must have been smiling as big as Ezra right now, trying to keep a steady pace and walk up her front steps as if she wasn't so extra specially happy.

"Grandma, can I go watch a movie tomorrow? Sam asked," she called, throwing her bag down on the couch. She could hear movement from the kitchen as her grandmother tried to find room for more jars and packets to cram into her cupboard. Spare groceries, she called them. You never know when you'll need them.

"What time?" she called back.

"Not too late. We'd be back before seven, I promise."

"Sure, Carrie. But you have to go see Ezra first, don't forget."

Carrie's shoulders dropped. "I can't," she protested, coming to lean against the pantry door frame and stick her lip out. "I'm going to go have dinner after."

"You can still have dinner. Have it right after the movie. The hospital cafeteria serves until six and you can take Sam up to see Ezra." Her grandmother pulled her head out from a musty cupboard and looked up to smile condescendingly.

Carrie glared at her. "Ezra's embarrassing. He tells dumb jokes that don't make any sense, and he says yes to everything I ask him."

"I know," she said.

"He's not my friend, Grandma. I don't want anyone to think he is."

"I know," she said again. She got up, brushed the dust off her skirt, and went to collect the rest of her shopping from the car.

Saturday

Carrie explained to Sam, before they climbed up the stairs to the general ward, that Ezra was different. She tried to come up with the most natural way of saying it, and all that came out was, "He's a bit weird, but in a good way, I guess. You just have to get used to him. He's got some quirks: there are creases right through the middle of his palms and white spots in his eyes."

"White spots in his eyes?" Sam said skeptically. There was annoyance in his attitude, though he didn't say anything about it.

"He's got a condition," Carrie ended, almost defensively. She really did like Ezra's eyes. She could admit that to herself.

"Oh," said Sam. Carrie wasn't sure if it was because he didn't know what that meant or because he just couldn't think of anything better to say.

The last slip of sun was flooding the second floor and lighting up Ezra's hair as he turned to look at them with the usual, large smile he gave visitors. His mother had told Carrie that when Ezra was little, he'd gasp when he saw new people.

"Hey," he said.

"Hey," answered Sam. He was looking at the chair and then at Carrie, and she knew there was no chance he was sitting on the bed, that close to Ezra. Most likely he'd been warned about germs, too. Not that there was anything infectious about Ezra—it was his heart that was the problem. Carrie wondered if it was too big, if that was what was wrong. Could be.

"Wana sit?" Ezra patted the area beside himself obligingly and looked at both Carrie and Sam. Carrie sat. It was softer than the chair. Some statutory introductions, and they all fell silent. Sam's face was rigid and his hands were resting tensely on the arms the same way Carrie's had the first day she came into the hospital; she'd forgotten how intrusive and odd she'd felt. Ezra's face was blissful. It was radiating happiness like sunshine. She could tell he was thinking how marvelous it was to be surrounded by good friends.

"Sam?" he said, with a symbolic glance at Carrie.

Please, Carrie begged silently. *Don't say it. Please.*

"What?" Sam asked.

"Nothing," said Ezra.

It was raining when Sam's mother came to take him home. She peered hesitantly into Ezra's room and saw the three of them sitting there, pink cheeked amidst the blaring white of sheets and curtains and floors, watching ravenous lions tear into prey on the television screen with big eyes and straight faces. Ezra was fixated. Seeing her standing there, Sam leaped to his feet in relief, throwing a hasty, "See you, Carrie," over his shoulder.

"Who's 'at?" Ezra inquired rudely, pulling his eyes away from the program and focusing on her instead.

"It's Sam's mum," Carrie answered half-heartedly.

"Hey," said Ezra, giving her a brief nod and a smile.

"Hi," said Sam's mother.

Carrie could see his thoughts sticking straight out of his face. He was evidently thinking Sam's mother looked relatively nice and pretty but lions were more interesting, and he turned back to the screen, still smiling. Carrie glanced at Sam and his mother as they turned away, wondering if Sam would look back, but she should have realized by now people don't look back just because you're wishing that hard. Is it better not to look, so as to avoid disappointment? Or could that lead to someone else's disappointment? Her grandmother came to take her home in the little gray Volkswagen Squareback so she wouldn't get wet; Ezra could see it out his window, in the parking lot, and he admired it and said in an indicative manner that he'd love to inherit a Volkswagen Squareback from someone nice. Grandma smiled. She'd never part with that car. She said she wanted to be buried with her arms crossed angelically over the steering wheel lying on her breast. Ezra laughed his deep, warm laugh and gave Grandma an amiable pat on the arm as she stood by his bed, and she kissed his cheek and told him to get better. He said okay, he would, he had to be out by his birthday so that he could have a party and Carrie could come celebrate being thirteen together. Grandma was good with him. Carrie couldn't see why she had to sit in the hospital with Ezra every day when Grandma liked him better than she did, but Grandma said she was too busy and Ezra needed a young person like herself. She didn't call Carrie a little girl anymore. Sometimes Carrie wished she would.

Tuesday

All Carrie could think about was those confounded waxy monkey tree frogs. She found herself typing waxy monkey tree frog into the search bar of her laptop during history just because curiosity got the better of her and she couldn't stop imagining what they would look like. Someone behind her stifled a laugh, and Sam, sitting a couple of desks away, craned his neck to see.

"What are you doing?" he whispered.

"Ezra likes frogs," she whispered back.

And why do you like Ezra? She knew he wanted to say it. When she walked back home after her visit in the evening, he was skateboarding again. He offhandedly asked, "Do you see your friend every day?"

"Ezra? We're not really friends. . . . My grandma makes me go see him. It's just because he doesn't get many visitors and he's lonely in the hospital. He spends a lot of time there."

"And he teaches you about frogs?"

"He likes frogs," she said again. She left him standing with one foot on the curb, holding his skateboard, and walked up the front steps to find her grandmother. Her phone was dead, and she went to sleep that night watching the weak light of its charger on the wall, contemplating the ugliness of waxy monkey tree frogs and the stars dotting the oceans of Ezra's eyes.

Wednesday

The edge of Ezra's bed was preferable to the chair, Carrie knew, and there was no point suffering any more discomfort than necessary. She sat close to him and thought about how much longer these visits would continue—would he be sad if he got better and she didn't come to see him anymore? His smile was so big it shouldn't have fit on his face, and yet it did every time, perfectly. He was just so glad she was there.

The monitor continued to beep through the silence. Carrie reached for her pocket and her hand touched nothing but the fabric of her jeans—somehow she'd forgotten to slip her phone in that morning. The TV channel had gone static, but Ezra liked watching all the little gray grains of nothing on the screen. He'd hum to himself, serenely, as if creating his own discordant theme song for a world only he could see.

"You know, I'm really lonely," Carrie said suddenly. "I try to make friends, but everything seems so empty. I feel small. Almost how small a frog is. Everyone else is going somewhere, and I'm just Carrie, sitting around, waiting for life to happen."

Ezra blinked, pure innocence.

"You don't understand," she sighed.

"Yes," said Ezra. She couldn't be sure whether it meant yes or no.

"You say yes to everything," she told him.

He paused and blinked again. "Yes," he shrugged. It was still raining.

Grandma went shopping on their way back, and Carrie's feet unwillingly dragged her along the aisles, her eyes blurry with tiredness, the kind of tiredness you get from being alive, she guessed. What if she just expired one day? Disintegrated into a million miniscule pieces and floated away on the wind? Maybe all the loneliness would blow away with her, attached to the very fibers of her dust. The raindrops traveled thin, invisible roads down the windows of the Squareback, and Carrie and her grandmother sang along to the radio while Carrie traced them, watching them glisten in the red and yellow streetlights. It was nice, singing. Carrie used to do that with her mum, before she left. *They all leave*, she thought.

Friday

Carrie wondered when the rain would end. It spattered Ezra's window relentlessly, joining the monitor in discreetly filling the silence between conversation, running down the gutters of the street below, forming shadows on the floor as the weakest light broke through the clouds before disappearing again. She watched Ezra's hand out of the corner of her eye to see if he would lift it towards the remote, but it lay almost lifeless on the sheets beside his leg. His face was pale. She thought again about skateboarding, and whether or not she should have brought her phone; maybe just sitting there was alright, maybe she should suggest they see whether there was a wildlife show on at that minute so they wouldn't need to think about what to say.

The nurse came in, red and pudgy, with an expression that made it clear she'd been made for some other line of work and she knew it. She tried weakly to start a conversation with Ezra, using words too lengthy for him to process while administering his tablets, encouraging him to swallow them in halves as he shook his head and set his mouth in a firm, angry line. It didn't suit him to look that way. It was as if God had designed his face specifically to accommodate a smile and to see any other kind of expression on it would make anyone want to bring it back. Carrie stared out the window again, feeling uncomfortable, and reflecting on how busy and yet unimportant the world looked from up on the second story.

Everybody was moving and moving, and here was Ezra, lying in a hospital bed, taking it all one day at a time and being considerably light hearted about it. It had been months since he'd been at school. One illness seemed to develop into another. He'd get sick just like that, and his heart would refuse to settle, refuse to just work properly and quit bugging him.

His arguments failed, and he submitted to swallowing the tablets, pulling horrendous faces as they traveled down his throat, so that the pudgy nurse would leave him alone. It made Carrie feel aggrieved somehow, the way the presence of that nurse and her tablets seemed to suffocate the happiness in the room. She stuck her tongue out at her back but didn't let Ezra see, figuring he'd laugh too much and mimic her. The trolley carrying plates of steamed and boiled food for patients who would do their best to cram it down their throats came rattling down the hallway and into the room. An ugly, steaming dinner was laid out in front of him, and he started to eat, holding the fork in a clumsy fist grip, sliding the usual tub of ice cream over to her with the back of his free hand and choking on pale mashed pumpkin as tears started rolling down his cheeks. His wet eyes shifted to meet hers. She wanted to look away. She hadn't seen him cry about anything before.

“Gonna be an Olympic gold medalist when m'heart's good,” he whispered. He sniffed and wiped his nose and mouth with a baggy white sleeve. The complicated words were a little struggle, but it was a pretty good sentence, Carrie thought. “

Okay,” she answered. “That'll be brilliant.”

“I know, right?” He sniffed harder.

“I'll come and watch you, if you like,” she offered. “My grandma likes watching the Olympics on TV, but she said one day she wants to go see them in real life. So maybe in a few years, do you think?”

“Yes.” He brightened. Just like that. Like someone had snapped their finger and Ezra had come back to life. “But if I don't do Olympics,” he added, “I might do food in hospital. You know, push the trolley? I'd like my own trolley.”

“I'd like a trolley, too,” she said, for lack of inspiration.

“Caroline?”

“Yes?”

“Nothing.” He chuckled. It was as if he hadn't cried at all.

She swallowed and peeled back the top of the ice cream, pushing it back towards him. The rest of the meal didn't look so appealing, she decided. “If you want to do any of that, you'd better eat it yourself,” she reminded him. “I know you don't like it, but it's good for you.”

“Okay.” There was that look in his eyes again, that love that couldn't be contained.

He closed them jubilantly as he stuck his tongue into the tub and lapped it up like a cat until he was finished. "It's cold," he observed and sighed. He went back to eating his dinner bravely, with that same tight-fist grip.

"You've got nice eyes, Ezra," Carrie said. "They're like the sea."

He looked up and patted her hand gently with stubby little fingers. "About time you said that," he replied.

The Volkswagen Squareback was drawing into the parking lot, wiping the raindrops away furiously, its lights glowing dimly in the grayness. When Ezra was better, maybe they'd take him for a ride and get real ice cream somewhere, Grandma said. Carrie had heard plenty of maybes in her life, and she didn't think they meant very much anymore. Sometimes she told herself maybe her mother would decide to come back or her dad would find a better job and they'd be together and maybe her phone would heal the little hurts and maybe Sam would come around and ask to watch another movie.

"Caroline?"

"Yes?"

"Your grandma's here. I see her car."

"I know."

"When I'm older, I'm gonna drive a car. We can drive to the zoo. There's frogs there."

"Sure are."

"You're really nice, Carrie," Ezra said. "I think you're my best friend." He lay back on his pillow and closed his eyes, and the rain and the monitor persisted, and Carrie could not remember what she had been thinking about because the room was warm and the loneliness had begun to slowly ebb away.

The Last Living Ash

John "Borzoi" Chapman

"Ask, if another branch smacks me in the face, I'm going back to find some merc's gun. Do you know what I'm going to do with the gun?"

"I don't know," he replied sarcastically as he pushed his way through the brambles uphill under a chilly black morning sky. "You're going to shoot me with it?"

"I'm going to shoot you in the face with it," I added.

Ask was serene to my death threats. He'd heard them a thousand times before. He heard them at the Birdcage, and he heard them stack up now as we trudged through this forgotten nature trail outside of town. My moaning about how wet grass and dirt was seeping into my stolen sneakers gave me nothing, but I was as used to that as he was to my violent promises.

"You wouldn't do it anyway."

"Yes, I would." I was obviously bluffing. I had no idea where we were going or where we had come from. I had no leg to stand on. If anything happened to Ask, I would be dead by daylight or back in handcuffs soon enough. I don't know which I'd prefer.

I did feel some relief from this sweet summer night clinging wetly to my skin. The last time I had been outside at night had been years ago, and now having the buzzing of mosquitoes in my ears brought back sudden memories of childhood on my grandmother's lawn of cupping lightning bugs in my tiny hands. Being out here had shaken a lot of memories loose. The screens at the Birdcage make you forget a lot, but what's worse is they make you forget what they mean.

Ask, I had to admit, helped me to think a lot more ever since we met in the Birdcage. The Birdcage was what we called the juvie. I don't know how it got its name. When he came into my cell, I was already on year two of my sentence and I'd been through three cellmates already. I always made death threats to every single one of them when I first met them. Doing the same thing online landed me there in the first place. Ask was not only the first one who didn't care about what I said, he was also the first one I shared skin color with. Maybe that meant nothing. Ask said it means everything, even for teenage scumbags like me. He didn't want to fight me though, and that was something new. Ask being how he is was why I was here with him now, following him up this mountain in darkness.

“Aidan,” I announced to him when we met. I wanted to size him up.

He gave me the briefest glance while he made sure his bed was made and mumbled to me, “Evan Ashley.”

“I’m going to kill you in your sleep.” I needed him to know I was nuts.

He didn’t respond at first. That usually gets them going. Usually, the other kids get up in your face. They’ve got something to prove. They need you to know they’re wilder and crazier than you are, or they just sheepishly back down. They never give you nothing like he did. He just carried on, asking me what our daily routines were and what got me in here. I was so surprised by the reaction that I gave him an honest answer.

“Wake up. Make the bed. Breakfast. Go to classes about being a productive member of society. Go to classes on privilege and diversity. Lunch. Free time unless they got other plans for you. Dinner. Lights out. That’s basically it. As for why I’m here, I threatened my teacher online. Almost got tried as an adult too, but they said they could save me. You?”

His reply was mysterious. “Being who I am,” was all he said, and he made himself at home.

Evan wasn’t like any of the other kids in there. They’re all animals. So was I, because you have to be one. I got into the habit of calling him Ask because everything was always “just ask me” with him when he caught me staring at him with something on my mind. I had no expectation I would ever get to know him, because when you’re in that cage and you’re not hard like the darker kids, you tend to snap. I couldn’t stand to see another White boy in there with me because they almost always went crazy and broke down in some way. Everyone there was meaner and rougher with us, and they looked for every way they could to take you apart.

That was when you weren’t dealing with the corrective officers, counselors, and computers that tried to do worse to you in their classes to reform you. I wished being here was actually just about punishing you and making you hurt so you wouldn’t do it again. Our days were constantly filled with activities that were designed to change our behavior. The computer programs and videos were worse than the sharing circles because at least then you could talk to someone who was real instead of being talked at by something that wasn’t. We rarely saw the outside. We were kept inside all hours in front of screens being told to be good. It would be one thing if we learned anything. What we usually got was classes on diversity and acceptance and identities, especially if the identity was being a real freak. Kids like me and Ask got classes on our privilege. They also always pulled Ask in to something that seemed to be more one-on-one. Guys who talked said that it was a “deradicalization” thing. They seemed to have a special interest in Ask, but he wouldn’t talk about it when I prodded him about it.

It was a month before I really got to know anything about him there. I kept trying to find out what got him in the Birdcage because he just wasn't the type that should be in there. He was too quiet and way too serious. He answered every question about his life outside there with silence. It was always like he was a world away from us. We were lying in our beds when he finally said something to me in pitch darkness.

"Did you know your grandfather?"

"Which one?" I was too taken aback to ask where this was coming from.

"Either, I suppose." There was a pause in his voice and he added, almost hesitating, "It's just one on each side, right? No more or fewer than that?'

I stifled a laugh out loud because of the danger of being heard. I couldn't help myself. Ask had never been this chatty or personal in the full month I had known him. "Nothing like that in my family, but we had our own problems. I don't know my dad's dad that well because I didn't really know my dad that well since my mom did everything she could to keep me away from them. We were friends online, my grandpa and I. He added me and wished me happy birthday and stuff like that. My mom's dad I remember when I was a little kid, but he was killed when he was doing delivery driving stuff."

"Murdered?"

"Yeah, murdered. His life cost seven dollars and a cracked phone." I tried to see him in the dark but couldn't glimpse him. I needed to know now what he had been hiding. "Yo, Ashley, you been in here for a month and have been giving me the silent treatment unless I badger you with something. Can't get a word out of you about anything real with you especially what got you in here, and all of a sudden, you're asking me about my family? What gives? What's going on with you?"

There was a long silence. I thought maybe he'd clammed up or gone asleep. "My mother did her visitation with me today."

"Oh yeah, I noticed you were gone a while. Well, wasn't that nice of her. Wish I had a mom that nice."

"While she was here, we talked about when I would get out of here and what we would do and where we would go, as we can't stick around. I asked her about Grandpa's grave and she said we could always come back to see it when we could. Now all I can think about is getting out of here right now so I can visit my grandfather's grave. I can't stand the thought of never seeing him again."

I was frustrated hearing this. I felt like I was being jerked around. "Okay, Ask, enough. You can't talk like that and not tell me what the hell you did to get yourself sent to juvie."

I waited. He finally spoke after a minute.

"I was sent here because of a hate crime charge they tacked onto a littering charge. All I did was tear down some dumb political stickers in the park and some of that trash happened to touch the ground that was already covered in garbage and drug needles. They targeted me because of who my family is. They're still mad at my grandfather and my dad is dead, so I'm the last Ashley male they can punish. Maybe some of them think they can break my will in here and turn me against anyone they think I might know, but I think most of them know that's not going to happen. It's just about hurting and humiliating me and letting me know they'll bury me in holes like these whenever they please. The moment I get out of here, they'll find another thing to hit me with and drag me right back after I get a little crumb of freedom. That's why my mom wants to whisk me away from our home the moment this sentence is up, assuming they just don't find some way to extend it indefinitely. That's why I don't talk to any of you in here. Why risk it all? Why get any of you in trouble for talking to me?"

My head was spinning from all of this gushing out of him. Guys in here always talk about persecution, but when you asked them what they actually did, it was always some stupid fight or vandalism. Sometimes even just a straight-up murder. This was the first time I had met some kid with a story like this. I needed to know more.

"Whoa, wait, what? Hold up. That's a lot you're dumping right there, Ask. They're punishing you because of your granddad? What did he do? Blow up a school bus or steal millions of dollars? Are you running with a gang or something like that?"

"Not quite. My family are all radicals. My grandfather, Evan Ashley, was the brave and honorable man I was named for. He was an activist for our people. He protested wars, and he protested the murders of our people. He organized all kinds of aid and assistance. He kept it all nice and legal when he was young but when this country started really falling apart and getting violent, he became a real pain for the system. Probably the worst thing he ever did was he somehow got a thousand people to show up and protect a guy who had a warrant on him for trumped up charges. When the police came, they were completely unprepared for the show of force my grandfather assembled. They made the pigs run in fear at our show of force while the guy they protected was hidden from them. They spent years arresting as many people as possible who were involved in that, but they could never get to my grandfather or find him. He knew how to stay hidden, and he died in his home, surrounded by his family and unpunished for his crimes against the system. And they never forgave him for that. My dad died before they could take out their rage on him, so instead it became my turn."

"Bro, you have got to be playing me. What you're saying is crazy. I've never heard of anything like that. Thousand people fighting the cops? That would be all over the news."

"No offense, Aidan, but you don't really strike me as the type of guy who was really following the news."

I laughed. "Yeah, yeah, you got me there."

"Quiet! That's your only warning!" shouted the voice of the corrections officer, which put an end to our conversation.

I didn't really understand Ask, but in that moment, I knew I couldn't help but like the guy. I'd never met anyone like him. I'd say that most people are pretty simple to figure out. We're all chasing the same things: chasing money, chasing women, chasing highs, chasing fame, or chasing respect. We're all running after something. Even brainy types. They're all little pretzel people twisted up inside who don't know how to live because they're so afraid of everything, but they're so certain they've got everything figured out. At least with someone who does you wrong, like hit you or steal your girl, you know what they're about. These people say one thing and then do another. I hated them the most because they liked to tell you just how smart they are. They weren't. People like Ask were smarter than them, but they never showed it and they always put those brainy people in their place.

Ask was the kind of guy who life has it out for, and he dealt with it without whining to anyone about it. Ask was the guy who could end up homeless and would never beg anyone for help. Ask was the guy who always had the answer but never made you feel dumb about it. Ask was the guy who saw things we couldn't see, and he was the guy who had your back no matter what.

That's why with less than a month left on his time here, when he told me we were escaping, I went with him without a second thought. He had it all worked out and didn't even announce it until everything was set in place. Anyone else here would have been all talk.

I had no idea how shoddy security in juvie was or how easy it would be to escape. Every other kid could do what Ask did to get us out if they had two brain cells to rub together. The moment he got us out of the office window and past the outer security system we ran as far into the night as we could without looking back. It was two miles or three before we stopped to get our bearings that I finally wanted to know what was next.

"What do you mean? We part ways. You go wherever you need to go. I've got my own path."

"Oh," I said, surprisingly crushed.

"This is your chance to really get away, Aidan. They're going to be more interested in me than you. If we split up and they know we've split up, they're going to search for me first. You'll be an afterthought. They will catch me. That's unavoidable. As bad as this country is now, they still have the means to find me."

"So why run at all?"

"I want to see my grandfather's grave one more time. Before my mother tries to take me away and before they completely put me away."

I knew there was something more to it than this. I didn't believe for a single second that someone as persuasive as Ask couldn't get his mother to make some stop at a grave in between sentences. I knew there was something more to this, but I also knew Ask wasn't going to say anything until he was ready.

"I'm going with you then."

"Are you sure?" He didn't seem surprised. Ask always seemed to know what anyone wanted or was going to do before it was ever said and done.

"Yeah, I'm sure. You're too much of an egghead to survive on your own. You need my help."

He chuckled. "Whatever you say, Aidan."

We spent the next few days surviving on our own, eating whatever trash we could scrounge up and stuff our faces in. Dumpster diving was nothing new to me, but Ask clearly never did the deed before. My problem seemed to be sleeping. No matter where we stopped, I barely got any rest. The hardest part of getting away from the Birdcage was getting back to an actual city.

These country roads were dangerous because any teen walking it alone was suspicious. Everyone in the area knew about the Birdcage, and word about our escape must have spread.

It's funny how fast the outside world can change when you're on the inside. We knew the area outside the Birdcage well enough that we knew what the first real city we were going to hit was. What we didn't know was how bad things had gotten in this part of the country since we got put away. Without any phones on us and with so few newspapers around, it was impossible for us to know that we were walking into an actual warzone.

We reached the outskirts and were creeped out by how few people there seemed to be. The few vehicles we saw sped by at illegal speeds while the sounds of shouting and gunfire could be faintly heard deeper in the city. We stayed off the main road and kept close to wherever any residential and business areas might be. It was clear looking into many of them that a lot of this city had been temporarily deserted while the few people we did see threatened us with their own firearms to move on and to move away from us, protecting whatever it was they had to hold. Eventually through the eerie carnage we found a dollar store ripe for our pickings. We scarfed faces with more cheap carbs and put on our new shoes and clothes as we tried to make sense of the gunshots and fires that had been burning throughout this once cozy, colonial town.

“Any idea what’s going on?” Ask looked at me like I might know better and then said more to himself, “Maybe we might have known if we had listened to the correction officers’ gossip a little closer.” He cursed himself then looked back at me.

“I saw some blacks with guns roll by in something like an SUV,” I mentioned, thinking back to when we were avoiding the cars that were zooming by.

“Like a gang?”

“Nah, they were uniformed. They looked way more organized than any gang I’ve ever seen. They looked like mercenaries in a video game.”

“Black. Uniformed.” He tapped his face and furrowed his brow. “There’s two groups of mercs that use that many Africans that I’m aware of. One’s the revised NATO group propping up the government and the other, well, no one really knows who the other group is or who they work for. They might just be here for their own reasons, picking through what they can in this country. The former pretend to have rules they follow, but the latter are complete savages just short of being cannibals. Neither is really better than the other since the NATO goons also do political policing to pick up the government’s slack. Could be the Chinese alliance, though I’ve never heard of them getting into this territory or using that many Africans.”

He looked at me and stopped once he realized he was mostly talking to himself since I had no idea what he was going on about. All I knew is that ever since I was a kid, sometimes a city had mercenaries from all over the world fighting because either they were resisting the government or because they were supporting it. I don’t ever remember the fighting getting this far out here though. That always seemed to be a world away from me. It didn’t really feel like a war as I’ve spent my whole life missing it. Unsurprisingly, Ask seemed to know everything about it.

“We should try to find some girls while we’re out here,” I said to break the tension.

“I don’t think we want the kind of girls that we would find out here.”

We laughed and finished our looting.

We spent that entire day just barely avoiding getting killed. We had no choice but to go straight through the city as his granddad’s gravesite was a bit out on the other side of town. Block by block we moved in terror, dodging at every sound of gunfire or a moving vehicle we heard. We hid as little as we could, afraid we might get stuck in place and be found. We weaved in and out of deserted alleyways and climbed through boarded-up businesses. When night fell, we snuck into the backroom of a nail salon in a strip mall. Being here felt unreal, like I was walking through a waking dream.

We tried to sleep, but I had no chance of it. Ask seemed to doze off without a problem, but I was jolted awake by every gunshot that I heard. It was sporadic but consistent throughout the night. I was used to staring off into the nothing of the night from my time in the Birdcage, but as awful as that place was, you knew what to expect. This was the tyranny of freedom. Anything could happen now, and we were truly on our own. I wished I had a woman or an angel by my side.

"You still awake?" I eventually heard Ask call out. I had no idea how much time had passed since I lay down.

"I couldn't sleep. I don't think I slept at all."

"We will need to leave soon." I could feel he had more to say. "Why couldn't you sleep?"

"I don't know."

"Most people live in constant stimulation of their senses. So they don't want to sleep until they're too tired. They are so terrified of that space between waking and sleep, its silence and the darkness, that they need something to keep themselves from being in the dark or hearing their own thoughts. They leave on lights or they listen to music or they drink, anything that keeps them from facing bitter realities and the truth. It's ironic because they're in the dark and afraid of the dark but want to be kept in the dark. When you remove all the stimulus though and just let yourself be, really be, without fear or expectations, then the secrets of this world may reveal themselves to you."

I didn't really know what to say to that. I watched as Ask laid his body out on the floor, keeping his ear to the ground. I've seen him do weird stuff in the Birdcage, but this was strange even for him. I wondered if the place had made him snap in some way. He turned his head to me knowing I wanted to ask him about it.

"What are you doing?" I obliged.

"This strip mall was built over what used to be a Confederate soldier cemetery."

"What, like the Civil War?"

"Yes."

"Are you even allowed to do that? Destroy cemeteries, I mean?"

"They did it. People who weren't in charge weren't happy about it. They did it anyway. The people they brought here didn't care. Why would they? They got a retail store and an Indian restaurant out of it. All it cost them was the memory of someone else's war, people they had nothing to do with but were rewarded for hating, so they joined in and reaped the benefits. Why wouldn't they?"

I felt like I was starting to understand why Ask always seemed so mad. I never thought about these things. I never really had the time to think about it, and no one really taught me or taught me how. I knew about the Civil War, but I didn't know if I was from the North or the South. I didn't know if my ancestors were here when it happened and if they fought in it. For all I knew, it might have been my own great-great-grandfather, or however many greats, buried beneath the linoleum. Was I robbed? There are many things that are crimes but shouldn't be, like what Ask did, but there are also things that I don't think are crimes but feel like they should be. If I was robbed of my history, then that should be a crime.

I was in a daze thinking about these things and watching Ask. It looked like he was mouthing something, and I felt outside my own body. The more I talked to him, the more I didn't feel quite like myself.

"I can hear them," I thought I heard him murmur, "their forgotten voices drowning in even more blood."

"I'm sorry?"

"I didn't say anything." Then he added, as though he changed his mind, "Just mouthing a prayer."

I shook my head and rubbed my eyes. Ask was staring at me, waiting for me to say something. "I think I'm hallucinating from the lack of sleep."

"You're going to have to suck it up. We need to start moving again."

I felt delirious just getting up and walking. We somehow made it out of that town unscathed, and after we crossed the deserted highway, he was dragging me up this mountainous hill through the wilderness. "We're getting closer there," I heard him whisper. This went on for hours, and was punctuated with my tired threats and desires to stop. They were always hollow words, that was true, but they felt hollower now as I felt I had changed in these few days following him. I looked up at the sky, and the first sign of daylight was beginning to show itself. Instead of blackness and stars blocked by city lights, I could see little waves of midnight blues and deep purples painting themselves for my exhausted eyes.

A hint of light emerged as we came into a clearing somewhere on the side with a lone ash tree and a stone that was placed before it. I realized this must be it and that I had no idea how we got here. It was like we had stepped through a portal to some old magical place untouched by the world outside it. It seemed so hard to find, so out of the way, but now it made sense to me. If Ask's family was this big a deal, then they would desecrate his grandfather's grave like the soldiers' graves.

Ask went ahead of me and knelt down next to the stone. He touched it and spoke down to the bones that were buried there. I turned away from him. It didn't seem right to look. I sat down in a spot where I could somewhat see the road we'd crossed. I could see the town from here, and while it looked peaceful from this far, I wondered if people two hundred years ago during wartime thought the same thing, armies of brothers fighting each other just for all of us to arrive at this same point. I reached down into the grass with both hands, grabbing clumps and tearing some of it up. If robbing people of history is criminal, then criminals must be punished.

As I watched the sun rise, Ask came and sat down next to me. He stretched his arms out then lied back into the grass. His eyes were closed, and his smile was content. I lied down next to him and put my grass-filled hands to my chest, rubbing it. My brain was racing with too many thoughts, but I needed to know the truth now.

"I know you didn't run from the Birdcage because you thought you might never get here again. You're too smart for that, Ask. So, what's the real reason you ran?"

"I did think I might never be here again, but you are mostly right. It's not about my mother. It's about proving a point. I want my oppressors to know they can imprison me seven times and I'll just escape eight. I want them to know they can put all their screens in front of my face, with all of its humiliation and hate meant to break me, and I'll still find a way out here and feel this grass between my fingertips and this sunrise on my face. They can't make me forget who I am, and I'll still be here when they start chopping off limbs. I'll keep coming back here."

"Do you really think you can win?"

"I might not ever win. I'll probably never get anything I want. Every hand I get dealt is a bad one, so I have no choice but to flip the table and draw whatever else I have. All that matters is they don't win. Not one bit. What's funny is I don't matter in the grand scheme of things. I'm just somebody's grandson. They'll die seething anyway."

That was good enough for me. I sat back up and stared back at the ash tree. If the earth could swallow us up right now, I'd die in peace. I never felt this feeling before, and I might not ever feel it again. I felt like the secrets of this world were revealing themselves to me. Was this how Evan felt all the time, this most serene silence? If it was a dream, then I should close my eyes.

In the distance we heard the sirens, as inevitable as death. We waited. So could death. I took a deep breath and counted the seconds. I opened my eyes and woke up new.

Rumspringa

Kleetis Conrad

Thirteen

"*Thou shalt not make unto thee any graven image or likeness of that which is in heaven above, nor the earth beneath. Thou shalt not bow down thyself to them, nor serve them; for I, the Lord thy God, am a jealous God. I visit the in . . .* visit the in. . . ."

The word always escaped me. My father took a long, loud breath through his nostrils. The candle on the nightstand quivered in his ogling eyeballs. His thistly beard perfectly framed his pink, bony face. "Iniquity," he exhaled. "*I visit the iniquity of the fathers upon the children unto the third and fourth generation of them that hate me, showing mercy unto those that love me and keep my commandments*. Have y'been doin' your recitin'?"

The crickets outside went silent as did I. Disappointing my father was not without consequence. Though I knew the punishment would be mild, I remember feeling shame, having forgotten my verses. "I have been," I shrugged, standing there in my button-up undergarments.

"Well, it certainly doesn't sound like ye have been," he answered. "Go and get to bed now, Will." His old, brown Bible made that satisfying *thud*, and I scampered into the sheets.

He exaggerated a groan as he stood from his chair and knelt next to my bed. He glanced at my hands, signaling me to intertwine them as he had.

"Dear Lord and Heavenly Father, ye who sees our hearts and hears our prayers, have mercy on us, O' Lord, just as a loving father has mercy on his *children*."

He cleared his throat and rubbed his face quickly with folded hands, something he did mechanically in prayer.

"Lord, grant us the courage to live humbly and remain unblemished by this world. In Jesus Christ, your only Son, our Lord and Savior. For His namesake, Amen."

A cool breeze shot the smell of fresh dirt and manure through the crack in the bedroom window and pressed against the tiny flames. Our German shepherd,

Hanz, could be heard barking. Father rose to shut the window. He stared out into the dark.

"Wilhelm, you *must* practice your verses. There's much to be done in the fields, but God sees your heart. He wants *you* to know *Him* through His word so He can protect you. Do you understand?"

"Aye, Father. I'm sorry," I yawned.

"You needn't apologize to me, Will. Just to be makin' time for your studies. We must strike a balance between our heads, our hands, and our hearts. 'Tis the way of our fathers before us, the way of the Amish."

The old chapel was atop a grassy hill overlooking the flat farmland. The aging, white paint seemed to chip away in real time. The church sat in eerie silence—row after row of uniform suspenders, spring-colored dresses, bonnets and beards, all with heads bowed and eyes closed. I turned to see a woman, wearing a red shawl with twinkling charms, seated in our family's pew. She cocked her face towards me, smiling, and batted her long lashes in a strange fashion. A tingling, hot wave of fear came upon me, and my eyes darted frantically from the pulpit to the balcony and back again. She was gone. The elegant and wonted stained-glass Apostles began to morph into ghastly, distorted monstrosities. Then, the woman in the red shawl reappeared outside the chapel, looking in through one of the windows. Her face was different now: a long nose; a wide, gangly set of teeth; and finally, a pair of coal-black blinders found my gaze through her wiry, gray hair. She lit a match between her rumpled, yellow fingers and smiled devilishly at me. I was screaming, shaking, and tugging at my mother and father, my brother and my two sisters, but they were frozen in a trance. Black smoke began to billow out from the floorboards, and flames followed. I felt the warmth of the hellish incandescence on my cheeks as fire quickly surrounded the congregation. I cried out—so loud I thought my throat would burst—but not one of my beloved church family looked up from their prayers. I watched through tears as their bodies burned, their flesh swelling and crumbling into ash. Staring still, the haggard woman outside raised a single finger to her grinning lips. *Shush.*

The crowing roosters finally tore me from the horrors of my subconscious. I was surprised my blankets weren't soaked through with sweat. Even the worst nightmares fade swiftly in the morning, only to haunt one's reverie for years to come. My elder brother's bed was still made.

The screen door creaked and snapped behind me. Grandfather was waiting in his rocking chair, as usual. He grumbled quietly, and his boots clomped on the porch planks.

"Good mornin', Will," he said as he stood and squinted into the horizon. "Best get to it."

The land was blue and still. Chirping crickets and our dusty steps were the only sounds on earth. We made our way down the dirt road from the house to the pastures. I broke the peace. "*Stand therefore, having girded your waist with truth, put on the breastplate of righteousness, and shod your feet with the preparation of the gospel of peace—*"

"Bit early for recitin', boy," Grandfather heckled me.

"Father told me I must make time for His word. I shan't disappoint him again. *Above all, take the shield of faith with which you will quench all the fiery darts of the wicked one. And take the helmet of salvation, and the sword of the Spirit, which is the word of God—*"

A loud squish cut me off mid verse. We both stopped and gawked at the heaping mound of horse manure I had carelessly stepped in. Grandfather cracked a smirk.

"Best to watch where you're goin', there, Will."

We arrived at the cow stable, and I collected the pails. Grandfather pulled the small stool over to old Weibsy. I sat down carefully and began tugging on her soft udders. We sprayed milk into our buckets with loud, metallic spurts.

"Grandfather, why do we live out here on our own, away from all the others?"

He cleared his croaky throat. "Why do we keep Zicke away from the heifers?" he asked.

"Because he's ornery and mean and he tries to buck them with his horns?"

"Yes," he answered, "'tis the nature of a goat. The animals are all unique, Will. They have different preferences, different temperaments. 'Tis true for man, as well. Today, we're all expected to live on the same big farm. It's best we keep to our kin. Keep separate."

The cacophony of warbling birds crescendoed as we made our rounds. Grandfather's commentary continued as we fed the fowl and the livestock.

"The swine stay with the swine, the sheep with the sheep, the ass with the jenny, and the colts with the mares. The same is true for the feral beasts of the wild. They mate with their kind. They give birth to their kind. Would you ask a caterpillar to lay with a bear? Or a chicken to build a home with a snake?"

"Nic!" I chuckled and dumped some scraps into the pig troth.

"Some men would try," he said and spat to the side.

"What men?" I asked.

"Ack, they're more akin to rats than men!"

We went to fetch a couple of horses. For a while, all was quiet, save the flies and the cicadas. I brought Felix and Bruno around to the south field and strapped them into the rusty plow. "Grandfather, why do y'always leave church during pastor's sermon?"

He stepped onto the platform and took the reins.

"Pastor doesn't know his knee from his elbow n'more. That's why."

Both horses nickered and eased forward, hauling the plow through the dirt. I climbed up to join him.

"What do y'mean?" I asked.

"The church has been corrupted, Will. Perverted . . . by Jezabelle and Molech. That new pastor is a wolf in sheep's clothing. With a silver tongue! Always makin' excuses for sin and modernity. The Amish ways need protectin'. Enough of this dribble about tolerance and acceptance. 'Tis the feral offspring of our pacifism. I say, enough."

The sun came over the faraway hills, flashing from the windmill to the weathervanes. I led the horses back to the stable, then returned to see Grandfather, kneeling in the fresh, cool soil. I approached tentatively and stood just behind him. He leaned over and plunged his callused hand into the dirt. He squinted as he did, when the sun met his brow.

"Does God ever talk to y'boy?" he asked the horizon.

"Yes. Sometimes. Sometimes, I can hear a voice . . . not in my ears or my head. . . . It's. . . ."

"In your heart." He spun his head around to me.

"Aye," I nodded and hung my head, ashamed to admit something so silly.

"'Tis the blood of our people that pumps through y'Will. The blood of your ancestors. Here." He struck his chest with his fist and a puff of dust left his shirt. "If we allow the corruption of our people, we contaminate our blood. We sever our connection to the past and that voice . . . will be forever silenced."

He grunted as he tried to stand, and I lurched forward to help him. He released a loud, short, raspy breath from the depths of his lungs, as he tended to do. He patted my head.

"Good boy," he said.

He retrieved his pipe and fixed it between his teeth. The familiar scent of his homegrown tobacco soothed me as it did him. We gazed ahead for some time, tracing the fields down to the forest at the edge of the farm. Eventually, we heard manic barking and Hanz came running past us, quick and determined, heading straight for the old hay barn. I shuttered. Though it was once a favorite hiding spot of mine, I avoided the old hay barn like I did my gospel studies. I couldn't reason it. Suddenly, the large, wooden door creaked and crept open. I gasped quietly and winced at the rolling sound of the track wheels. From where we stood, I could see my elder brother, Samuel, emerge from the hay barn, followed by two other kids his age. I wanted to call out to him, but something wasn't right. His stride was wonky. He stumbled and lost his footing a few times coming up the road. His shirt was unkempt, his face pale and soulless. His friends staggered behind him, crowing and snickering.

“What. . . .” I managed to whisper.

Grandfather blew smoke through the corner of his mouth and put his hand on my shoulder. “Rumspringa,” he said.

Seventeen

“Go around the other way, dude; they’re gonna flank us!”

“Shit! Who’s shooting at me?”

“Caleb, I’m at the green door, get over here!”

“Damn it! That bastard with the retro skin just blasted me, boys! I’m out.”

The voices from the gaming headset were the only friends I had made after moving in with Samuel. The latest combat simulator was an addictive fantasy realm complete with colorful, life-like stages, tough-talking avatars, an orchestra of gunfire, and seizure-inducing muzzle flashes. It satisfied a young man’s primal lust for blood, conflict, and victory over his enemies. I found myself fully immersed in this digital purgatory. Initially, when I left the farm, I enrolled in public school, but the other students were hostile and sometimes violent. Even the teachers made fun of my accent. I dropped out within a couple of months. My parents were not pleased, but I told them I would get some kind of job in town soon enough. Sam said school was stupid and there was no good reason to attend. He also told me not to worry about work either, as he intended to start selling weed to pay for the apartment. The hot summer sun sizzled outside, and we lounged in our fortress of soda cans and pizza boxes with the air conditioner cranked.

“Cover me, guys! I’m goin’ in! Ahh!” I bellowed into the microphone and smashed the controller, gritting my teeth. Sam’s phone started to vibrate the plank of wood and crates we called the coffee table. “Samuel! Your phone! Someone’s calling you!”

Sam coughed hysterically into his filthy, brown bong, mid rip, spilling water and hash chunks all over his wife-beater undershirt. Hacking and wheezing, he managed to set the glass on the kitchen counter and shuffle into the TV room. He grabbed his device and swiped right to answer without checking the screen.

“Yo, what up, playa, what took you so. . . . Oh, Father! No, no I thought someone else was callin’.”

Sam’s whole demeanor flipped, and he reverted back to his accent. I paused my end of the game play and removed the headset to listen in. Father had taken to calling him every other week from the new landline at Moses’ saddle shoppe. I could just hear Grandfather grumbling to himself or hollering about technology and Amish birthrates.

“Yes, everything is fine, Father. Will is doing just fine. I’ll tell him. Yes. We’re fine. Tell Mother we . . . we love you both. I’ll try, Father. We’ll see come harvest time. Father, I have to go now; I’m getting another call. Yes, Father. Goodbye.”

He thumbed the phone a few times and put it back up to his ear. “Yo! Yeah. Alright, I’ll be over. Yup. Peace.”

He squeezed the little, black square and slipped it into sagging jeans.

“I gotta go,” he mumbled, fitting a baseball cap to his head and scrambling to find his keys.

“Here.” I snatched them up off the discolored carpet and tossed them.

“Good lookin’, bro,” he said and shot out the front door.

The sidebar chat overflowed with curses and question marks from my video comrades. Alone, now, staring into the sign-out screen, I felt the pit of my stomach churn. Sadness crept over me as thoughts of my mother and sisters pressed their way into my mind. My cheeks began to ache. I set the controller into the lawn chair cup holder and hung the headset on the back flap as I got up.

Samuel once referenced a shoe box full of “porno” that he kept in his bedroom closet. Though he was kidding around with a friend at the time, I was convinced it was in there somewhere. I pulled the folding doors open and stood on tiptoes to search the top shelf for the forbidden treasure chest. After carefully removing and rifling through a few containers, I spotted a reddish shoe box in the upper corner. I grabbed it, set it on the floor and removed the lid. Inside was a small stack of DVD videos and one of those portable DVD players. The disc covers displayed women bending over, spreading their butt cheeks and legs and holding their breasts. One of them was surrounded by erections and donned the title: *Super-Sluts 4*. I ran to the window to make sure Sam’s car was still gone. My heart started racing as I cracked one of the cases and popped the disc into the little player. An FBI disclaimer flashed on the screen, followed by a startup menu featuring some trashy rock music. I sat on the bed with the player in my lap, but before I could press the play button, I felt a strange, sharp pain in my chest followed by a cold tingling in my fingers and my face. I realized I was no longer breathing. In an instant, I was outside of myself, transported into the past.

Seven

With all my might, I heaved and slid the heavy barn door open just wide enough to squeeze inside. The familiar smell of old hay permeated the dark, musty outbuilding. Specks of dust and bugs floated in the bright, yellow stripes that spilled through the wooden slats. I climbed the rickety ladder up to the loft to hide from my big brother, the seeker. I plopped down between two tall hay bales and tried to slow my breathing so I could disappear effectively. Samuel was surely finished counting by now and would likely check the stables first. Then, I heard the barn door slide open and footsteps enter. The door roared shut and the barn was dark again. I covered my mouth, waiting to hear if Sam would check the dry bales or go straight for the ladder. Instead, I heard the bizarre sound of muffled music, a man groaning and a woman crying out, over and over. The noises were microscopic, as if played from a music box inside a jar. I crab-crawled vigilantly to the edge of the loft and peered over the beam to see Father standing in the corner. He was holding something, gazing into it. His face was lit by a glowing, blue light. His breath was heavy.

Twenty-one

"*There is no one righteous, not even one; there is no one who understands; there is no one who seeks God. All have turned away; they have together become worthless. Their throats are open graves; their tongues practice deceit. The poison of vipers is on their lips. Their mouths are full of cursing and bitterness. Their feet are swift to shed blood; ruin and misery mark their ways, and the way of peace they do not know. There is no fear of God before their eyes*."

The pastor's voice reverberated from the pulpit through the archways of the chapel. I let my eyes wander, and I took stock of the remaining church members. The pews were no less crowded then when I was a child, but the members themselves emanated emptiness. I felt as though we were all going through motions, without fervor, without spirit. Perhaps my trials in the modern world had tainted my faith and condemned me to a sort of limbo, a life-long Rumspringa. I was shaken from my thoughts by the pastor's words:

"*There is no difference between Jew and Gentile, for all have sinned and fall short of the glory of God, and all are justified freely by his grace through the redemption that came by Christ Jesus.* So sayeth the word of our Lord."

"Praise be to God," the congregation chimed in unison.

My father glanced at me with tired eyes.

After the service, I stood with my parents and my two sisters just outside the chapel, greeting and well-wishing the other members as they filed out through the large, double doors. I was, indeed, the only one in modern clothes. My father sidestepped to me.

"Forgive me, son," he muttered in between handshakes and forced smiles.

"Eh?" I thought maybe I had misheard. He didn't answer.

We walked together, Father and I, back toward the house from the chapel. The farm was the same as I left it after my last visit. Somehow, he had kept up the work without us.

"I meant to tell you earlier, Will," he began as we slowed our pace.

"What's that?" I asked.

"Your brother is in jail." His voice trembled slightly. "He was able to call your uncle Mose yesterday." We stopped in our tracks as the wind picked up the dirt.

"I'm sorry, Father."

"I don't know where I went wrong. All we can do is pray and ask God for forgiveness, aye Will?"

I sighed involuntarily and looked away. He cleared his throat, and we continued along the road.

"Well, you've got yourself a good girl, now, eh?" he nodded to the house where my girlfriend, Amy, was helping Mother with the laundry. He patted my back. "You two thinkin' about rejoinin' the church, Will? Mother asks me every day."

The women spotted us from the yard. They both smiled and waved. My two sisters came running around the house, giggling and yelling.

"We'll see, Father."

Grandfather's grave was next to the big oak tree on the south end of the farm. After lunch, Amy and I decided to walk there together.

"You go ahead," she insisted as we approached the humble stone.

The grass was soft and cool underneath the tree. I took a deep breath before kneeling, just short of where I pictured his feet to be. The crudely chiseled, gray rock stared back at me.

"My whole life, I heard that voice. For a time, I thought it was God talkin' to me, watchin' over me. When I left, I tried so hard to block it out, but no use. It never went away. It stuck with me. It haunted me. But that voice doesn't speak in verses or riddles. And I realized it wasn't God. It was you."

I stayed there for longer than I could fathom. My face welled up, and my nose started to drip. I took in another breath and stood up to face my future wife. She understood.

"You okay?" she asked me.

"Yes." I sniffed, and I took her hand.

"You ready to go?" she smiled.

"Yes, let's go."

Never spent

Paul Dempsey

Hermann woke up to the sound of the delayed alarm clock. The ceiling above looked completely smooth and monochromatic in the yet dark winter morning. The sky was brightening through force. Perhaps it did not want to get any brighter. Dull clouds formed another ceiling over the whole city. Across the street, the new university building made of metal and glass merged with the sky, as if supporting it like a pillar. Hermann got out of bed, went to the kitchen, and made some coffee. The coffee was bland—he had opened the pack a long time ago.

After getting dressed, Hermann went out, closed the door, and got into the elevator. It took twenty-five seconds to go down seven floors. Then he was out into the street, cold and windy and with winter dust in the air. The road to work took thirty-five minutes, most of it by Labiauer Street with four lanes always full of cars. The view of the King's Gate was Hermann's only reward on the way to work. It always stood out of the surrounding landscape with grim, Soviet-era, Khruschev houses and the noisy Labiauer Street with many new, tall blocks of flats on both sides of it.

Hermann entered the office building that stood just across the street from the King's Gate. The office of the company he worked for was on the third floor. He went up there.

"Good morning," he said, twisting his mouth into a smile.

There were some twenty desks in a T-shaped room. Hermann's was beside a wall, with no one sitting next to him at least on one side. Two monitors helped to fence him off from the person across the narrow passage. There was only his colleague on the left that could see him and his right monitor. That was not really a problem since the man was out on business trips most of the time.

Hermann turned on the computer. His first task for the day was to write a spam letter, the kind he would never read himself, something about "the best strategy out there" and "earning millions in five easy steps." It worked in Thailand, they said.

Then there were ads. Hermann had to write them all unique and creative and somehow the same as the day before. He forced the words out of himself onto the screen.

A meaningless meeting followed where nothing important was discussed, but you had to listen to the voices that you'd got sick of over the years. Hermann watched the talking heads, and the sounds were blending into a monotonous hum until he could not understand what they were saying.

When will lunchtime come, Hermann thought. *Want to smoke*, he formulated his only desire. You could probably smoke in the office a hundred years ago. Hermann looked out of the window at the other end of the room and saw only the bare trees on the Lithuanian Shaft.

Lunchtime finally came. Hermann went out of the building and crossed the street to a small kebab place. He ate there, looking out at the gray street with some old cobbles showing from underneath the asphalt. Then he walked along the quiet alley that went all the way from the King's Gate to Rossgarten Gate between the canal and the shaft. The canal was calm, as always, with occasional ducks swimming in the dark water. There were trees in the canal that had fallen there a week before, during a storm, but no one had since taken them out. The pipe smoked too hot because of the wind, so Hermann put it away in his pocket. It was not worth walking there now without a pipe. He went back to the office.

Again, he had to write something. Another empty text, a waste of letters. Hermann could not force himself to write it. He sat uneasily at the desk and stared at the screen, watching time pass slowly, minute after minute. A meeting brought him out of this state of numbness, only to immerse him into the incoherent noise of the talking heads. He could not escape it. Hermann remembered the trees that had fallen into the canal behind the Lithuanian Shaft. *Who will take them out of there?* he wondered. *It's no place for them.*

The work day ended at last. Hermann put on his coat and went out into the already dark, cold street with car lights and street lamps and all the evening sounds of the city.

His two legs were moving with great difficulty. His body wanted to collapse right there, in the street, and never to rise up again. It felt as broken as a toy, when children stop playing with it, and no one ever thinks of repairing it. There lurked somewhere at the back of his soul a disgust for his life, but he had forbidden himself to complain long ago, and so he did not quite know what he felt, or if he felt anything. There was only emptiness and winter without snow and the strange desire to collapse right now and become one with the darkness of the evening, a shadow, a void.

Hermann came home and sat down on the couch without undressing. For a long time, he watched the shadows of buses and cars moving on the ceiling from one side to the other and back again. Then he looked out of the window at the cloudy, yellow-gray sky that reflected the city lights. You could not see the stars because of them. The last time he had seen stars all across the sky was on Kurische

Nehrung several years before. He remembered old stories about the fishermen's houses there and how children used to hug big porcelain stoves in winter, with the snow and the pines and the stars outside.

Hermann glanced at his radiator and grinned. Maybe he could go and see the spit himself, he thought. The next day would be Saturday. He had to go to sleep. With much effort, he put his coat on the rack and got into bed with the rest of his clothes still on.

Morning came unexpectedly. Hermann lay in bed and wasn't sure he could get up and go to the spit. After some time, he dragged himself out of the bed. He put on his old coat, took a pipe and some money, and came out into the street. The gray sky was all over the city. Hermann went to the bus stop and got on the bus going to the center. The city was changing rapidly. Everywhere there grew ten, twelve, fourteen-storied houses. None of them were nice. Hermann got off the bus on Steindamm and headed towards Kneiphof. He lit up the pipe and crossed the bridge to the island where the cathedral still stood after eight hundred years and all the wars—gothic, grand, and beautiful.

Hermann recalled his youth in the park that had been planted on Kneiphof in place of the houses. The girl he loved, the picture of her against the cathedral in Autumn, looking at him with eyes full of love, rum and kisses. *Those were very old memories*, he thought. *When was it? Ten years ago?* He was seventeen then. That was gone. He had started many things. His book had to save the world, but he wrote less and less every year, even though he told himself he would start writing properly tomorrow, or the next week, or on holiday. And the proper writing never happened. He had perhaps a third of the book written and an infinite amount of notes taken for it. He still took notes. Recently, he noticed there were many that repeated each other.

"Farewell, Kneiphof," Hermann said. "Farewell, cathedral."

He crossed the bridge again and went to the Nordbahnhof through Steindamm and Hansaplatz. There he took a train to Cranz. The fields out of the window had all the russet colors of late autumn, but now they were cold and hard. In Cranz, Hermann bought a bottle of rum and got on the bus to Kurische Nehrung. Soon there were dunes and pines and firs and spruces all green for many kilometers. He got off the bus halfway from Rossitten to Pilkoppen. There he stood for a minute, facing the forest, uncertain.

Finally, he entered it. Quickly through the forest, up a dune, and there it was. The sea. Metallic, cold, and lifeless. Hermann came down the dune with the sand creaking and whistling under his feet. There was no one at the beach as far as he could see. *We shall surrender on the beaches*, he thought and grinned. He came closer to the sea past the line of small pebbles, past the wet sand, down to the water. Hermann checked his pockets, but there was nothing to forget. He slowly got into the quiet sea, making short steps, up to the sheen, up to the knees. It was cold, but not too cold. He stopped. Suddenly, he felt warmth around his feet, coming up to his knees. In front of him was endless water. A few more steps and he would feel it hold him up, then drag him down. Then he would gasp.

Then everything would end. There would be only a bloated piece of meat on the sand. Hermann turned, made a few steps parallel to the beach and looked at the dunes. He imagined how he looked from up there. *What are you doing?* he thought, turned once again, and waded ashore. At the beach, Hermann instantly got very cold. He took a drink of rum and briskly walked to the forest.

He looked around. The forest was green and warm. He used to love Kurische Nehrung and its pines. He'd spent a lot of time there as a child. Another drink of rum. It got warmer. Hermann felt soft moss under his wet feet. He breathed the air. It was fresh and smelled of pines. The moss was so soft that he wanted to lie down. So he did. Now he saw only pine tops and the sky above. The picture didn't seem real. Too far away from the office and the city, disconnected from that reality. Hermann watched the pines sway and the clouds float endlessly up in the clearing sky and suddenly felt very calm. The legs did not bother him. He needed nothing. He became one with the forest, immersed in it, sleeping and not sleeping, losing the sense of time. His body was now part of its stream of energy, its life. It was not quite his body anymore. Hermann didn't move and didn't want to move. His mind could now think clearly and properly as he watched the pine tops swaying gently against the blue sky with rare clouds. What if that was how one died? The fever was building up inside his body. So peacefully. He wanted this peace to last forever. An end to misery, failure. Remember the dreams of old. Going to the sea. Travel. Write. Read. Live a meaningful, colorful, interesting life. Live the life of a writer. It was too late, though. It was all wasted. He did not want anything anymore. Had no strength to do it. All spent. Even that feeling that he had when reading how Parisian mist smelled like wild strawberry. Where was this Paris now anyway? Gone. Life too. Peace. Quiet, peace here in this forest where it's so good to lie on soft moss. Pines creaking lightly and that pine top swaying calmly there and back again, there and back, and there, there, there, there. . . .

After what seemed like hours for him, with his mind pure and empty and numb, thoughts started returning to Hermann. The fever subsided. *The forest is quite all right,* he thought. It's alive. Remember? "But for all this, nature is never spent." Yes. The spirit of the forest. He used to believe in such things. Spirit or no spirit, the forest was alive. After all, maybe he wasn't spent completely. He no longer felt like he needed peace. Besides, it was stupid. Stupid all along. Could he go on, then? Not spent yet. Could a man be spent? No. A man is like nature. A man is never spent.

Hermann got up, much to his surprise, and walked somewhere aimlessly, just to use his body, all of it. Around him was a bright forest with patches of moss on piney hillocks glimmering in soft sunlight. "There lives the dearest freshness deep down things," he recalled again. He saw a tall pine and started climbing it, branch by branch, to the top where the sun shone on it mildly, eveningly. Hermann felt some pleasant fire go through his muscles as he clung to the branches, used his feet to test which of them were strong enough, and pulled himself higher and higher. At last, he was up among the pine tops, hot from the climbing. The sun caressed his face. He felt cleansed, born anew. The dirt on his soul was gone. There was an old Prussian house with a porcelain stove and a clear desk waiting for him somewhere. His hand was itching to take a pencil.

The world around Hermann was glowing with hope and life. The lagoon on the left and the sea on the right, the forest around him and the sun going down into the glistening waters still kept the freshness and the power of the first day of creation, and he could handle anything. Besides, the sun would also rise.

Touch Grass

Froskaz

It's been three days since I buried myself in the ground. Not completely in there of course; vertically, only up to my chest and armpits, my arms and head are free above the soil. I can get out if I want, I think. The spade is a little too far away, but I can probably dig myself out with my hands if enough force is used. I had fit comfortably before when I first dug it, a little snug—then the rains came, heavy and hard, beating me like pellets. I held my arms around my face and cradled into the soft ground before me. It beat the ground too, like a million little drums, and by the time it was soft enough to raise my head to feel the gentle drops, the wet mud formed opaque rivers that had flowed into the tiny gaps between me and the earth until it had encapsulated me, holding me tight like a primal embrace. I haven't tried, but I think I could get out if I wanted. I'm not sure I do.

My body is sore, and something gored my leg earlier, I believe a large mole or a small badger. Came through the ground, bumped into my thigh and just started savaging. I didn't move. I felt as if I was a tree in that moment, unable or unwilling to stop it. But trees have their own kind of retaliation or survival strategies; I had no mycorrhizal system nor chemical defenses. I also couldn't regenerate a limb from just a stump. But the attack didn't last for too long and soon the creature left. My leg was pretty numb beforehand, but now there's a dull stinging biting through the nothingness. The wet mud packed back into it though, I think, but I don't know if it's good or bad. Does that help the wound recover or does it increase the likelihood of infection? Don't mud baths promote healing?

I haven't eaten in a few days, obviously, though that stopped feeling like an issue yesterday. The wanting just went away. I've drank the rain whenever I felt the need. I'm sure it never stops. Occasionally I'll just loll back with my mouth open, drinking my fill—the process becomes relatively automatic pretty quickly. And it's a good stretch for my back considering how much of my time I've spent leaning forward while sleeping. I've adjusted quickly to that too. My back is limber in all sorts of new ways; all it took was a little necessity. I'm not sure if I'll need that if I ever get out. I didn't before. But maybe I will. My posture was pretty awful; surely this can't hurt? I never realized how little I lifted my chest up until I needed to drink. It was difficult at first, using muscles I've never used, but now it's easy and natural. That's how we're supposed to be, right? Chest up and proud. It's fair to say I didn't have a chest before. Now, halfway in the earth, I have one.

The rain has made my bare skin gnarled and wrinkly. I wonder if anyone would think I really was a tree if they happened to pass by, which they wouldn't do anyway. I'm far out the back of my land, and it's just me for miles. No one else wants to be here, to live here. I'd bought the land for everything I had left, even knowing it was worthless. Felt like everything else was worthless too; at least some land with some trees and boggy earth was cool. Plus, I could dig a hole and get in it and nobody would stop me.

I've been feeling a sense of peace I haven't felt, perhaps ever. A sense of agelessness as if I had stayed in this mud for countless eons and would remain in it for longer still. It had only been three days, as I said, yet these three days felt longer than the rest of my life put together. There was the past and there was now. I didn't want for anything. I didn't feel pulled to anything. I didn't want for enjoyable things in the same way I didn't want for awful things. Both were memories of the past; both were foreign to me in the same way; both would equally destroy my peace.

Some more days passed by, though I stopped counting. Each day felt endless as I faded into the background of the field I was in. There is so much animal life here that I absently watch day in and day out. It was so bursting, so insistent. The construction of molehills felt rapid. I watched the flowers move in real time. When the sun finally appeared from behind the clouds and rain, I unfurled like those flowers and basked in her wretched glory as she teased me into movement—though those flowers opened up quicker than I, hungry as they were for her.

When the stars come out, I watch them too, as they travel through the sky: burning, whirling vortexes that dance across the blackness of the void. The great river flows up above me, them the little eddies in its endless stream.

And there is now something more. I feel something moving very slowly, impossibly slowly through the soles of my entombed feet. I had forgotten I could feel through them. There's something growing, something building around the bottom of my feet, something sending signals very slowly, very weakly through the floor of my feet. I don't know what. My sense of touch has become strange, numb, and yet hypersensitive. I wonder if this was what trench foot feels like. But it doesn't disturb my peace, so I let it lie. My body has two forms now, I find: opened up, arms unfurled, palms and chest up for when I bask in the sun or drink the nourishing rain; or arms closed, head down, palms down, and shoulders hunched for when I sleep the time away. My sleep is strange though, and I feel more and more as if the boundary between awake and asleep blurs. My dreaming visions are surely the same as my awakened ones, and I transition between the two states effortlessly. Moving takes me an impossibly long time now, and the connection between moving and not moving, awake and sleeping seems to become more and more like a strange and obscure memory. Why should one be awake to move? Why should a sleeping one stay still?

The movement at my feet is growing. I've become hyper-aware of my body, even as I remain in this tranquil state. I feel the earth around me and the deep connections flowing through it. The stars seem to stare down at me in a way I hadn't noticed before—a vast, interconnected tapestry, connected to me too. My throat swallows, and my muscles flex, though I know it must take an age for them to do so. A million eyes look at me from the depths of the night, and I feel open now, exposed. Reborn. My knees would tremble in glorious terror if they could, and I stare in awe until the reddish pink floods the sky with the dawn's entrance. My feet twitch in response—no. Something touches my foot in response. It's hard to know the difference by now. The appendages on the bottom of my legs feel as much a part of me as the rocks in the field. Still, I felt something from them, a pushing from the outside coming in. It was insistent, constantly repeating. It made me think of morse code. It was very weak. I couldn't feel it at all unless I truly concentrated. But it was there. There was a certain predictability to it, a pattern. A message?

I did not dwell on it overmuch, fascinated as I was by the world around me and in such a state as to find any kind of exertion overstimulating. The message continued coming through, slow and insistent. I did not have to concentrate to feel it now; knowing it was there had broken some sort of barrier, and my sensory systems had adjusted in kind. I had not moved my feet in the many days since I had first felt the message coming through. I wasn't sure I could, if I somehow remembered how. But movement had been replaced with a higher order of sensitivity, and now I could feel a distinct pushing, pushing at the soles of my feet—not at, *through*. That alerted me slightly, making my eyes open wider than they had in days. They had been heavy lidded, seeing everything as a blazing rush of life and movement through the periphery of sight, but now they concentrated. This was anathema to me now though, and I felt it an invasion of my peace. My eyes rested on a small, lone tree not too far from me before I fell back into that heady daze, awed and one with the violent circulation of the earth and the sky.

I woke slowly, confused to the boundaries of awake and dreaming still. The pushing I had felt earlier continued, and I realized I was right: it was through the soles of my feet. I could feel energy rushing through the bottom of my legs, slowly making its way up to the rest of me. It didn't come from nowhere, and I realized too that something had connected itself to me through my feet and was delivering that energy. I felt the progression of growth from my feet upward. My sensory system was developing rapidly, or so it seemed, as quick as my thoughts, though many days passed as I comprehended what had happened to my legs. The pattern felt like a drumbeat now, sending itself up through my bloodstream and hitting my heart, resonating against it. It had continued unchanged. But maybe that's because it really was a message? And messages are sent to receive a response, right? But if it was a message, then there was something sending it. I fell back into my restful position, far too exerted for all that thinking. It was a couple more revolutions of the stars before I took up the mantle of thought once more.

My eyes scanned the field slowly. The small tree I had gazed at before seemed less innocent now. I was beginning to feel it had *reoriented* itself towards me in a way I hadn't been aware of back then. This was the one ruining my peace. It wasn't moving, not visibly, not even over the span of many days—I'd have noticed—but it had a certain directionality to it now, almost as if it was pointing at me. It shook in the wind. The morse code through the bottom of my foot continued its endless tattoo. I would fix this. My feet had now adapted to their hypersensitive state. If I could feel a message, I was sure I could send one. Through a momentous and herculean release of effort I managed to signal back. I could feel the electricity move down my spine and into my legs and then through my knees and down further and then into my feet and then . . . not gone. I could still feel the electricity as it continued outside my body. It passed through me, went underneath the ground and kept moving until it reached the small, lone tree not so far from me. It was then, as that message kept spreading that I realized it was not alone, not at all. It was part of a vast underground network intricately connected. And now so was I. The message on my foot stopped. A different one came. But the enormity of my undertaking had pushed me beyond my limits, and the fog over my brain descended as I fell back into my trance state, following the sun and the stars.

When I next awoke, I felt energized. A heady rush flowed into me from the outside world. Energy in its purest form transferred up my legs and into my spine. My body creaked strangely as I unfurled in the rising sun. My feet, conduits for the outside world as they are, were under siege. Before I had been receiving one strange message through the ground. Now I was receiving hundreds. I looked around my land once more, and the whole forest had changed. Every tree and most every plant in sight was *reoriented* towards me. I could feel it, feel them through my feet. The great deluge of energy I was feeling came from them, transferred through the ground directly into me. I truly appreciated now the immense power of the glorious sun. It was incredible feeling the energy flow directly into the plants I was connected to. And it was amazing when some of that was siphoned off into me—a tiny amount, a miniscule percentage. But it flowed constantly as the sun's power continuously fed into the plants. They could only store as much as they could handle, and that was filled up quickly. So, I decided to pull more from them, to figure out how. It happened in bouts. It was an intense activity to push myself into movement, into moving my electricity through my nervous system and into my feet. Every time I sent a new message, I would fall asleep, passed out from exhaustion. Often the messages I sent would receive no response, and the amount of energy I was getting received no change, no confirmation that they had been read. Why would they be, when I did not know their language? This was trial and error. Every time I fell asleep, I wondered if I had accidentally sent the wrong message, asking them to stop sending to me, cutting off my energy source. It was entirely possibly that I would, firing random signals into the dark ground as I was. I found the thought of death did not bother me overmuch. But as fate would have it, every time I woke up, every time I survived. And then one day, I got truly lucky. I hit the right one.

I woke up sooner than I usually do, feeling more powerful. I had discovered the word I had been searching for, the word that would elevate me. *More.*

And more surely came. *More.* Rivers of lightning coursed through the underground, through the soles of my feet and into my spine. From there it shot out across the rest of me. *More*, I demanded hungrily, until the plants and trees connected to me were giving as much as they got.

But I was not made for this. Now that I had the energy, now that it flowed so intensely through me, I had to move. Still, I could not dig myself out, could not break myself from my energy source. I didn't know whether it was possible or not and was too entranced with the power to try. But with what I had above the ground I chased the sun across the sky and danced with my arms and head frantically and nervously underneath the baleful glare of the uncountable stars. My body used up some, but my mind took most of the energy. It was like I was a biological super-computer. Immense calculations were nothing to me, and with my intense imagination I felt I lived the life of every plant and creature in my lands. I calculated their lives. I watched them play, and in my mind saw it through their eyes and the eyes of all the other lifeforms in the fields. The whole world was created anew in my mind, and I was every part of it.

When one thing killed another, I was both prey and predator. When something dug, I was both digger and the soil. When something flew, I was both flyer and sky. I had become part of the whole and was the whole. I was this corner of reality. It seemed to me I almost lived an eternity like this. The passage of time was nothing as I lived and died a hundred times over, living as all manner of creatures, then fed on my own corpses first as the fox and later the worm. I was the buzzard in the tree. I was the adder in the grass. I was the loping hare. I was the croaking frog. I was the spiraling life, a mixture of every living thing here. In my field I was endless; I felt and observed everything, and from other eyes, and I observed my body dancing to the strange rhythm of the sky as I did so. Its guidance had become subconscious and my responses to it instinct. When the sun came out, I chased her. When the rains came out, I thirsted. When the wind whipped, I howled. When the moon rose, I held eye contact. And I danced the whole time. Endless movement, endless action, endless life and death. New rose and fell, birthing more new. Everything grew and decayed. Everything rose and fell, just to rise again.

I knew the earth and the sky more intimately now. They who appeared first as passive observers had become in my mind the movers for the entire play. Their clashes and romances were sometimes impossibly slow and sometimes tempestuous and violent. They were minuscule and hard to see; they were overt and impossible to ignore. Every life was mediated through the actions of these two, and I became so full of awe as I observed the play of the majestic. I almost became absorbed in trance once more, though this time it was the trance of action. Overaction, endless thought, and stimulation as I gazed up in wonder at the immense powers around me. But something else was swelling in me, taking over me, something I was unable to ignore.

I was not taking part in the great play. I watched life and death but did not live life and death. Upon this realization, one of my toes twitched. It was a shocking and frightening feeling, strange and awful—completely foreign by now. Strange responses came from the multitude I was connected to, which I interpreted to be confusion. Why not? To move is to send electrical signals after all. I imagined I had just sent a very odd message. But perhaps it did not matter now. I knew what the toe twitch was. It was a recognition of myself as life, as something that moves. I had to move; I had to get out of this hole. But I had felt something else when I twitched my toe: I had hit something hard. I moved my foot now, just slightly, all I could manage. It hit something hard also. I moved it the other way and felt the same. I was beginning to grow concerned. There had been no rocks down there before. I moved my foot up. It hit something there too. The various roots must have reached out to me and coalesced around me—no wonder I had been able to communicate to all the trees; they had me in their grasp! I began to scratch at the earth around me, muscles weak but bursting with energy. I knew well the motions of the sky and earth and could fathom from the divine play around me that there would be rain soon.

Rain there was, and storm and tempest! The wet mud was easier to claw, the shovel—long forgotten—still just out of reach. I just had to free myself enough that I could lean, really lean, and stretch and grab it. The wind pushed me to and fro, and I used its momentum, ripping myself free of the thick earth.

The rain was pelting when I finally managed to escape enough to grab the shovel. It had formed little rivulets into the slope I'd been digging as I freed myself, and the tiny current managed to carry the tool just into reach. From there the job became but a little easier, being able to use a lever to produce more force than my weakened hands would allow. By the time I dug down enough to reach my waist, another revelation was waiting for me. Black lines ran up my hips and across my legs, emanating from a spot about halfway up my thigh. I knew what they were: roots under my skin, climbing through my body. There had been a wound in my leg, I remembered—that must have been the entry point. I cleared more earth, and sure enough there was a strange wooden cast around that part of my thigh, seeming for all the world to be an odd mix between wood and flesh. I dug around the other side of my legs, launching mud as I did so. I was granting myself some room. I knew it would be easier to extract myself from it rather than destroy it. And besides, I was filled with curiosity as much as revulsion. And I wanted to see what was going on with my feet before I tried anything drastic.

So, I dug deeper and deeper as the storm clouds clashed above me. By the time I got down to my feet, the dance of the sky and earth around me was in full sway. Spiraling cones of white, made of that strange wood and flesh mixture stuck out through the ground. It had grown thickly around my feet, and when the lightning crashed, I could see the tinge of red and the movement of blood through veins within the odd structure. I crashed my shovel on top of the pale root cases around my feet, but that strange substance held firm. It was just soft enough to absorb the impact, yet hard enough to resist whatever damage I was trying to impart. I yelled again and again as I hit it, but it was to no avail.

Strength did not work. I tried a different route. The cones did not completely encase my feet; there was room to pull my ankles out, almost as if they were some kind of strange shoe, far too tight and unable to be removed. I moved my feet mightily now, pushing and pulling this way and that. A sharp pain emanated out from my thigh where the roots penetrated. I moved my feet more, and there was a wet, ripping feeling as something—some kind of skin or membrane—tore within the spiraling white cones around my feet. It hurt slightly, but now I had more freedom to move about the cones. Still, I could not get my foot out, could not remove myself from its trapping.

I felt the grand play take another turn and knew this was my moment, what I'd been waiting for, an explosion of pure energy and movement. I held the shovel up above me as lightning flashed and thunder roared as one—

Blinding light, burnt wood and flesh, and the smell of scorched hair. Lightning had struck right through me, striking the heart of the root system I was encapsulated in. The white wood peeled back just a little, flinched back in response to the fantastic destructive power of the lightning. There was just enough room now to remove my shaking feet from their would-be tomb. It was a painful struggle, but I fought and fought and managed to squeeze through. I saw my feet were red with blood, though it was quickly washed away. I flexed them a little and was more than grateful to find them looking not only normal and hale, but working also. There were little cramps, and movement was not easy, but that was far more than could be expected. The next part would be difficult.

Using the shovel as leverage once more, I managed to slowly climb out of the hole, step by step. The white cast about my leg protested as I moved, but I overpowered it. The roots embedded within my foot as they were removed, so deeply entangled were they with the rest of my system. It took me a very long time, moving centimeter by centimeter and slowly moving the roots this way and that, before they were finally pulled free. The slick rain helped. I was shocked at the sheer length of the root system: it was at least twice as long as my arm and had more strands than I had fingers. It must have been coiled extremely densely within me to have only gotten as far as my hips. I noticed that the roots I had thought were black were in fact red with blood, which dropped from the open ends. With that removed, I finally freed myself from the hole.

It was an incredibly odd feeling, losing my direct connection to the plants and trees I had been so intimately connected with—but it would always be there in the back of my mind—and to not feel encased in the earth as I had been for who knows how long. I did not think it a shame though. I had lost my power source and security but gained my legs, weak as they were. And I had not lost my connection to the earth and the sky.

I barely managed to stand up and observed the land around me. The lightning flashes revealed my body to me, in full. I had become extremely skinny; each muscle and tendon could be accounted for with but a simple look. I moved my legs from side to side and felt a power flowing through them I had not felt in a while—my own.

Through the blinding rain and whipping wind, I looked in the bottom of the hole I'd crawled out of. Hundreds of white, fleshy roots stuck out from the mud into where I had been—connected deeply, intimately to me, to what remained of me down there. Thick, wooden versions of my feet lay in the epicenter, stumps clearly, but there was the red tinge of veins underneath. I checked the bottom of my feet: some little blood holes remained there where root had been ripped from flesh but were otherwise fine. That wasn't the only remnant of me down there. There was the cast of my thigh in root form, created where the wood had penetrated the open wound in my leg, where I had ripped it out. Red blood dripped down my leg from the small hole that I'd pulled it from. The surrounding skin was covered in a heavily calcified scarring, thick and indented like wood itself. But I was fine. I looked down at the strange scene before me. It was time to be done with this.

While the rain hammered on my back and my legs shook, I raised and plunged the shovel again and again until I filled the hole with the wet mud, burying my remains. I passed out from exhaustion then, atop my once would-be grave.

I awoke with the morning sun as usual and flexed my whole body as I unfurled beneath it. I stumbled up, feeling extremely weak. Adapted as I was to the energy source of hundreds of life forms, what I generated myself seemed very little. I knew I would never go back to how I was before that though; I would rather die than become that slow, slumbering being. I hadn't eaten in a long time; food would be my fuel now and once more. It would not be easy, as absorbing the energy from the trees had been.

I wondered what had happened to the immense energy diverted from them to me and whether it would continue to flow into the bloody remnants of me down there, those layers of skin intertwined with root. I was sure it would keep coming though. The flesh I left behind wouldn't die, kept alive by that energy from the trees, and I knew nothing but the correct signal back would stop the process.

A plant may grow back from any stump, but a human may not. What then, would be formed from a strange mixture of the two within the bowels of the earth? I didn't wonder too much. I had other things to do now, other places to be. My nervous system was strong, but my muscles were feeble. My stomach roared and clenched. My metabolism had been incalculable. Now so far from my energy source, my hunger was no less. I needed food: energy dense and in huge supply. I could not return to the slow-thinking, slow-moving person I had been before I buried myself in the ground. Nor could I be the trancelike, seedlike being that did naught but observe the violently moving world. Neither could I be the powerful and vital beast stuck in the ground, fed with huge rivers of energy but unable to move. Movement was my creed now. I could see the endless energy in the world around me. I had felt the awe from the venerable power of the sky, the strength of the lightning, the dance of the stars, and the soothing, life-giving strength of the sun.

And I wanted it for myself. The more energy the better. And I knew where it was. I felt as the first predator felt. The sun's gentle light had become more refined and more concentrated in the body of the plant. It was further concentrated in the rabbit that ate it, then in the fox that ate that. I was salivating at the thought. I knew I could not stay here long. Move, I had to move. I had stayed still in the earth for far too long; now the ever-moving sky would tell me where to go.

I left the shovel there, too weak to carry it as I stumbled off. But just in case there was something growing down there, I made sure to drop the shovel where it would be just out of reach.

Untitled

Gomes

The young man knows something's off. Maybe the air is too thick; is the ventilation even on? A colleague passes by, and their eyes meet for a brief nod of mutual acknowledgment. It's a regular day; it's Tuesday. He knows it's Tuesday because yesterday was Monday and he was off the day before. Impatient and a little fidgety, he's only been there for an hour, and it seems the workday has been going on forever. He reaches for a sip of coffee; it's part of the morning ritual, but the mug is already empty. Has he had enough water? *I should really drink more water*, he thinks to himself. Caffeine messes with the body's retainment of water, or something to that effect. He knows this. He read it somewhere.

As he continues about his day, he occasionally wriggles in his chair, more so than usual. Perhaps the lights aren't bright enough, or maybe the lamps were changed overnight. Things feel different but in a just-the-same kind of way, as if the repetitiveness of this day like any other was just being re-discovered, but he does not quite reach the point of contemplation just yet. Sighs punctuate the numerous pauses in between bursts of meaningless work that appears more meaningless than usual: the tapping of the foot; the playing with the pen; the simulation of untroubled normality at the coworkers that make irregular contact. Maybe he's just getting a little burnt out; it has after all been a considerable streak of months without any sort of holiday.

It's alright, he thought, finally beginning to put his reason to work. *I'm just trading my time for some money*. But this mantra that often serves to summon forbearance toward his unexciting condition falters the more often he resorts to it. Irritability slowly sets in, but not even that is anything new, for this cycle of feelings is accompanied with a nagging self-awareness, a latent rationalization, like the motion of a tide coming in, each wave inching further toward the coast. At some point, it's the little things that make up his orderly surroundings that bother him the most once he starts noticing them, and he is overcome with a need to rearrange things, to fiddle, to re-position, to bend, and sometimes even to damage and to destroy. Another colleague's approaching steps snap him out of these intrusive thoughts, pleasantries are exchanged, and back to his salaried tasks he returns.

The rest of the work day progressed as usual. When he thinks back on it, there's nothing to think back on.

The restlessness that had characterized much of the day on the job did not stay behind as he left. It accompanied him on his way home, souring the usually bland landscape of people and buildings that made up the long journey back to his neighborhood. The weather was gray, cold, and humid, nothing new as it had been the trend for the past three or so weeks. Had he not been so absorbed in his disquiet, he certainly would have lamented the obvious signs of the coming showers, as thick gray clouds slowly rolled in from the horizon, but that urge to alter, dismantle, kick around, and reorganize now seemed projected over all which he laid eyes on.

It was something about the arrangement of houses, the flatness of the asphalt on the road, the neatness of the sidewalks that were at the same time too dirty. The cars sort of all look the same, and the few patches of grass here and there are mowed and sterilized. None of these features are new, and the young man is perfectly conscious that the observations now bothering him constitute neither discovery nor epiphany. These things are there and are the way they are by some other person's design, meant with purpose and function, and despite recognizing through reason their usefulness or reason to be, an inexplicable mixture of tiredness and antipathy was aroused. In a bid to avoid the increasing vex, he took a detour through a less densely populated area, passing by the edge of some woods. He felt tempted to take the trek through the forested area and obliged the urge to do so. The area was known to him as he had hiked there often the previous summer and had begun resorting to paying it short visits during particularly tiresome days when he thought necessary to fill his eyes with green and his ears with quietude, and so, with a ceiling of canopy swaying with the rising winds over his head, he made his way in.

"This is more like it," he exhaled. Here the air wasn't too thick; it was cool and breezy. An earthy smell emanated from the humid ground covered in a cushy leaf litter, and he many a time couldn't help but to stop and run his hand over the cold, wet, fluffy mosses that adorned rocks and trunks, in vivid luscious greens and of notably varied types when inspected from up close. Wherever there were mushrooms, he would kneel by to observe, as they often stood out from their background. He couldn't tell you what any of the multitude of fungi were called, nor whether or not any given type was safe to eat. He always wondered about that but never followed through with the curiosity to learn about foraging. *Maybe one day*, he lied to himself.

A small creek ran by the poorly defined path; he did not remember seeing it during previous excursions, but he was thoroughly enchanted by the sound of the running water. The general area around him was not one he recognized, and the shrubbery and abundant trees on either side of the trail made it impossible to see far ahead in any given direction. He made note of the now dimming daylight, a stronger rustling of the verdant cover of the trees as the wind gained strength, and the first drop of water that met his cheek, coming from above.

Perhaps it was the result of his absentmindedness, or a consequence of his overconfidence in his knowledge of that place. *I'm lost.*

As the pitter patter turned into a drizzle, and the drizzle turned to thickening rain, the young man tried to find his way back to no avail. It seemed that in either direction things felt new and untreaded, and repeated back-tracking back and forth only served to further confuse him. Clothes became soaked, hands got colder, and his hair was drenched as the rain got denser and the winds picked up, causing the tree trunks to sway and creak with its sustained heavy blows, as if the wood groaned under strain. The noises of the downpour and of the continuous gusts were all he could hear; it was as loud as his own thoughts, which had now become hastened and upset. These woods were small—he knew that in his mind—but his heart on the other hand lacked the support of any attempted logical reassurance, as the rumbling of thunder approached from a distance, from every direction. It was under the threat of the falling night and in the hurriedness of trying to reach the end of this something he was lost in that his feet gave way. The young man lost contact with the ground for a second, tumbled, slid, and rolled through mud and brush in a brief but disorienting fall.

Here water no longer showered from above, but rather flowed along the muddy ground, and as he regained his wits, he realized he had slid into the mouth of a shallow cave, offering him respite from the storm above. Only a very dim light made it into this small space, but the darkness there was momentarily nullified by a bright flash, then quickly followed by the shattering clap of thunder, close enough that it shook the ground and raised the hairs on his arms. It was during this impromptu recess from the tribulation of the elements outside that he realized that his chest beat rapidly, not out of fear but out of lively excitement. Adrenaline coursed through his veins; he felt stimulated and tested, untethered by tedious predictability but rather enthused by a daunting unknown. Each roaring thunderclap splintered the woods outside, brightened the cave and raced his heart. He felt frigid, but the air was filled with static and this electricity animated his spirit like he hadn't felt before, and overcome with this lively feeling he let out an excited titter. It wasn't until another flash of light later that he noticed by his side a small, brown toad just a couple of feet away, facing him, seemingly unbothered by the little water flowing under and around him, just stoically sitting there.

The two maintained eye contact for a minute, until the young man blinked. He wasn't scared of critters, and the idea of having lost a staring contest to a toad drew a smile upon his face. Of course, he never stood a chance, however; toads don't normally blink unless they're eating. The company of the animal brought an unexpected sense of companionship and guardianship over him, and as the time passed, and the storm outside died down, the young man's weary eyes slowly closed, and sitting with arms and head over his knees, he drifted into sleep from exhaustion.

He woke up to the sound of chirping coming from above. The toad was no longer beside him, and with the light of dawn chiming in, his place of refuge seemed much smaller than he had thought it to be. He crawled up the slope he had fallen through and was greeted with the most serene of feelings. The sun-crisped woodland was dampened from the night before, but the colors seemed brighter and more vibrant, and golden god rays shone through the scattered branches above. It seemed obvious to him that the sun had just recently risen and the day had just barely started, but the blissful feeling was quickly interrupted by remembering that he was still lost. He made his way in a direction he was the least unsure about, and to his surprise it was only a matter of a few minutes until the edge of the woods came into view, along with a familiar neighborhood not far from where he lived. This of course was absolutely bizarre, but the young man did not find himself inclined for big inquisitions. He was hungry, tired, his clothes still wet, and the damp cold was now felt down to the bone. He felt miserable, but he also felt triumphant.

Away from things and places built and shaped by the will and intent of Man, away from the day-to-day nursery provided by the architecture of utility and efficiency, he stumbled onto a sobriety that was as cold as it was magical. The galvanism of that storm animated his body and spirit in such a way that, upon meditation over his ordeal, he could only describe his daily lifestyle up until that point as more of a deathstyle. But the young man did not become flustered with the following days that came, as full of that exchange of personal time for money as they were, as he put it. On the contrary, it seemed as if the discovery of this reality that he felt as if it were more real than the day-to-day "reality of life" meant that there had to be much more to existing than thick air and the morning rituals of productivity. The mosses, the toads, and the storms would remain outside, independent and unaffected by the restlessness of rearranging things, of fiddling, re-positioning, bending, and sometimes even damaging and destroying.

He knew he would soon have to go back to work; it was Wednesday after all. He knew it was Wednesday because yesterday was Tuesday, when we lost his footing but found his grounding.

Soon It Will Be Light

Andy Hunyadi

I had figured out how to kill myself.

Conscientious to the end, my biggest concern was not leaving a mess for the people who would have to clean it up. Perhaps mostly out of vanity, my second concern was leaving a presentable corpse. Having seen enough gore vids of suicides and jumpers online and then in person overseas had given me premonitions of how my face might look like blown open, and something about it seemed humiliating. Unlike my boomer relatives who constantly smirked and squawked about "Why should I care? I'll be dead!" whenever you tried to impress some time preference on them, I had some care about things after my physical death, intimations towards continuance, a vague sense of the spiritual, I guess.

With no access at the time to a gun and no desire to go out violently, I had it narrowed down to hanging, slicing wrists, or gassing. I had immediately dismissed pills as they seemed too unlikely to work correctly and there was something inherently feminine about it to me. Ironic considering I was looking to check out because "I was sad," but the thought of being roused by some disinterested paramedic, covered in vomit while the cop and his partner exchanged knowing looks—"What a faggot"—didn't appeal to me. Neither, actually, did the bleeding out in the bathtub. Too dramatic, too Sylvia Plath. I flirted with goths in high school, but even this seemed a little too on the nose. Hanging seemed out; another downside of renting a shoebox to live in is the lack of sturdy overhead beams like you might find in a garage, just smoke detectors and contractor-special clearance lights dotted with fly corpses. That left gassing.

I had worked out the details sitting in traffic one day, stuck watching the red tail lights ahead of me wash down the windshield in the sleet. The drive took about as long as it did to walk, given the traffic, but I preferred the relative comfort of a plastic and imitation leather, steel-cased bubble over the dreariness of the cracked concrete, featureless blank panels of steel and glass, and the chaotic mishmash of angular shapes that made up the few blocks from work to home. I had come to view this ugliness as purposeful as opposed to incidental. It was tailor-made to crush what vestiges of soul one had left. Seeing the exhaust billow out of the car idling forward in front of me was the eureka moment.

There was a vacuum repair store on the corner—for those who would repair something rather than throw it away, unlike myself—and I put two and two together and came up with a mobile gassing machine. A length of vacuum flexi-tube from my tailpipe into my car, which was the only comfort outside my home I knew, and I could quietly pass into the hereafter, wherever it may be. No fuss, no mess, just a pretty corpse, a quiet ride and an easy cleanup for the taxpayers. They should bury me in a hero's grave with the key to the city for this. More irony, that only in death would I be appreciated, seen, maybe. There's those high-school goths again.

I had joined the infantry right after graduation out of a misguided sense of patriotism, which I felt was lacking in my fellow countrymen. After 9/11, the beginnings of the good team (me), bad team (you) divisions began to coalesce and become obvious to even the most checked out, apolitical normie. My region was full of those that thought it was gauche, taboo, low-status to support your country. I grew up in the farmlands outside the city and had always been an outsider, and eventually started leaning in to it, internalizing my family's strong conservative leanings as moral superiority and figured I'd show these liberal hippy fucks what's what by Serving My Country™ and Making Something of Myself™. From high-school loser to hometown hero, that would be me.

Two tours in Afghanistan later, I did not renew my contract and left back to the city. I had seen two men I would gladly call brothers die in front of me when their carrier flipped over after detonating a roadside bomb and they got crushed by and in it. Nothing I did there made me feel heroic. Nothing I saw there served my nation. Home could not have cared less: a "Thank you for your service; have you seen the new episode of *Big Bang Theory*?" and that was it. The boys who had made my life a living hell in high school were now family men, living in homes their dads bought them as wedding gifts for them and their prom dates, now fat, but homely and tending to twins. I had a green duffle bag with shirts that no longer fit and memories I repressed.

I ended up back in a city I hated—since my folks had sold our childhood home once I was out of school and moved to an HOA in a southern state where the leading cause of death is collision with golf cart—and was working a minimum wage job whose hours were oh dark thirty to stupid early, five days a week starting Wednesday. This meant my time off was me, wide awake at three a.m. on a Tuesday in February in a city that rolled up its sidewalks after supper. I only saw the sun in fleeting auras on the horizon as it retreated or as I pulled the towel serving as a blackout curtain over the two by three-foot window above my bed so I could sleep. I would have turned to drugs to numb this, but I didn't make enough money to even start. I tried to numb it with alcohol, but thanks to, on my dad's side, a generations-long tradition of alcoholism, quickly even a mickey didn't make a dent on my smooth brain. I couldn't afford a bottle and a half of whisky every night to get a buzz, so I stopped bothering.

I told myself this was all temporary, just while I found something more, something worthwhile, something with dignity. Turns out my work experience in the infantry didn't translate to much beyond the civil service, and I had been turned down three times now by various police and government services. Officially, my applications didn't quiiiiite rise to the top of the "extremely high level of applicants" they had received this fiscal year. Unofficially, but in reality, it was because they were no longer hiring White men at this juncture. A retired recruiting sergeant in a nearby police force who was neighbors with my folks let that one out of the bag after a frank discussion with me when I went to him for advice.

With nothing else to pass the time, I would pull my pre-deployment era laptop, with its broken lid hinge and grinding fan ball bearing, into my bed and browse online for eight or ten hours at a time. Online I could disappear into a world and environment of my choosing and try and seek the brotherhood I had last left bleeding out screaming in the dust of Kandahar. Here, a comforting numbness.

Online, I quickly found groups and pages of things I was actually interested in, conversations with people, the sort I couldn't have with the few I knew in reality without getting some dead-eyed, bovine stare back at me, or a nervous chuckle when their (merited) fear of my tenuous grip on reality shone through my poorly socialized ranting. I had enough leeway as a veteran to blame my social missteps and faux pas on "that's just how we were," but that excuse was wearing thin and I didn't believe it anymore either. People online either couldn't tell as much or didn't care. I could get into arguments about errata and minutiae, things that would leave me steamed for days, long enough to think up some clever remark and then return to the thread or conversation and lay it all out just as I practiced in my head for the hours I was stuck at work, staring unseeingly at a form or screen. On at least one occasion I had dissociated entirely in the middle of a phone call because I was mad that some forum goer had the temerity to disagree with me about some minor abstract political point that we both approached from the same side of the aisle, just one a little askance of the other. I finally had something to occupy my time and distract me from the daily repetitious treadmill that was slowly but perceptively grinding me down.

Coming home from work and throwing my bag behind my single bed, I would immediately flop onto the mattress with my laptop and then browse in a loop the same four or five sites, the same chat program, the same DVD of season five of *The Simpsons*. I was mostly eating what I could swipe from the shared break room at work where often bruised apples and pink oranges would show up, stale raisin bread, Subway from across the street. At home I had a hotplate and a mini fridge, so I mostly had eggs and toast or simple pasta and sauce. A carb heavy diet, but not enough calories in a day to make me gain weight, so I began to soften and grow cloudy minded, a stark change from my field years where I was hard, angular, and sharp-eyed at all times as a matter of survival. The Warrior returns, not to beat his sword into a ploughshare, but to read Wikipedia articles on different kinds of swords until he passes out in a haze of seed oil cookies and Diet Coke. This would repeat itself day in and day out, and the gnawing pit in the depths of my soul that echoed that something was seriously wrong yawned larger and larger, growing in ways I was unable to fill. I had begun to think of ways out, and here the germ of suicide had planted firmly in this pit.

While I prolifically chatted online, I realized at some point that I had commonly gone days without ever talking out loud. With nobody to talk to and no interactions with people, I simply had no need to utter anything. I had been surprised one day at the hoarseness of my voice when to the register girl at McDonalds I ordered fries, craving salt, unaware that I was in the midst of seasonal allergies and my throat was closed up. If she noticed the shocked, confused look on my face, she didn't mention or betray it. I felt like a wild animal that had just seen its reflection in a mirror, not understanding what it was perceiving but knowing on a visceral level something was wrong. I tried to call my parents and tease a conversation out of them, if only to practice talking again, but ended up more frustrated than I started:

"Hi, Mom."

"Oh! Hello! Sorry your father and I were just playing lawn bowling with the neighbors. What's up?!"

"Oh, nothing much."

"How's your weather?"

"Cold, gray. Snowing still."

"And how's work?"

"S'fine."

"Did you go out with your veteran's group?"

I wanted to tell her that I couldn't stand being around them, a group I was strongly encouraged to join by a veteran coordinator as I transitioned back to civilian life. Most hadn't seen combat; most were a decade or two older than me; most didn't consider the action we engaged in as "real war" like their grandfathers had fought. Most were dire alcoholics or without any direction in their lives post-military. Still getting a high and tight; still sitting rock backed in a chair; still miserable about their third divorce. I didn't have anything in common with them outside of the beast we served.

"No."

“Oh, you should. Okay, well I’ll tell your dad you say hi! Talk to you later!”

This was the extent and depth of almost all our conversations, and I quickly stopped bothering. Theirs was a world entirely alien to mine, and mine to theirs. To them, I certainly would be fine because I checked all the boxes they laid out for me, as their generation had; any deviance from that was simply indication of low character on my behalf and resolvable with empty, frustrated platitudes. “What do you have to be sad about?” Everything had worked out for them in the end, even if they had to work part time for an *entire* summer to pay off the Corvette they crashed drunk driving in the sixties. If they could do it, so must I.

Online I didn’t have these tortured conversations. Online I could relax and be at ease, I thought, with people I would consider friends. I didn’t know their names, who they were, anything about them, just that they responded to me with the same sort of humor or consternation about how things are, how things were, and how they ought to be. I conversed with funhouse mirrors. The pit grew.

Eventually I was just in a rut, a well-worn groove between my bed and my desk, back again and then to the ever shrinking internet, walled in by my own desires to pad my surroundings with comforting familiarity: anger, rage, whatever chemicals the brain releases when the blood is angry at injustice or disgust. I would spend hours just clicking in loops of things that knowingly upset me, just so I could be upset, just so I could look at things that upset me more, and so on. Eventually my online life became indistinguishable from my living reality, just another part of the decay and ugliness I endured day after day outside the stucco walls, no longer an escape but another stop on the racetrack of indignities my day to day became. I was now acutely aware of the aching loneliness deep within me, and more and more I found less and less reason to count myself among the living, imaging the relief the novelty of death would wash over me, perhaps to take me to a place I might know happiness again, or at least comfort. Shortly thereafter, sitting in traffic, the idea of a flexible length of tube would pop into my head and from there I floated in what felt like relief, although was most likely numbness of my soul confronted with the egregious sin I had consigned myself to.

I had considered where I would do the deed. Doing it in the alley behind my apartment seemed more depressing than the idea of killing myself, and I didn’t want to get caught. Quickly I settled on doing it down by the lake at sunrise. A last moment of beauty, peace . . . then nothing. I figured I was owed at least some respite from the gray ugliness and oppressive claustrophobia I experienced day after agonizing day. It was already late May, although I felt I had just worked through Christmas mere weeks ago.

The lake was about an hour north of the city, with plenty of wild land around it and long stretches of beaches. The surrounding soil was too soft and sandy for development, so there were big swathes of wilderness peppered with logging roads and ATV trails that melted into a rocky beach and the cool, gray-green water. I had been to the one beach town there a couple times last summer, once with my veteran's group who spent the entire time at the local beach bar on the patio getting progressively surly and accosting of the college students, and once alone just to go swimming, although it had rained earlier that morning and it was fairly cold and unpleasant.

I figured I would drive down one of the side trails, park overlooking the east bank, obscured and hidden from view by the trees, and eventually drift into a peaceful sleep as the sun rose, bathing myself in sunlight and sure to be discovered not too long thereafter, presentable enough for my family, draped in the flag. Something to pass on to remember me by. I had sent enough of them off to sobbing widows and mothers for men who also died uselessly, too young. A lump formed in my throat.

I read my favorite forum one last time, seeing but not retaining any of the information or threads. More topics designed to anger me, more trash seeping in from the corporate internet, demanding to be part of my online and living cultural experience. A newish poster was in the midst of the exact same argument I had had months ago, making the exact same headway I did. The group chat was sharing YouTube videos of progressively higher series numbers of squat, autistic debate nerds calling screeching, clown-haired grad students losers. I didn't feel like I was saying goodbye to my friends or leaving a place of great importance and cherished memories. It felt like I was turning off a TV show rerun I wasn't particularly interested in.

Although night had fallen and dawn wasn't for a while yet, the alley was illuminated with harsh, bluish-white, LED security lamps and a flickering sodium lamp casting a fire exit in sickly orange light. I had to keep my curtains drawn at night, as it was brighter than the daylight but more disruptive; my brain didn't know what to do with the unnatural colors. I hopped in my car and pulled out of the alley onto a dead street. I wouldn't see any traffic for the entire twenty minutes it took to drive to the outskirts, yet I would still somehow end up at a red light every intersection—one last series of indignities.

Eventually I passed the little strip mall on the very edge of town and opened up the engine a bit on the highway. With the windows down, the cool air was refreshing. I breathed deep. Part of me was confused that I didn't seem to be bothered or second guessing my final destination. Was that normal? I would have figured my soul would have been ignited in flame of doubt, of anger, of self-preservation. Instead, I was just numb, and thinking about things I had read while mindlessly scrolling. Instead of immolating myself, my light had simply extinguished. I drove on.

Presently the skies opened up as the light pollution of the city receded. It was a clear night, as most of spring had been, and the stars were beginning to reveal themselves. I leaned out the window and took in the magnificence of the sparkling glitter against black velvet. The arm of the Milky Way was visible when I unfocused my eyes a bit, a cloudy tendril of millions of tiny individual diamonds visible in my periphery. The time travel effect of the stars struck, how one can see the light for centuries after the star itself has extinguished. And instantly I was back in high school, in my dad's enormous Buick, pulled off the side of a country backroad with my girlfriend, a farmer's daughter. She, like me, lived out in the sticks where such skies were the norm during the summer. We were on the hood, simply lying there, both too afraid to make the first move, staring at the millions of pinpoints, trying to identify constellations, spotting satellites, watching the wing lights of a jet liner thousands of feet above us, and suddenly she was kissing me, her hand pressed into mine, the shock quickly wearing off as I pressed back, harder, pushing my face into hers, pulling her in to me, denting the hood, feeling the warmth of the small of her back under her summer shirt—

I violently swerved back into my lane, chirping the tires, realizing I had nearly gone off the opposite ditch. Back in the present, back on Earth, I briefly thanked God I hadn't hit anyone before realizing the irony. I was on my way to kill myself, and this would have been a natural and blameless way to go and I . . . didn't want that? I didn't dwell on that. My heart was racing as the adrenaline dump was flushing itself through my system, and my breath started coming to me in ragged gulps. All I could think about was my first kiss.

Farm barns and houses passed silently in the night, some warmly lit in that soft yellow light on the porch. I imagined for a son they were waiting to come home from Afghanistan or Iraq, like me. My folks never left the light on or tied a ribbon around a tree for me, but I couldn't go home again. Briefly an intrusive thought of pulling in to one of the lit porch homes, knocking on the door and . . . what? Be welcomed in as a returning son of the soil? Sat at a country kitchen and given a hot cup of strong coffee and warm slice of homemade apple pie and told the town's proud of me and I can rest now? What I sought was saccharine even for a Rockwell painting, but I still wanted it. The doubt was starting to seed itself, filling the pit and pushing the suicidal desire out. Off the internet I was in my head, a chaotic, tumultuous place, but it was my own.

Sooner than I expected I arrived at the little, dirt-road turn off into the forest. I turned off and slowly trundled deep into the darkness of the woods. Despite growing up out in the country, I never experienced its darkness alone, or far from home, and I was not prepared for the overwhelming awareness that seeped into me. We had no wild animals or predators around here—the lakes were home to nothing beyond small minnows—and yet I was hyper aware of the scene illuminated in my headlights. The world only existed as far as I could see ahead; it was so dark all around me otherwise I might as well have been in space, a star whose light had extinguished long ago, the image still making its way to be observed fading to nothingness. This was an odd sensation because I wasn't used to it, but I wasn't scared. I was more aware than I had been outside of those convoy patrols, without fear that something was coming to kill me. I was coming to kill me; I already knew this. I just felt . . . alone, but not in a lonely way this time. More like as the last survivor of a battle, just the last man standing by wits or skill or grace of God alone. It was a refreshing feeling.

I slowly crept my car out of the tree line and onto the rocky shore that dipped down into a placid lake of flawless glass. I shifted to park and set the brake and turned off the car and headlights. Darkness surrounded me, but I felt illuminated. In contrast to the darkness of my apartment alley, the lights here were comforting. Starlight above, moonlight reflected almost still off the lake. Wet leaves glinted in these rays like the metal flake in my car fender. The sky almost fluoresced as ink blue against the total black of the trees. It was so still I could hear the blood in my ears, my breathing, the creaking of my vinyl upholstery as I leaned forward to stare at the moon. The stars had set my mind into a swirl of memories, and snippets played in my head as I zoned out. Where was the farmer's daughter today? I got lost hiking once in the woods near my house and didn't get home until sunset, and the forest got super dark then too. I watched the moon in the desert night thinking how clear it was on the opposite side of the Earth as well. The vacuum hose in my trunk would need to be duct taped to the tailpipe.

I stepped out onto the rocky ground and felt each individual rock shift under my weight, crunching and shattering the silence I hadn't heard in almost twenty years. I forgot how loud true silence was, and how it seemed to act as an amplifier for my thoughts, as though a custom-built amphitheater for them to project from. I mantled off my front tire and lay down on my warm hood, condensation already developing in the cool, late, late night. Surrounded by darkness, washed in the cool air and staring off at the pinpoints of light, I realized I hadn't actually experienced my own thoughts in the years I had been living in the city, burrowed online.

Here in the clearing at the beach, with no artificial light, no noise, no visual pollution, no modern distractions, I looked upon nature for the first time in I couldn't remember when. Clearly, I had always existed in or around it, but never being of it, until now. This little pocket of reality seemed almost unreal from where I had been an hour and a half ago, but I was here, and I existed now. The tree line circled the lake and enclosed me here, hugging me. This was fine. I felt . . . fine, which was a surprisingly large improvement on where I had been when I started.

Sitting in the serenity of the cool outdoors brought me back again to my long ago past, a connection made beyond time, and I was in the woods again as a ten-year-old, with a stick in my hand standing in for the German rifle and my dad's old, olive-green, surplus army jacket I was convinced was camouflaging me from the Americans hiding in the brush as I sat by the creek that wound its way behind our house. The last time I remember being calm. I hadn't sat with my own thoughts in years, and now as I stared at the water my mind was five, ten, fifteen, twenty years outside my body. I thought of my brothers I lost. I thought of the missed connections, the lost relations, the regrets, the mistakes, the stupid shit I said and did. I thought of the jokes and the pranks and the laughter and the firsts and the rites of passage. I thought of the non-stop stress I felt in the city. I thought of the deep unhappiness I had been stewing in for years. I simply thought my thoughts for the first time in a long while, now that I could hear myself think. I didn't have a computer screen to blot out my thoughts or invade with shallow anger and outrages and culture rot, nor urban ugliness to distract me. I had to experience my mind, and the emotions within it. I inhaled raggedly the cold, fresh air, needles in my lungs, and in shuddering breaths exhaled a vapor cloud that swirled like a galaxy forming, spiraling, dissolving, disappearing. I did this for hours.

I watched the sun rise, orange, neon, and pink against the black of the pines, turning the lake into a mirror reflecting light into my face, touching me more tenderly with more warmth than another person had in months. The bright, saturated colors faded to cotton candy, tendrils of steam rising off the lake now as the sunlight broke through the tree line, dotting the water with golden drops. First light broke, and the grayish blue of the sky began to fade in from the dying pastels of the sunrise. Dew was forming on my car. My mind wasn't as chaotic as when I arrived. I had felt things I had been ignoring, refusing. Remembered memories, relived experiences, took up the space that was my birth right.

Briefly I thought of the tubing in my trunk and the notion that this would be the last time I saw the sun rise. I slid off the hood and sat on the bumper, still thinking, feeling. If not now, then never.

Later that night, by the unsteady flames of the little beach fire I built, I watched the sun set.

New Swabian Blues

Dairyian Hyperboreanist

He had done this a thousand times before. It was so easy it bored him. He opened up a viewscreen to play a new game while he performed this chore. His power-armored boot easily turned the rotted hovel door into flinders. His voice boomed through the speaker system built into the suit, amplifying his sub-vocalized words to somewhere in the range of one thousand decibels. "I am Lord Megacommander SturmFuhrer Countonius Augustulus Von Himmler XIV, the Bruce, Champion of the White Race, Centurion of New Agartha, 4th Legion. By right of the Supreme Aryan Reich, I claim this hovel and the land between it an inner earth as my own by right of colonization. Face me and receive a quick death by my White Hand. Hide and be obliterated by fire." Silence. The smarter of the brownoids had learned to gouge their eardrums out so that the deafening blast of the white voice did not immediately disable what little brains they had. Maybe this hovel would prove to be worth his full attention. Augustulus closed the viewscreen on which he was playing the latest game in the hyperborean-super Anglo-survival-based building-battle royale-inventory management-real time strategy-casual-TND-sim-4x-masseuse-retro fps genre to give this job his full attention.

Somewhere behind Augustulus a flurry of shots pinged off the back of the neck joint of his suit, followed by a bang. His Vril-based, semi-intelligent body glove informed Augustulus that the bullets' velocity and grouping suggest that the shot came from an older-style volley gun manufactured in Greater Melungia. The weapon fired about four hundred two-inch, melanated bullets in the span of one second. More than sufficient for the Melungeons to hold back the brownoid hordes of Mer'ica and the Kangdome of Yakub, but unable to even scratch the paint of his Version 14.88, Hyperborean steel, Colonization Class Powered, TND Battle suit. The Vrilsuit pinged his HUD to indicate where the shot likely came from: about five miles away, still well within his claimed land. "Better deal with this problem first. Suit-chan, rearrange my clearing schedule to accommodate this change in objective," Augustulus told the body glove.

"Yes Zaddy UwU," the suit responded.

Augustulus changed the suit to lynch mode and ran in the direction of the shot, when suddenly—

Darkness. Everything had gone black. Brian Smith jumped at the sudden loss of haptic feedback from his Noxulus Brift™ Gaming bodysuit. A very loud and ethnic voice pierced his ears: "Hullo saar, thees is American racisms offisar James Sangdulluulooloobad, for crime of racism your accounts has been repatriated to oppressad races of yewnided sdades of America. Dank yew and have neice dey."

Brian's heart began to pound, his mind racing. "Wait, what about my inheritance?!" he subvocalized, in the correct way for the gaming body glove to output as a shout. No response, as officer James appeared to have ignored Brian's legal right to an explanation and ended the call.

His accounts contained his family inheritance, which was large enough for him to live comfortably off the dividends and not have to work. Brian could not even remember the last time he had left his home, much less spoken to anyone. He had swapped his grocery delivery service over to drone-based as soon as possible to avoid the possibility of having some brown person use the service as an excuse to get his house access code and both mug and stab Brian.

Bills, all my bills are due tomorrow! thought Brian. His pulse rose ever higher as he stood up for the first time today, an occasion only reserved for the most extreme of biological needs. Brian had splurged and bought the top-of-the-line gaming bodysuit that had the self-cleaning diaper (good for over two hundred uses before needing to be changed) *and* the soylent IV that gave him more than enough nutrition to game on through the most extreme tactical combat gaming scenario competitions. He became vertical too quickly for his body to react, and the lack of blood to the brain caused him to pass out.

Brian was not sure how long he was unconscious. He knew for sure it was at least long enough for his bills to go unpaid, as his power was out. He was also naked, likely meaning his subscription lapsed for the gaming body glove, as it had detached itself from his body and made its way to the nearest reclamation center. It was unlikely that he was robbed as he could not feel any obvious stab wounds, meaning he wasn't robbed by some random noggaloid, nor could he feel any fresh scars, indicating that his organs had not been stolen and he did not have the misfortune of being a viable organ donor for a thugtel boss in need of a new kidney or lung.

Cursing the once useful blackout curtains, Brian began to slowly right himself and make his way to where he believed the windows to be. It had been so long since he even thought about the windows, that it was a task to locate them on his very dusty walls.

After more time had passed than would be acceptable, and several painful falls onto formerly valuable, but still rather pointed and capable of bruising, collectibles, Brian found a window curtain and jerked it aside, letting light into his dirty and unkempt room. Mercifully, the sun was setting, so Brian was not blinded by the rays of the sun washing himself and his cluttered and dingy room with the light they had both been so long starved of receiving.

Brian took a moment to enjoy his first view of the sky in a very long time. The magmatic sun bled heat into the clouds blanketing the sky. It was as if one threw a quilt over a campfire and the flames tore jagged rents in the beautifully patterned cloth. Shamed by this barbarity, the sullen sun hid behind the tree line on the hilltop, its embarrassed red face glowing through the trees.

His bruises aching ever so slightly less, Brian turned to face the interior of his home. It was quite a shock for Brian to see his room under this new light; he had long gotten used to trudging along the small trails he kept the larger toys out of so that he could get from his bed to his computer and to the door to the rest of the house. It is surprising how many action figures and playsets one acquires in thirty years of life; even more surprising how hard it is to find somewhere to put them all, so inevitably the less valuable, bulkier ones must lie on the floor. *Maybe I can sell some of these to pay some of the bills*, a thought that surprised even Brian, as these were his most valued possessions, after the computer and its associated gaming body glove. He almost felt guilty for even considering selling his 1st edition Boarglaive Wargaming battle station set piece UberPOC Premium Gold Plus Club Collector's Edition™ that is one of only two million made on the second Tuesday of the first month of production (so it has a pretty good chance of being the last one made by the third generation robots that had the all-red color scheme, so it's actually quite rare), as it is the centerpiece of his collection that he keeps on the floor and has only accidentally stepped on like twice, so it's in near mint condition.

But what good is a "rare" collectible when your pantry is empty? His soylent IV bags would last another fifty years, but it is very difficult, never mind illegal, to get it into your system without the body glove. He was already in enough trouble. He didn't need the phone-home microplastics that saturate the soylent converting the nutrients into diuretics before calling the Department of Food and Seasoning Enforcement agents to bust down his door.

The stress of his situation weighed heavily on Brian. Every thought was weighing him down and adding to his problems rather than solving them. He couldn't forget about them, as he couldn't play videogames, so it was time to think about what he did *before* videogames. Was there a before videogames? He hadn't thought about anything other than videogames in a very long time. Just waking up, gaming until it was boring, catching up with his racist internet friends, and scanning the headlines they shared around until he fell asleep before doing it again the next day.

Sitting on the edge of his bed, his feet wedged between unopened boxes of toys, Brian turned to look outside and let his mind wander: *The sun is getting lower and lower; it will be dark soon. I better get my walks in while I can still see. That's it! A walk! I could go for a walk! That should calm my nerves.* In happier times, Brian would take a walk around the backyard to take a break from studying. Before. . . .

Realizing he was naked and his window blinds open, Brian scrambled over yet more toys and collectibles to reach his long-forgotten chest of drawers. It was a laconically beautiful item, made of now extinct hardwood. It wasn't painted, but rather stained and sealed; the knobs were made of the same wood. It was about chest height to Brian and was wide enough for each drawer to hold an ample supply of whatever clothing one wanted to put within its drawers. It was built by his great-great-grandfather and passed into his possession as a gift for earning his first PhD.

Mom and Dad had said it would look great in his future super-studio, meaning extra small, communal apartment. That's where the plucky young PHD grads moved into after college way back when. But Brian never moved out. The economy took another downturn, and even though Brian had racked up six PhDs, he still couldn't find a job in his field that would take him. It probably didn't help that he insisted on taking a principled stand on the application, listing his race as "Pure Aryan" and his gender as "Gogachad." All the other jobs he was either unqualified for or were excessively dangerous because they necessitated brownoid interaction. Instead, he stayed home and did chores around the house, caring for his parents as they aged. It became a full-time job as he was an only child and the chores kept piling up. And when they died. . . .

Brian picked out some clothes sufficient for the weather and began the slow process of fumbling through each room to find the window, dodging floor-based collectible items-turned punji sticks along the way, opening the blinds, and moving on to the next room: rinse and repeat. Finally reaching the door, Brian began to tremble. He kept a very close eye on the news, and he knew how bad it could be out there. News on the national level anyway, he didn't know much about local conditions. He stepped over to the window facing out to the street and let the sunlight wash over him while he tried to assess the situation outdoors.

It appeared that his neighborhood was abandoned, with the forest slowly reclaiming the surrounding houses. That was not surprising given the "Walkable Cities for BIPOC Respiratory helf [sic]" bill basically ended private transportation, and commercial vehicle rentals to what were once suburbs were prohibitively expensive. Brian felt a little more comfortable going outside but decided he would try to stay on his property to see how the backyard had held up. Since he was at the front door and it would be a chore to find the back door, he opted to just walk around the house. *I'll get more fresh air that way anyway*, thought Brian. *Heh, I'm a sunlightpilled outdoorcel. I'm going fresh-air mode*, Brian chuckled to himself, the first time he had smiled in what was probably years.

Brian's home was an absolutely decadent four-acre plot with a two-bedroom house. Back when White people could flee the cities, this house could easily be sold for a king's ransom. Now though, it was more to simply maintain. While it is technically legal to grow your own food to eat or sell, the regulations around it make it impossible to do so at all, much less profitably. As per the American Food Freedom Bill to Make Food Cheaper and Safer for Americans bill, all food items have to be quadruple checked for thetans contamination prior to sale. The process for scanning, say, a single apple for thetans takes about one week of nonstop gamma radiation bombardment. So, the only foods that are legally edible are ones that can safely discharge all that radiation and remain uncontaminated.

Brian was pleased to discover that the old pecan orchard had survived the total lack of upkeep he had imposed upon it. The blackberry bushes were also thriving, taking over what used to be the vegetable garden that was formerly adjacent to them but now thoroughly within the domain of the thorned menace. The greenhouse could just be made out beneath a sea of vines. The rainwater collection tank was easy to spot since the grass surrounding it was particularly lush and particularly green. Brian had many happy memories on this land, in this garden: helping his parents plant carrots; watching dad build the greenhouse; hauling that dreadfully heavy stone bench right where mom wanted it, and then stifling his complaints when she decided it needed to be moved about a foot this way, then six inches that way, then another foot the other way before finally being happy with it.

With effort, Brian traced his old walking trail that went through and around the property. It felt good to be out in the air again. *Why did I ever stop doing this?* he thought. Brian walked and walked, tracing his path through the four-ish acre wood again and again. Afternoon turned to night. His feet aching in that ever-so-pleasant way that only a good workout can produce and out of breath from his sedentary life, Brian found a spot to lie down that wasn't too overtaken by thorns, where the view of the sky was unobstructed, and decided to look at the stars.

There was at least one upside to no more cars and no more neighbors: the sky was clearer than he ever remembered it being. The ocean of little white dots was vast and uncountable. Some of the dots blinked and buzzed in unusual patterns, marking them as anti-anti-satellite satellites. Some of the lights moved rather quickly, meaning they were either passenger jets or police spinners. Seeing these little dots buzz in front of this great, dark backdrop gave the appearance of ants marching to and from their latest prize and back to the anthill. Some of the dots were perfectly still. Those were the beautiful pearls that Brian's ancestors used to navigate the seas. What was particularly striking was the North Star. It was impossible to miss, try as the artificial lights might to cover it up. The Big Dipper seemed to complete its orbit around the North Star before his very eyes.

After stargazing for a while, Brian remembered the events from the other day. Losing electricity and access to his games and his internet friends now seemed so insignificant that he couldn't help but laugh. But alas, problems were problems. First things first, food and drink. It had been quite some time since he ate. *Well, the pecan trees seemed pretty well-stocked, and the rainwater collection cistern appears to still be holding; that should take care of me for now. Legal or not, I have to eat and drink*, thought Brian. Next was the problem of money. That was a more difficult one. *Maybe I can find a wagon and haul some of those stupid toys to town and resell them. Not a great plan, but a plan nonetheless. Hopefully I can make enough to get the electricity back on and get some digital work*, thought Brian. And with those problems sorted, Brian drifted off into sleep in the field, getting his best rest in years.

A Hand Beckons

Peter Iversen

A cold wind blew across the plains, and with it rode the men that stalked the herds of buffalo-cattle that had dominated it for a hundred years. Humanity had begun to wane, inhabiting the silence that follows a concerto, and where once the landscape bore the unmistakable mark of human intervention there was now wilderness. Mankind had once stretched across the surface of the earth like a shroud, but it was now reduced to bright islands adrift in a deep and hostile darkness. The men of the plains were something other than human, a sort of evolutionary lost link between chimpanzees grooming each other for ticks and the sort of man who enjoys molecular gastronomy. While they lacked the inescapable control of their domain that Man had enjoyed in ages past, they were sufficient to scare what was left of Mankind into their hovels in the deepest hours of the night, when the wind blew from the west.

Two figures sat on horseback on a ridge overlooking the City: the oldest men who sat around the fire and smoked and spoke dreams into being said that it was once called "the city of many waters," but now it was a mausoleum in steel and glass inhabited by strange creatures with bulbous bodies and spindly limbs, pale and horrible to look at. The lights still came on when the sun went down, though as the years went by, more of the spires remained dark, and those that lit up blinked out before the sun rose again.

"You ever think about what it must've been like when the City was still alive?" whispered the boy, mostly to himself, his gaze on the steel with a mixture of awe and trepidation. The man, who had been watching the color of the river turn from black to red as the sun began its descent, snorted.

"Can't have been good." The younger looked at him expectantly, but no elaboration came for a long time. The river had changed from red to black again as the moon began its ascent, and the only sound between the two was the sound of the wind and the far-off thunder of the buffalo-cattle. "You haven't been in the City, but there's nothing that grows there. It's a dead place—bad land, bad air—and only evil people can live there." The boy was dissatisfied with that answer, but did not complain. They rode into the City along the river as the stars opened their blinking eyes to gaze upon their journey, and the closer they got to the City, the more the boy realized that the verdant undulations of the landscape were being replaced by gray figures shaped with geometric perfection. They ceased to glide along dirt and grass and began to clunk noisily against what seemed like granite, some pale gray and some nearly black. Up until that point, their approach was lit only by the moon, but they began to notice the yellow glow cascading down from above them higher than they could reach, even standing upon horseback.

They had gone like that for quite a while, their path lit in some places, dark in others. They were the only living beings on that strange trail, but still the boy had a feeling like he was a mouse being stalked by an existence totally incomprehensible to him. "I don't like this," he hissed, and almost as if he spoke a long-dead dream into being, a strange light appeared before the pair, first murky and thin as fog, then condensing into shapes, then into the silhouette of a person, then taking form. The light was a human—a woman, glowing in the pale purple of the aster flowers that grow across the prairie. She was beautiful to behold, and the boy, not quite a man, was transfixed by her appearance, the smooth curve and gentle sway, the hair that fluttered in a breeze that did not exist, the gown that hung close to her body and accentuated her rhythm as she moved towards them like gliding on ice, and he was consumed with a desire that dried his throat and made his jaw hang open. The older man, perhaps seeing a past self in the younger man's temptations, grabbed him roughly by the collar and shook him awake. "Keep your wits about you," he admonished. "She's not real."

The woman pouted for a moment, then smiled coquettishly. "What a rude thing to say!" She disappeared for a moment, then reappeared in front of the boy, sliding forward as if to crash into him, then burst into a scattering of light, the motes dispersing like a fog bank crashing against the bluffs. She reappeared some distance away and waved the pair toward her before blinking away again. "Don't trust her," the older man cautioned the him. "She's a *sorcière*, a *wicahmuga*. They steal men's souls to sacrifice to the Rotten Thing, and no medicine will bring you back." The boy looked sufficiently chastised for his satisfaction, and they continued on their ride. As they did, the glow of the witch appeared from far away, and each time it did the older man would *cluck-cluck* to remind the younger man of their goal.

As they moved deeper into the City, the buildings hemmed them in and the horses complained of having to walk on the gray stone. Under the flickering lights that hung mutely above them, they dismounted to spare their horses and tied them securely to the light posts. "We have to go on foot this soon; it's a bad sign." The boy instantly trusted the older man's judgment when he turned back the way they had come and saw the glowing eyes of dozens of the pot-bellied inhabitants of the City ruins staring down at them, thin fingers tracing on the windows. The older man shook his head at the disfigured observers and shook a spear at them, sending them scattering from the window. Chuckling to himself, he told the boy, "They're the least of your worries."

They stalked through the empty streets, the man calm and the boy frightened, and the soft padding of their leather slippers sounded like rockslides in the imagination of the boy. At any moment, he imagined that one of those creatures, eyes blazing like the lightning dogs that prowl the plains after a storm, would appear as if out of thin air, or grab him from behind. He held the shaft of his spear more tightly, and if the older man noticed, he didn't comment. After a long while, they arrived to what seemed to be the center of the City, an open plaza marked with dry fountains and a white building surrounded by bright lights that was distinctly shorter than the rest in the City: this white building had only three rows of windows adorning its surface, while the rest of the buildings had over a dozen. The boy was relieved to see that there was finally a bright feature in this gloomy place, but it still felt ominous. There was a carving across the top of the building in a language he did not recognize, and two carved men rode horses larger than buffalo-cattle, positioned as guards to the building, curved scimitars raised in the air as if commanding a charge. They were not pristine, however, and both bore the scars of some old indignity: the horse on the left was missing a leg and was painted with a glyph that he did not recognize; the other rider had lost his head.

"This is the place." The older man wasn't looking at the boy, but it was clear that he was the audience. He couldn't say why, but something in the pit of his stomach roiled, and he wanted more than anything to be out of the City and back on the plains. The old man waited a moment as the boy struggled with his fears, but turned after some time to impel the boy forward with a stiff smack on the back. The boy jolted back to reality, and although he was still reluctant to enter, his feet were no longer frozen to the street. Flinching away from the statues, almost as if he feared that they would come to life and trample him, he crossed the plaza to the entrance of the white building. The doors were closed, but they opened as he approached them to reveal the dull white gleam of a pile of bones, broken and scattered across the foyer floor. Alarmed, the boy looked at the older man, pleading, but the older man shook his head. "You have to go in. Alone."

The boy desperately did not want to leave and go where the man could no longer look after him, but this was the purpose of their journey: the man would not permit them to return without completing their aim. Slowly, begrudgingly, he went to the doorway in stuttering steps. The foyer held only a wide desk and the bones of an unfortunate man who had become a meal for the creatures that stalked the buildings where he dared not go. Behind the desk was a single door, which too opened with a gentle *whoosh* as he neared its threshold. It opened onto a long hallway, interspersed with doors that remained closed as he passed them, and terminated in a door that hung ajar, red light spilling from within.

Inside the final chamber, bathed in that red light, which made everything seem unreal, like a dream under the blood red moon that follows the summer fires, were five pods that laid along a curved wall. Their surface was a translucent dome, and beneath the gossamer lids were four figures, too desiccated to be truly human. He was sure that they were mummies, the restless dead of the civilization that fell to the monsters that ruled the City, but at length one twitched its fingers, then another, and he realized that these "mummies" were alive. The fifth pod was empty, and he stood near it, unsure what to do next, when the gentle trill of a woman's voice came up from behind him. "Get in," it said, and he spun around to find where the sound had come from. It was the witch, but under the red light she looked sinister, and her eyes were deep black. "Sit," she whispered, and the voice entered his head, and she floated over to him and was upon him in an instant.

For a moment, all he could see was the deep burgundy that made up her form, and he could smell flowers, sickly sweet like the roses that grow along the marshes and catch rabbits to fertilize their roots. He gasped, struggling to breathe, and then he could see again, and she was standing by the pod. She gestured to it, and the lid gently slid open, inviting him in. Something in his mind spoke in the voice of the man, saying *Sorcière! Wicahmuga!* but he was powerless to defy her, and his limbs moved with a desire of their own. She smiled as he climbed into the pod, and she giggled as her hands pulled the lid down to seal him within. The moment it sealed shut and separated him from the laughing woman, he felt overwhelmed by a deep fatigue, and though he tried to keep his gaze on the witch, his eyelids first closed, and then he drifted off to sleep.

When he woke, he was no longer in the pod, and he was no longer under the red light of the pod-room. He was standing on the gray-lined path of the City, but it was no longer decrepit, and the buildings were covered in panels that bathed him in neon glow. The panels held images that moved, not just the way that a cave painting appears to move when a flame is passed across it, but more like the way a human or animal moves. A woman brandished a white block toward him on the panel, then she was replaced by a man cutting vegetables, and just as quickly he was replaced. There was something about this place that was distinctly unreal, and his heart started to race and his hands searched for the comforting heft of his spear, but found only air.

The witch appeared before him, still beautiful, but seemingly more solid than she had been when he first encountered her. "Welcome to my world," she cooed. "I've been waiting for you." The boy felt a flitter in the pit of his stomach, and although he remembered the man's warning, he couldn't help but feel pulled toward her.

"What is this place?" he squeaked out, trying to sound brave and failing miserably. The witch giggled and threw her arms around him, like before, but this time they felt like they had weight, and he could smell the perfume of spring flowers.

"This is cyberspace, my little mouse," she whispered into his ear, her hot breath raising a tingle down the length of his spine, "a place where anything is possible." She pulled away, and he felt regret for just a moment, wanting that moment to last. "Come on," she called, waving him after her, "I'll show you what this place can do." Half reluctantly and half excitedly, the boy followed after her and through a wall that turned into a door as he approached it. The other side of that door was a large room that stretched up as high as the trees, and it was covered, floor, walls, and domed ceiling, by panels that each displayed a different person speaking to him. When he tried to focus on one voice, he found that he could not hear it over the noise of the panels that surrounded it. "These are the images and sounds of the world, little rabbit, hundreds and thousands of happenings and goings-on from the past and future, chewed up and digested with commentators and pundits and critics." A sly grin spread on her face as she reveled in the boy's confusion as he struggled to imagine hundreds of fireside tales being argued and interpreted without stop.

"Come, my dear," the witch cajoled, her voice soft and persuasive. "There is so much more for me to show you." She slipped through the far wall, but the boy hesitated to follow. He knew that he should be cautious, that he couldn't trust her, but her allure and the confusion caused by the surrounding images prevented him from being able to resist. He took a breath and plunged through the door that opened before him.

He proceeded through a dizzying parade of colors, shapes, and sounds, all totally foreign to him: a room that screamed in mechanical whirrs as black belts moved brown parcels back and forth, and clear tubes shook as dark, metallic cylinders shot through them, this way and that. The air was thick with the smell of oil and metal and something reminiscent of damp logs.

Another room was a vast, round chamber with a curious automaton in the center: a many-sided chef whose dozens of arms flailed about, chopping and mixing and flipping and turning, and hundreds of pounds of food rested on the surface of an enormous griddle that surrounded it. This strange kitchen was watched patiently by a crowd of figures that seemed to glow the same lavender as the witch, but whose form seemed to have a solidity that his guide lacked. He went close to the robot to see what sort of food it was making, and one of the figures turned upon him, and the sight of the distorted features of its face, only humanesque, startled the boy so badly that he fell back. The witch smiled at him, but he wasn't sure if it was meant to be sympathetic or sadistic.

Another room was lined with rows of altars, more than he could count, and many were attended to by a shimmering figure similar to the one he had seen in the commissary room. As one figure approached an altar, it reached out an arm and the hand seemed to melt into the altar, fusing into it. The boy approached one of the altars near the periphery, and it began to thrum as he approached it. The sound was rhythmic, like the sound of singing and drums, but there was a tone he didn't recognize. Hearing it, like a war song drifting on the wind across the plains, made his heart race. He went on to the next altar, and the song was slow and somber, like the dirge sung for the re-burial of the sacred dead. Excited, he went to another altar, but there was no music, only a rude noise and cacophonous screech that made him wince and step away.

The next room, though, was different: it was covered with panels and moving images like the first room, but the images were a roiling mass of flesh and disembodied limbs and body parts that didn't seem to have a coherent function or connection. The air was suffused with the sound of heavy breathing and moans that alarmed him, but as he continued to look at the panels, he began to pick out flashes of nude bodies and he realized what he was seeing. He swallowed, but his throat was dry. He grabbed his shirt to steady himself and found that his hands were sweaty. His stomach churned and a wave of nausea washed over him with the singular thought that he was seeing something that he should not.

From deeper within, though, there was a fluttering that kept his gaze fixed to the moving pictures. He knew that he should turn away, but he found himself unable to, and it frightened him. The witch noticed his fascination and whispered into his ear, "It looks nice, doesn't it? Come, see for yourself." She pulled him deeper into the labyrinth, and all along the way he saw the figures, slack-jawed voyeurs, splayed out on the floor or hugging their knees. The images turned perverse and degrading, and the moans turned into groans, and then screams. The fluttering faded, and his disgust grew, but still the witch drew him forward with an iron grasp. He shut his eyes and eventually he was out, but the witch was laughing at him and mocking his apprehension.

The witch was still dragging him through the dreamscape that was no longer a source of excitement for him, but now of shame and violation. He knew that he had to find a way out, but he was powerless to resist the witch's pull. He was dragged into another room, laid out with moving pictures like the last, but where the last room had been lustful, curdling into violence, this was pure mayhem and torment. His mind swam as he was assaulted by the odor of blood and rot, and his ears rang with the sound of screams and loud thundering booms from all around him. The witch wore a malevolent smirk as she held him in thrall, and though the boy tried to resist, he was too weak. She dragged him to a central rostrum, and though he tried to close his eyes, her hands seemed to wrap around his head and peel back his eyelids.

It was a rapid succession of images, none more than a few seconds long, of killing, maiming, torturing, gore, viscera, and the spilled innards of a thousand unfortunate souls. If he felt ill in the last room, he was now overcome with the desire to purge himself, but he could not. He wanted to run, at least turn away, but he could not. The witch's voice was a hiss in his ear: "Look at them; this is what happens to the weak. The strong do as they will; the weak suffer what they must. Blood. Pain. Death!" The hot breath on his face made him shudder with revulsion, and he could feel himself becoming numb, as his vision grew cloudy and his limbs slackened.

The witch was powerful now, and he was carried like a drowned cat into the final room where the overwhelming chaos made him gasp. It was unbearable, with blinding flashes of light, deafening sounds that seemed to come from all directions and from within his own skull, and a dizzying kaleidoscope of colors. He could feel himself slipping away into a dark oblivion as he tried, failing, to make sense of the incomprehensible tumult that enveloped him.

Slowly, the swirling mass coalesced into the witch's face. She was beautiful, almost enrapturing, but there was a cold wickedness in her smile that sent a shiver down his spine. He felt as if he was floating in the river, being imperceptibly carried away. She began laughing, and it echoed around him, doubling and tripling over itself, adding to the cacophony and the throbbing pain beginning to grow in his head. Her laughter only grew, but her beautiful face began to contort, her pale skin turning a sickly shade of green, and her eyes splitting, and splitting again like soap bubbles on the water. Her grin widened, then split the sides of her face as she revealed a yawning maw filled with hundreds of razor-sharp teeth. In that moment, he knew that she was incarnate of the Rotten Thing, and he tried to scream, but it caught in his throat. He tried to struggle, to get away from her, but his muscles were numb. The witch-monster came ever nearer to him, and he felt himself slipping away; even his struggles to scream faded as he became unable to do anything except stare into the rolling eyes and gaping maw. He drifted away like a dream, the sort that sneaks in silently and unseen to seize upon the senses so that one never knows when he enters slumber or awakes, and the sound of the witch faded.

When he realized that he was awake again, he was back in the pod, and the translucent lid peeled back to release him. As he clambered out, he felt sore, and like he wanted to vomit, but he was relieved to have finally left the irreality. The man was waiting for him in the plaza and rushed over as he stumbled out of the building, a look of concern etched on his face. "Are you okay?" he asked, grabbing his by the arms. The boy took a few deep breaths and nodded, though his voice was still caught in his throat from the shock. The man sighed, too. "You're a man, now. That was an artifact from the ancient City, a trial for you to face the depraved past and return unharmed. You saw the mummies in the pods? Like as not, a few would have been the old denizens of the City, kept just barely alive by the profane technology of the old City, but there would have been the men of the plains, too, the ones that failed to escape."

The boy shuddered, thinking of the witch-monster, but the older man patted him on the shoulder in what he must have thought to be a reassuring gesture. "Don't worry, it's done now. You faced it, and now you go back to the plain a Man." The boy nodded, but he shivered as a cold wind blew across his small frame.

"Can we leave this place? Please?" the boy pleaded, holding himself to keep warm. The man laughed and nodded, leading the boy back to their horses. It was a short ride out of the City, shorter now that they knew the coming dawn would keep the creatures of the City up in their buildings. They had mounted the ridge overlooking the City as the sun rose, painting the sky with shades of orange and rose, but something inside the boy compelled him to look back. When he did, he was startled to see the witch, now grown gargantuan and stooping over the City, her thousand eyes spinning wildly and toothy grin dripping. He was frozen with fear as she noticed him, and a deep rumble rolled out across the plains. She was laughing.

I Remember Grass

T. B. McGill

"I remember grass."

The old man's eyes sparkled.

"But what does it mean?" asked one of the many youths gathered around his repose. "'Touch grass'?"

The old man laughed. It was a laugh that was full. Full of both wistfulness and melancholy.

"It meant . . . well . . . it meant a lot, and so little." His eyes were wet with a long-passed memory.

"Grandpa, you're saying two things at once," the youngest among them quipped.

Grandpa was obviously a colloquial designation. To properly encapsulate the man's true relation to any of those gathered would require a tiring procession of "great, great, great, great . . ." and "Grandpa" was just easier, and less cold, less clinical. The man lying in front of them was perhaps the oldest extant member of this world. Even his name was lost to time, and himself.

He remembered grass.

He laughed, a soft, warm laugh. A laugh in the process of remembering. "Touch grass. . . ." He gave a little snort. "It was similar to saying 'kick rocks,' I suppose."

"But what are rocks?"

Grandpa chortled at this question. It looked like he might roll right out of his stasis chamber. Though something seemed to strike him in the middle of this revelry, and his laughter was choked by a sudden teary arrest.

"How do I even explain such a thing?" He seemed to be genuinely asking himself, waiting for an answer as much as the children gathered around. "Grass. Rocks. They were the decorations covering the ground. The land. Earth." He gazed out of the viewport at the clouds. Silvery and opalescent, they shimmered in the sun. Like anything that had the look of nature, they were a simulacrum, woven out of an aerosolized concoction of modern chemicals and elements. Not quite oxygen, not quite water; not quite clouds, in truth.

"Grass was a type of plant. It grew out of the ground, alive. It used to be everywhere. People surrounded their homes with it. It was soft, but kind of itchy, in a nice way. If you grabbed a handful of it, you could scatter it like confetti in the wind. I guess you could say we took it for granted. Really, 'touch grass' was a mild insult; it was like saying 'You need to get outside.'"

"Sounds like more than a mild insult," opined one of the youths. "You'd die!"

Grandpa smiled. "Back then, outside wasn't so inhospitable. You could lay in the grass and watch the clouds overhead. The real clouds." His gaze was far, far away, as if he were looking upon them now. "It always seemed like such a shallow thing to say to someone, back then. I guess we all ought to have taken heed. None of us imagined there was any risk that it wouldn't be there the next day, that we wouldn't.

"Even touch. Touch itself is now just something they've tricked our brains into experiencing. It used to be something you did with your body. . . . Oh, a body"—he shook his head in the memory—"a body was a physical avatar. Everyone had one long ago. Everything now is a reflection of how it was then. We are like an artist's interpretation of an artist's interpretation. Yes, something like that." He paused. "Back then it used to be optional, to be inside or outside, online or offline. . . . Now there isn't an option at all. There's only one side, and we're all on it."

The children listened intently, but it was clear they didn't really understand. Terra Firma is nowadays little more than a pretty legend, remembered only by the eldest of the elders, the stewards of bygone knowledge. They knew of things lost to us a thousand years hence. These ancient, persevering relics of the old world were well respected and carried with them the faint memories of time past; though in truth, most believed their memories were a patchwork of wistful inventions and reinterpretations.

The natural flow of the interaction seemed to have faltered a bit. Grandpa was staring further and further into the distance, and his words were beginning to trail off and miss their meanings. The children were growing a bit listless.

"Grandpa?"

"Yes, Kaliyu?"

"Touch grass."

All the youth laughed uproariously.

The smile that crossed Grandpa's face this time was unlike any of the previous. He grinned the sort of grin that had seen something completed which was long, perhaps too long, in its creation.

"You know what, Kaliyu? I think I just might do that. Thank you for listening to this old man ramble on about old times . . . very old, now."

The children filed out of Grandpa's server stack. A robotic schoolmarm servitor clanked ahead of them, reminding them to be courteous and to keep their voices down while making their way through the most ancient wing of the Grand Database. This was where the oldest souls in the stack were etched upon network.

The next day, Grandpa logged off. There had never been a member of the stack who'd done so. Until Grandpa logged off, it was assumed that it wasn't even possible to do so. For one thousand years, no members had entered nor departed the Grand Database. It was presumed eternal and unchanging, but Grandpa had just left.

On his block, he had inscribed for himself what served as an epitaph: *Outside, Touching Grass.*

Sundowner

Ndabaningi

The group forms a line, a little column, to clamber through another rocky outcrop. Then it disgorges onto the flatter land beyond, spreads out, and the conversations continue. The autumn sun is ahead, leading them on; its tempered glow warms bare skins, keeps jackets and jerseys open or tied around the waist. They'll need them soon enough. When it moves, the air is cool and will get cooler yet. The wisp of a path tends ever upward through a profusion of grass and sandstone. From time to time a climber will straighten up and squint uphill with shielded eye. Grass and stone, the red clay columns of anthills, draw them on. The path lies beneath, invisible; they follow instinctively.

It's the best sort of mixed company—diverse, in fact. Drawn from town and country, different walks of life, they find themselves now and here on this hill of many hues. The younger ones occasionally draw ahead. They stop a while or double back to rejoin the ranks. With more determined, careful steps, the older set a steady pace. A middle-aged man carries a lively boy on his shoulders who slips down onto his father's back when they have to negotiate the boulders, suddenly unsure of his perch. A lanky, red-headed girl orbits them, her exposed skin daubed in sun lotion—swirls of chalk-wash vying with the pink of yesterday's sun. Two athletic men in their twenties exchange constant banter and the carrying of a heavy cooler box. It becomes progressively heavier but neither will admit it. Falling behind from time to time and with ragged breath, a stout man brings up the rear. Now he runs a pudgy hand through short, gray hair and wipes the sweat from his eyes; he waves a pair of flies away with a floppy hat. They return to buzz about his face. A bearded man with a pockmarked face lopes back toward him. He's broken off a stem of grass with spiky inflorescence. He turns it between thumb and forefinger and holds it up to the sweating man.

The man nods. "*Mannagras*, one of the setaria, bristle grass: it's good grazing," the cattle farmer confirms.

The other man is a hunter with an amateur interest. Bound by similar thoughts, they turn and stand for a while to take in the country below. It's a vast sweep of veld reaching as far as the eye can see, covered by a fuzz of thorn trees, broken by seams of natural bush crowding a few finger-like valleys, all disappearing into a bluish haze. Beyond that lie the mountains, so pale and gray that one could mistake them for the tufts and billows of cloud that surround them. Only their crenellations remain the same, marking them out, eternal watchtowers over this ancient land. They take in the dispersed kraals—the huts emitting faint wisps of smoke—the spidery veins of roads and tracks, the dots of cattle. There are goats too, but it's so far away that any sight of them would owe much to the imagination of the viewer. The farmer takes the grass and waves it gently. His forearms are strangely broad, more developed than his upper arms. He's spent a lifetime lifting heavy things, as and when needed, every day; he's never been to a gym. He plucks another culm of grass from a clump nearby.

"*Eragrostis*," says the hunter.

"Our people spread that." The farmer nods. "It's good country," he says. "Poorly managed, of course."

The hunter smiles. Overgrazed. There wouldn't have been so many thorn trees back in the day. The grass would have kept them in check, in balance. The taller man knows this too. For his part, professionally, it doesn't really matter. There are kudu in the natural bush, in the valleys. That's what's brought him here. It's been a good weekend. The client has bagged a nice sized bull after a not-too-challenging stalk and got to see a variety of game and birdlife besides. He's added a fair-sized tip in foreign currency over and above the fee and has left with a promise to return. The hunter scratches an ancient acne crater and wonders how much of that fee he spent on booze the night before. He smiles to himself. He's not as young as he imagines himself to be and is glad of the break offered by the ponderous pace of the older man.

"Rugby injury, my knees," says the farmer, as though reading his thoughts.

They're joined by a young man, who is also out of breath. He has no excuse for his rotund shape; neither age nor injury—simply a modern, sedentary life. They had been speaking Afrikaans. Now the hunter switches to English, equally fluent, but the farmer will continue in his mother tongue as he has all day. The young man, a post-grad student and IT manager, understands it well enough but, having spent all his life in Natal, doesn't trust himself to speak it.

"What are you looking at?" He points at the grass with his soft chin.

"Bristle grass," says the hunter. "Good for grazing."

"Isn't it all the same?"

The farmer shakes his head, and the hunter smiles. "Far from it."

The farmer glances up the hill, unclicks his knees, and starts to move again. The other two fall into line.

Above them the two men with the cooler box and their three female companions are drawing away from the group. For a moment they are silhouetted against the blue and then they disappear into a slight hollow. The hunter knows the way; he's been here before.

They had met the day before, a strange confluence of different waters temporarily pooling in the same pleasant place, before rushing off along their separate courses. An ambitious new marketing manager at the game lodge had organized a small beer and music fest. She'd invited a few friends and done some low-key advertising to draw in some locals. It was to be a test run, something the owners might find useful in the future. And it had gone off swimmingly. From the moment she'd made contact with the old varsity friends, it had all come together almost automatically. By the weekend, they'd rustled up three kegs of craft beer and two bands. While the beer was undoubtedly of an international standard—sourced as it was from a brew-house serving a well-trodden tourist route—the term "band" might have been an overstatement. However, the mix of cover tracks and Afrikaans folk rock that emanated from the guitars, concertina, drums, vocals, and lone accomplished trumpeter had made for an excellent afternoon. With the addition of hearty country food, what had been a rather hare-brained, last-minute effort had turned into a memorable party in the bush. And, mirroring the eclectic nature of the event, the guests proved an interesting mix. The marketing manager had welcomed her old friends, and they came with a number of their own new ones. Some were still slogging away at qualifications that simply refused to fall into the bag; some had moved on to their chosen professions; most had settled for less. The beer and the bands had brought a modest train of groupies. The guests of the lodge, a disparate group of holidaying families and travelers, found themselves happily caught up in the festivities. And then a number of the locals had dropped in, lured by rumor and FOMO. Acquaintances had been made; there was dancing and drinking and standing around braziers of burning hardwood that sent mirrored meteor showers into the starry sky. *Potjiekos* was dolloped onto steaming heaps of *krummelpap*, fiery sauces compared, kegs deftly changed and swiftly broached. A number of interesting conversations were struck up. Late in the night a group had coagulated around the main firepit and had most interesting discussion. A father of two had sent his reluctant children to bed; his wife, exhausted from the rigors of mountain biking, had preceded them, after declaring her intent to spend the following day at the pool. A hunter had taken leave of his clients, handing them over to the ministrations of butcher and taxidermist, and had begun to work through his windfall. A cattle farmer on his way back from the big smoke, relieved to be rid of the confusion of traffic and urban squalor, allowed himself a few extra pints to unwind. The marketing manager, gratified by the success of her party, had been loath to call it a night. A number of her friends had passed out or paired off; the others had moved on to brandy and coke and were slowly subsiding into comfort. An awkward, overweight, post-grad student and IT manager from a little tech start-up had joined them—silent at first, as though wincingly shy. The conversation, after flitting bird-like from sport to international news, from the incompetence of government to the electricity crisis with its interminable series of planned "loadshedding" blackouts, had finally settled on the land. One of the Afrikaans student musicians had been talking of the battlefield tour she had been on. Coming from the Cape, it was somewhat exotic to her—something from a story book—to have visited the site where British redcoat and Zulu warrior had given their lives for a vanished kingdom and a forgotten empire. The middle-aged father turned out to be something of an amateur expert in the field. While studying, he had done a history module under a professor who specialized in the Anglo-Zulu War. He had even supplemented his income with a stint of tour-guiding during the holidays. He quizzed the young woman about what she had been told. His old professor had been forced out of the country for not pandering to the shallow African triumphalism that had come to surround the battlefields with the advent of the "democratic dispensation" in 1994. The Battle of Isandlwana had become particularly imbued with simplified hero-worship, much of it ahistorical, and he wondered what tourists and local visitors were now being told. She confirmed his suspicions, and he shook his head and smiled as he listened. A cartoon-like tale of wicked Englishmen beaten back by brave Zulus, their absolute superiors in every way, had been presented to them by a young African with dreadlocks who mispronounced the few English names he'd bothered to learn. The father took up the story. Back in his day, some of the White tour guides had mispronounced the Zulu names, to be sure, but most had made the effort to learn them all, to familiarize themselves with the facts, and to present a balanced retelling of the events. As ever, history was more nuanced and, thus, far more interesting than the crass carping of today's propagandists with their garbled morality plays on the evils of imperialism and "settler-colonialism." Yes, the British had suffered a humiliating defeat—even that now had to be cast as Zulu victory, the mere suggestion that anyone could see it from the British perspective an insult to the Afrocentric zeitgeist—but the men of the 24th Regiment of Foot had sold their lives dearly. Even when all was lost, they had fought on to the end, and, what was always overlooked even in the "old days" when history was more balanced, they had broken the back of the Zulu army. Never again would King Cetshwayo field the *impis* that could seriously threaten the British advance. After a few months, the red juggernaut rolled up his kingdom. And that final victory had been paid for by the blood of the men who had fallen under the assegais and clubs at Isandlwana. At this point the farmer had muttered something about "the bloody English not having listened to their Boer guides." The father agreed. It was a common trope, but true nonetheless, that the haughty Victorians had spurned the advice of the Boers who had had years of experience fighting the Zulus, mostly notably at Blood River. And the mustachioed military men had come to regret the cost of their arrogance. One of the younger men, the concertina player, had brought up the British concentration camps that had killed thousands of his people. But the hunter, comfortable in a warm glow of brandy, steered the conversation on to more palatable aspects of the Boer War. Switching comfortably between Afrikaans and English, he wondered whether the group knew that, on this side of the river, this part of Natal had also played a role in that terrible conflict.

The father expressed doubt. “Surely it was too far south?”

No, and the hunter had something interesting to show them: the farm graveyard of a Scottish family and the wounded Boer they had harbored in those times of guerilla war and scorched earth. It would have to wait for the following day and would involve a long walk. The students had immediately expressed their enthusiasm; the father committed himself and his children (not his exhausted wife); the farmer grudgingly assented. The IT manager had demurred and mumbled something about not being an outdoors type and besides which he had some programming to do. The farmer, having committed his girth and dodgy knees to the proposed adventure, took umbrage at his lack of enthusiasm and gave him a dressing-down. The young man’s face reddened, and he was about to say something when the hunter laughed, put a firm hand on his arm, and answered for him. Of course, he’d come. It would do him the power of good. The hunter turned to the father and said how nice it was that one could find common ground. The father agreed in rusty Afrikaans. It wasn’t always so. Especially in this province. When he’d been growing up, old animosities had been nurtured. The English had prided themselves on not learning Afrikaans. There had been much talk about not speaking “code” and “dreaded throat sickness.” At that the farmer had laughed. He regretted that he too, as a younger man, had conversely made a point of never mastering English.

The boy and his father have reached the ridge; the girl bounds after them on gangly teenage legs. The farmer begins to heave himself up the final slope; a thousand rugby matches make their ancient presence known. He winces. The IT manager finds it even more heavy-going, and the hunter puts a hand on his shoulder to help him on. Soon they find themselves on the ridge. Behind them the vast expanse, an open world; before them a secluded grassy saddle. The others have made the short descent and wait for them, some sitting on the low remains of a wall of piled rock. One of the students is picking the *steekgras* from her socks, knowing she won’t get it all, the itchy grass, and that the prickling will continue until she takes the socks off. The hunter bounds down the hill, a sudden release of energy, a loosening of limbs. The farmer picks his way slowly, carefully through the tall grass, the young man following a few steps behind. The sun has edged closer to the distant mountains, the approaching reunion celebrated in a flare of gold and copper. The breeze flowing tide-like through the grass has a chill now.

Jerseys and jackets are put to their allotted use. The red-headed girl shivers slightly. Her brother is manhandled into a hoody, protesting in a flailing of arms. A younger woman sidles up to one of the cooler-box bearers and nestles under his arm; his companion pulls off the lid and starts handing out drinks.

The little farm cemetery is awash in a tide of tall grass. Most of the tombstones rise like high-masted ships. They're Scottish, the names etched into the sandstone all those many years ago. The hunter waits for the farmer to accept a bottle of beer, to take a welcome sip. He pushes a clump of *eragrostis* out of the way. The grave beneath is marked by a single, low, pale stone. "Here Lies an English Burgher," an unnamed Englishman who had fought for a Boer republic and had been sheltered by a Scottish family in British Natal. The father who had moments before been thinking of a sundown sing-along sighs. It no longer seems appropriate. They are gone now, all these people, all their struggles, their endeavors, committed to the silence of the veld. All that remains is the grazing and the encroaching African cattle.

The House in the Woods

C. O'Brien

Oh, to be a boy again on those blazing summer afternoons. Even now the memories fill me with overwhelming bliss. I can hardly fathom how I handled then. The summer holidays were best, adventuring beneath that sweltering sun, which was prompt to rise and reluctant to set so that the days felt endless.

I recall those times mostly as one grand mirage of fishing, tree climbing, and roaring fires in the evening when sun set the sky ablaze with orange light. Yet, among those times, there are days which were so wonderful that they stand out from the rest, adventures so adventurous that I recall every detail, from the breakfast I had that morning, to the last thought that crossed my mind before bed.

I have many such memories, for I was quite a curious boy. At any moment I can draw upon them and reexperience those magical days of my youth, feeling grateful for having lived. Sometimes I am taken back by surprise, the smell of freshly cut grass or the sting of a nettle stabbing me with nostalgic ecstasy.

One day stands out above the others, and it is the one which I would like to tell you about now. I was ten years old, and it was a cloudless Sunday at the dawn of those summer holidays which all children pine for and relish. I know it was a Sunday because after bacon and eggs for breakfast, our parents had taken my elder brother Edward and I off to church.

Ours was an ancient stone village on the banks of a stream in the heart of North Yorkshire's moors and surrounded on all sides by country. Everyone there knew one another. There was one shop, one pub, and one tea room. We had a community hall, primary school, and even a petrol station. Every one of these places had stood for centuries, save the filling station, though that had not been updated in decades. It was, and I am pleased to say still is, one of the most pleasingly English places one is likely to find, though I shall keep the name to myself so that it remains such.

Church was a joy. Our sermons were led by our priest, Mr. Guite, who was a warm man somewhere between Father Christmas and a hobbit in his appearance and manner. His greatest pleasures were Christendom and the works of Tolkien, Lewis, and Barfield. He delighted in pipe tobacco and ale and had the most wonderful library I ever saw. After the sermon one could always count on the old dears to swoon over us children, stuffing our pockets with sweets while our parents chatted, before we spilled back out into the village.

Ten was a fine age. At ten I still possess that sense of wonder which children are blessed with, but had grown sufficiently mature to be afforded a good bit of independence by my father, which seasoned the experience. This was fortunate because by that time my brother would not entertain my company. He'd been leading an outlaw lifestyle that summer since acquiring his dirt bike. He and his friends would meet at the petrol station, fill up, and ride off into the country, returning only when their tanks were dry and just in time for the Sunday roast. I longed to join them, but my parents felt ten too young an age for me to be let loose with an engine, and so I had to do with a bicycle equipped with a playing card—the ace of hearts if I recall—taped between the spokes so that it at least mimicked the sound of a motorcycle.

There was only one problem with Sundays. Many of my friends would visit with their grandparents, leaving me alone as my own came to us for their roast. There was one friend who stayed, however. Ryan Cornwell was a plump and peculiar lad, the victim of mockery from the other boys because he was slow and cowardly where boyish pursuits were concerned. I found him amiable enough myself, handy on Sundays because Ryan's grandparents lived in Brighton where his parents were from. I didn't know where that was, but I knew it was far and that it was a strange place because Mrs. Cornwell had pink hair and didn't believe in God.

When we made it home that day, my brother and I raced up the stairs to change from our Sunday best into tatty jeans and scuffed trainers. Edward was the swifter of us and had grabbed his motorcycle helmet and made off down the stairs before I had pulled on my shoes. Through the floor I heard his muffled exchange with my mother, then the door closing and his engine starting.

Strapping my pouch of ammunition to my belt, I retrieved my knapsack. It contained my catapult and other essentials like a book of matches and a length of twine, and with these I ran down the stairs.

"Charlie!" my mother yelled, appearing from the kitchen with my water bottle. "Stay hydrated. It's hot out. Have you got your watch on?" she asked. I did. "Good. Now, your father and I are heading into town so dinner will be late. I want you back here and washed for four o'clock. Do you understand?"

"Absolutely," I said, itching to escape.

"Good. We're having beef," she said, and with that she kissed me on the head.

I freewheeled my bicycle and followed the river, hanging back on the bars as though I were riding some big American bike along an open freeway like they did in the movies. A black bird kept pace and then flitted off like a dog fighting spitfire. The sun beat down as the breeze stroked my arms, and the horizon ahead was a haze of pollen and insects. I could not have been happier.

The ace growled in my spokes, and when I hit the gravel, I pulled my back brake and skidded across the drive. The car was gone, and all of the curtains were closed. I knocked at the door, worried that perhaps no one was home until, through the frosted glass, I spied a rotund figure that could only have been Cornwell.

The door opened, and Ryan peered at me like a toad disturbed beneath a damp log. He was still in his pajamas, and his hair was uncombed. He looked pale and vaguely displeased to see me.

"Oh, hello, Charlie," he said flatly.

"Have you just woken up?"

"No," he scoffed. "Whatever gave you that idea?"

"Well, you aren't dressed."

"No need. My parents are away for the day. What do you want, Charlie?"

"What do you think I want on a day like this, Ryan? I want to know if you're playing out! I have a new trick with a playing card, which makes your bike sound like a motorcycle. Look, I brought you one!" I said, producing the jack of diamonds from my back pocket.

Ryan twisted his soft face as though I were holding a cold dog turd. "I'm staying in, Charlie," he said sourly.

"Staying in?!"

"Yes, I have a new game for my PlayStation. Kingdom Hearts Two, Charlie! It isn't even out in this country yet. My stepdad brought it back from his business meeting in China." He smiled smugly.

"A game?"

"Yes, Charlie. There's nothing to do outside, anyway."

"But. . . ." I raised the card for him to see.

"I said NO, Charlie." And with that, Ryan closed the door.

* * *

We children lived in our own sacred world, one known only to us and with locations like "the pit," "the big hill," and "the watchtower." My favorite of these was the train yard because so few knew of it and those who did didn't care for the long journey to reach the place. It was a clearing in the wild, a graveyard for twentieth-century locomotives forgotten by the minds of adults. It was here where I went on this day, brooding and confused in my rejection.

Aboard the roof of a train car, I sat with my legs dangling over the edge and with the song of birds and grasshoppers all about me. Solitude was no problem. I had a good imagination and relished an afternoon alone. What had turned my mood was Ryan's manner. It was one thing for an adult to act strangely, but for a boy of ten to choose a computer over a day of such sublime promise, well, I'd never known it.

Taking the jack of diamonds, I struck a match and set the card alight, holding on until the flame grew too big. Letting go, I watched happily as the card fell, the smug face warping as it burned to ash. It was a petty ritual, but cathartic, and at its end, I decided I'd forget Ryan and enjoy the rest of the day. It was his loss, after all.

In one train car I had a hideout where I kept the contraband that my mother would not approve of. There was a firework, which I had brought from Edward, comic books of a gory nature, and the third page of a *Sun* tabloid, which I'd salvaged from a bin in the village. I was on my way to this illicit collection when, from the other side of a carriage, I heard someone whistling the theme tune to *Indiana Jones*.

I stopped and listened, wondering if I'd been followed? Perhaps it was Ryan having seen sense and come to find me. Dropping down to my belly, I peered beneath the carriage. Beyond the rusted wheels, a pair of small, dusty boots walking by and with hairless legs poking from them too small to have been an adult's, but too slender to have been Ryan's.

Lifting myself, I tracked the intruder with careful footing. They were headed for my den. With my tongue sticking out to aid stealth, I retrieved my catapult and picked a rose hip from a nearby bush. At the carriage end I waited, listening as the stranger slid open my den's door. When I was sure they had entered, I followed, setting the bud in the sling and pulling a full draw on the weapon.

The interior of my hideout was not revealed to me until I had stepped out of the daylight and into the shade beyond the door.

"Stay where you are!" I yelled. The unwelcome party was alone, smaller than I, and with their back to me. Jumping with shock, they dropped one of my very own comic books on the floor. But it was the scream which took me off guard, that girlish shriek of terror. Slowly they turned to face me, and I saw that what I had thought to be a pair of shorts, was in fact a corduroy dress, and that the face beneath the cropped red hair, which I had taken for that of a small boy's, was in fact slender and feminine.

"You're a girl!" I yelled, lowering the slingshot.

"I'm sorry!" she squealed, waving her hands before her face.

"What are you doing in my den!"

"I didn't know it was yours! I haven't taken anything, honest. I was just looking at your comic books!"

She continued to wave her hands with her eyes closed while she pleaded as though I were still aiming the catapult at her. It was such a fearful response that I wondered if I had not overreacted somewhat.

"Right, enough of that," I said, softening my tone. The girl steadied her hands and opened one eye. "Look, it isn't a stone. It's just a rose hip," I assured her and tossed the thing over my shoulder.

The girl relaxed a little and more again when I holstered the weapon. For a moment we stared at one another, and then she said, "I'm Mary Dobson," and held out a hand.

"I'm Charlie Birchwood," I obliged reluctantly and bypassing her retrieved my comic from the floor.

"Sorry about that. I didn't take anything, truthfully. I only found this place yesterday. It's wonderful."

"It's mine, and you'd better not have set my firework off," I growled, spotting suddenly the indecent third page laying upon the table.

Tossing the comic, I grabbed the page and stuffed it into my pocket. "What's that?" she smirked knowingly.

"None of your business!" I barked. "Don't you know not to go snooping around people's things?! Don't they teach you that where you come from?!"

"Oakwell."

"What?"

"I come from Oakwell. It's a little village just over—"

"I know where it is!" I said. I had grown flustered and awash with cold sweat at the embarrassment of it all, and Mary seemed to sense it and take pity on me.

"Look, I really am sorry. It's just, I'm new to the area. I've not got many friends here and so I've been exploring. I shouldn't have gone through your things." I nodded in agreement. "Here, have a bonbon," she said, pulling out a paper bag from her satchel and offering it to me, "as an apology." She smiled, and over her shoulder I spied my firework where I had left it, and so I accepted.

Friendships start over less when you're ten. I once called a boy my best friend for a year because we shared a birthday despite neither one of us liking the other very much. Mary didn't share my birthday, but she was ten, and she didn't visit her grandparents on a Sunday, or concern herself with silly video games, and so a friendship seemed quite natural.

I showed her my pen knife and Judge Dredd comic books. She shared her bonbons with me and then, aboard a train car's roof in the sun, I showed her my catapult, which I'd made with my father the previous summer.

"Are you a good shot?" she asked.

I laughed and reached into my leather pouch for a pebble. "See that sign?"

Mary nodded.

Giving the band a good pull, I sent the stone flying. The target burst into shards of rusted metal, which flew all about, pitter pattering like rain as they fell.

Mary gasped. I'd not noticed how pretty she was before, not until we were outside and the sun had set her auburn hair ablaze and flushed her cheeks a little pink, which were pale and freckled like a wren's egg, with Mary every bit as delicate as that little bird was, her bright green eyes fixed upon the destroyed target and her soft pink lips upturned ever so with excitement at my accuracy.

"That was good," she smiled.

"Thank you," I smirked. She was beautiful, and she enjoyed Judge Dredd, which I admired a great deal in a lady, and so I found myself happy to have impressed her.

Reaching into the pouch, I felt about for the cold, smooth sphere and presented the shining ball to Mary.

"What is it?"

"It's my good shot. It took me an hour to salvage this from an old pin ball machine at the dump."

"You mean old McLoughlin's scrap yard?"

I nodded. "I'm saving it. With this I can hit anything at one hundred feet."

"Weren't you scared of Taber?"

Taber was Old Man McLoughlin's bull mastiff whose temperament was every bit as genial as one might expect from a junkyard dog. Actually, I had it on good authority that Taber was at the vet's having his glands squeezed during the heist—my father was the vet—but Mary needn't know that minor detail, and so I simply shrugged coolly and Mary whistled approvingly, looking off to the shattered sign again and furrowing her brow.

"You must be very brave," she said.

"Well," I shrugged again.

Mary placed her hand on my own and drew a deep breath. "Do you know the big pine woods, just beyond St. Michael's?" she asked nervously, and with good reason. St. Michael's ruin was an hour out of Oakwood. The church was said to be cursed after a mad vicar had made a deal with the Devil, unleashing all manner of horrors upon that once holy ground. The woods beyond were dense, damp, and most uninviting. A gang of children had gone missing in them years before and so our parents had warned us from the place, telling tales of evil deeds done by ghosts and ghouls within.

Mary didn't know this and had ventured into that cursed place one week before we'd met, and alone, no less, and while she had made it out alive, she had not done so without a scare. In the woods she had come across a decaying cottage, which she had taken for abandoned. Entering, however, she had found the place distressed, but not without signs of habitation: a pot of rotten stew on the table suggesting a resident within the last week. Mary did not go beyond the kitchen before losing her nerve, but as she had turned to leave, she had spied the most terrible figure standing in the doorway of the cellar, which had jolted her with such fright that she had fled, running until she was out of the woods and her legs had failed her. Mary did not go into detail. All she said was that the being was a woman most grotesque.

To hear it was nerve splicing, as was the request that followed. While in the cottage Mary had held her necklace for courage and upon seeing the petrifying sight had snapped the chain in her fright and dropped it.

"My grandmother gave me that necklace," she explained. "I'd have retrieved it before I ran, but it fell between the floorboards. I suspect it fell into the cellar where the woman came out of. I know it's a terribly big ask, and I'll understand if you refuse, but I simply must retrieve my grandmother's cross, and you're such a terribly good shot."

Now, for a boy of ten, I would have said I was adequately brave, yet had I believed this story about the house in the woods, I likely would have declined. Then again, the history books and folk tales of England are filled with stories of men doing very silly things for very pretty girls, so who knows? As it happened, I was skeptical. Looking at it rationally I suspected that Mary had been spooked by a shadow or a curtain caught in a breeze, as girls often were, and so I agreed to help.

* * *

The forest beyond St. Michael's was like no wood which I had ever seen before, and too dense for travel by bicycle. Most of the trees were evergreens, standing tall as buildings and so close together that they blocked out the sun completely. From the branches, long beards of moss hung like decaying flesh, and there was a mist about the place and a chill in the still air so that when you were in it you forgot that it was summer at all.

The ground was mossy and damp where it was not blanketed with pine needles, and all about fungi of a gelatinous and poisonous nature sprouted. Every so often, as we walked through the pathless wood, we came across the leafless corpse of an oak, a remnant of the ancient native forest which had once stood there before it's felling during the Great War for some purpose or other.

We walked with silent steps, and because no birds sang and the trees had no leaves, and there was no breeze to quiver them if they had, there was a deep and unsettling quiet. Any courage which I might have possessed had waned, and all rationality had left me at the tree line. I was not altogether sure that I believed in witches, but if they did exist, then this struck me as a likely place for their residence.

My sweaty palm gripped tightly upon my catapult and good shot as I was tormented by the beating of my own heart, when suddenly Mary spoke.

"Look," she whispered, her breath adding to the fog. On a mossy rock sat a wonderful doll's house. In the elements it had fallen into disrepair, the wood rotting and wallpaper peeling with the damp. Inside, a family of five figures, each of them decapitated with a pair of seamstress scissors that rested by the house.

"I don't like this," I whispered, giving wholly to the presence of evil now.

"Do you want to go back?" Mary asked softly. I could see in her eyes her own determination to continue, and her hope that I would not leave her. I shook my head. Mary took my free hand in her own, though I was not sure if this was for my comfort or her own, and we continued.

The sight of the cottage worsened my unease. It was a stout building with walls once white that had succumbed to the growth of green mosses and lichens. The thatched roof was disheveled but appeared intact, as were the windows, though these were so dirty as to block any view of the interior. The rotten wooden door was open, and bracken and other foliage had claimed any plot of garden which might have been. The place looked medieval, as though it had existed long before the new forest had been planted, back when it was an ancient wood of oak, and ash, and thorn.

Mary gestured toward my catapult, and I set the ball bearing in the sling and readied to draw. By the door a black cat watched us with yellow eyes. It had no collar but was groomed and adequately fed, and as we approached it made no attempt to flee but rather growled in that low, rumbling way which cats do.

"I didn't see her last time," Mary whispered from behind me.

"It's just a stray," I answered, not altogether sure that I was right.

We crossed the threshold, the damp floorboards squelching beneath our weight. The light was little but sufficient to see about the kitchen. The place looked to have been abandoned as a functioning home, without a possession taken. There were rotten books of leather binding on the shelves and crockery and furniture all about the place. Everything was filthy and molded, and the air was stagnant and most unpleasant to breathe.

There were two doors out of the room, both of which led into blackness. One looked to lead to a living room, the other down into a windowless hole of a cellar.

"That's where I saw her," Mary whispered, her words shivering as she spoke them, "and this is where I dropped my necklace," she said, crouching down and running her hand over a gap. "Maybe we should have brought a torch," she said with regret.

Exploration breeds ingenuity. From a shelf I retrieved a rolling pin, from my rucksack a length of twine, and from my backpack two old socks which had plugged a hole. In a moment I had put these together to make a torch, igniting it with a match and handing it to Mary.

"Here. It won't burn for long. We'd best move fast."

Mary nodded, the flame flickering softly in the gloom as we made for the cellar door.

"Wait," Mary said, grabbing my arm, "the stew! Someone's been at it!"

The pot rested on a table with a ladle and bowl. With my breath held, I peered inside. The festering, mold-coated broth had indeed been disturbed, a ladle sized gouge missing from it, which had held its shape after the disruption. I drew back and looked to Mary with a grimaced face. Whatever could have eaten such a thing must have been unfathomably grotesque.

"Let's get this done," I said. Mary nodded, and together we stepped into the dark.

The stairs were wood, rotten and unsound, some so greatly that we dared not trust them completely with our weight. The cellar was one large space of rubble. All upon the damp walls were mad rambles, barely legible. Among the overlapped words I picked out "devil" and "flesh eater" before declining to read further. Already the torch was dying, and so swiftly we moved towards the spot where the necklace should have fallen, but found nothing there.

Above us was the gap in the boards, we were sure, yet Mary scanned the floor with the torch to no avail.

"It isn't here!"

"It has to be somewhere, Mary. Perhaps we're in the wrong spot."

"No, it was here. I'm sure!" she said still searching.

"Let's look about while we have light, just in case," I said, and the two of us moved through the room, waving the dwindling flame over the debris strewn ground until we were at the far side of the cellar with an ocean of darkness between us and the door.

Just as I was sure Mary's anguish could grow no greater, she suddenly yelled out, "Charlie, look!" and as she held the torch up my eyes spied the glint of the golden likeness of Christ upon the cross which hung from a nail up on the wall.

"However did it get there?"

"I don't know," Mary said, setting the torch against the wall. "Bunk me up."

Dropping the good shot into my pouch and holstering the slingshot, I hunched down with my hands clasped together, receiving Mary's foot and heaving her up. When she had retrieved the necklace from the nail, I lowered her, and so overwhelming was her joy that she squealed with delight and threw her arms around me.

“Oh, thank you, Charlie!” she yelled. Before I could offer a reply, a noise from the door startled us. It sounded like the cat, and as the tiny paws tip tapped across the floor, Mary lifted the torch out in front of us, but the flame was not more than a candle now and did little to light the dark.

The noise grew closer. I took my catapult from my pocket, but before I could rest my hand upon a shot, the most terrifying thing came wailing from the darkness, knocking me to the ground and spilling my ammunition all about the place. It was no cat, but a woman, blubberous, naked, and reeking of death and excrement. Winded and stunned, I heard Mary scream in horror as the ungodly hag set upon her, causing her to drop the torch, which thankfully remained lit, revealing the black space in the cellar wall which the hag was dragging Mary into.

Dazed, but still holding my catapult, I felt for something, anything to propel toward the witch. It was then that my hand fell upon the unmistakable smoothness of the good shot. Placing it in the sling, I drew back as far as I was able and sent the steel ball hurtling into the crooked teeth of that monstrous bitch, bursting them into smithereens, which fell like rain. The hag screamed in agony and released Mary, who scrambled into the dark as the burning eyes of Satan’s wench fell upon me, smoldering with hateful rage, the groom bubbling from her smashed mouth.

Then she was on me, the stink choking my lungs as she howled blood upon me, too heavy to escape from and with no other shot in reach. Panicked, I took the butt of the catapult and jammed it into the hag’s eye. As she recoiled in pain, Mary came up behind and with unimaginable force smashed the rolling pin into the back of the hag’s skull so that she fell from atop of me.

Mary pulled me up and we ran through the dark toward the door, scrambling up the stairs, heaving one another, and with several boards giving way beneath us. The Witch followed, though neither of us looked back as the sound of crashing filled our ears, followed by the infuriated shrieking of the hag and then the wailing of a cat.

Through the kitchen we ran, into the woods, and fleeing without stopping all the way to the ruin of St. Michael’s. Only once we were on my bike, with my legs pedaling as fast as they could, and with Mary on my stunt pegs and her hands gripping her grandmother’s necklace, did we begin to laugh manically over our escape.

I dropped Mary home that afternoon, and before she ran inside, she kissed my cheek, agreeing that we’d meet again. I was late for dinner, able only to provide the excuse that I had made a new friend. Mother took a disliking to this friend there and then, suggesting that I keep better company, and while it was not my practice to disobey my parents, on this occasion I did, though for this crime my mother has since forgiven me as Mary and I are married now and with three children.

Occasionally we discuss that day. It seems unbelievable even to us, though we both recall it just as I have told it to you. It was just one of the adventures which we've shared, and while I encourage our children to explore as we did in youth, I steer them clear of St. Michael's ruin and the woods beyond.

And of Ryan Cornwell. We grew apart as he retreated into the realms of the unreal. I saw him not long ago, and we chatted a little. He works in IT now and never married. He's grown paler and with a bad complexion. He seems nervous, his eyes flitting about like flies dodging the swat, like he's witnessed some unconscionable evil, which of course he has. His has been a life unlived, wasted peering into the digital abyss. It has sent him mad, as it must all men. His is a tortured soul, and he exists now only as a warning to others.

Gravity

Alan Schmidt

The dojo smelled of stale air and sweat. On the far wall stood a United States flag over bare white blocks of concrete. Even with its spartan amenities, the dojo had everything it needed, the floor covered with mats and the padded walls giving all the material support for the fighters. The instructor opened the few windows in the room to get some ventilation as the young boys tussled on the old, stained floor. Methodical percussion of bodies slamming onto the floor coinciding with heavy breathing permeated the room as some assistants calmly gave instruction and correction. Paradoxically, the activity gave the room a surreal sense of ambient calm amidst the violence of combat.

I, along with a few other parents, stood on the back wall to watch the skirmish. While most dropped their kid off and did errands, many stayed, and usually had the strongest compunction for their children to succeed. We wanted to see every move our progeny made, every mistake, every facial expression that expressed his inner dialogue amidst adversity. To those adults standing and watching, this wasn't just an after-school activity, or evening daycare.

This being a no-gi dojo, I could already see the strength differential in the young combatants. My kid was rolling with a new arrival who had definitely sparred somewhere else before. The child's long, sinewy arms and strong quads showed someone who already knew how to put his small body to powerful use. A red-haired, freckled boy with green eyes, he had made the ground his home, his lightning movement always a step ahead of my son. I shook my head in resignation that this was more a master class than a match.

A way down, I noticed the red-haired boy's dad observing the same fight. His arms crossed with a light grin on his face, he couldn't help but look pleased with what he was seeing. The eyes, however, betrayed his grim resoluteness. Underneath the easygoing exterior existed a fierce mind that wasn't satisfied with just winning.

I looked at my son, who just broke with his freckled boy after losing in another submission. My smaller, black-haired son had an olive complexion and brown eyes, like his mother. His facial expression showed resoluteness and patience, like he studied the loss, absorbed it, processed it, and prepped his mind to try again. An intellectual and stoic all the way through. I looked at the clock and noticed three minutes remaining, with the instructors content to stay with the current pairings until the conclusion. My kid had an admirable attitude so far, sparring with someone far superior, but I wished he could get a break.

I took another look at the father, noticing a worn face and bronze skin from long hours in the sun. He didn't notice me at all, his entire focus on the match. I liked everything about him, his posture, his confidence, his iron concentration, and wanted him as an ally. I strode over and gave a light tap on his shoulder. He turned his attention to me, like he just moved from being entranced back to reality.

"That yours?" I asked, nodding towards the ginger child.

"Yup," he replied. "And that's your kid?"

"Yeah. Haven't seen you around before. I'm Gary," I said, extending my hand.

"Jake." He grinned, giving a firm shake. "First time here."

"I can tell this isn't your first dojo."

"Haha, no. Had to move to get closer to work. Needed to find a new place. He's been training since he was six, took to it right away."

I watched the two, now with the primary instructor peering in and observing. My son lay in a guard position. This round, Jake's kid seemed to have lost some focus, impatiently trying to force himself into a better position. He leaned forward into my son, out of balance, and my son quickly took advantage, pulling him into himself and locking his arm, trying to get into position for a triangle submission.

Jake's jovial grin vanished, and he cursed under his breath. For a long few seconds, it seemed my son had the position to end the match but didn't finish fast enough and the red-haired kid wrangled free and back into a neutral position. He shook his head in disgust.

"I told him to watch that," he muttered. "Your kid had him dead to rights."

A whistle blew, and the sparring ceased. The students broke and congregated in a circle as the instructor went through the day's lessons.

"How long's your kid done this . . . oh, what's his name, by the way?" he asked.

"Tim. We've only done formal training for about six months. I taught him some stuff before then, but I can only teach so much. Best to get the professionals involved. This was never my thing until recently."

"It's a cool sport. Crazy what they learn at the start. Think they won when their opponent is on their back. Next thing they know, they're gasping for air." He said. "All about leverage. A lot to learn there."

"Shows how deceiving things can be on the surface."

"Yup. Hey, has he been in any competitions yet? There's one not too far away this weekend we're going to. You should sign him up."

"Not this weekend. He's signed up for anther competition."

"Oh, he in some other sport?"

"Not exactly, violin."

He looked at me like I was an alien for a moment, then chuckled. "Wow, that's night and day, isn't it?"

"I never thought I would be here five years ago, but I have the feeling he'll need both one day. Especially families like ours."

He processed what I implied, like he was going through calculations in his mind of how much of his inner thoughts he would give away to this stranger, and whether I really implied as much as I seemed to. Many thoughts and worries entered his mind as I suggested something he knew in his heart to be true for a long time, but only told in the most hushed of tones. He finally sighed and shook his head.

"Ain't that the truth," he sighed.

As Jake's kid came over, he took him aside, kneeled by him, and spoke to him. I knew that look, and that tone; I had already used it countless times when telling my child something of utmost importance. The kid looked at my son grabbing the bag and running to me, then packed up with his dad.

I gave Tim a pat on the back. "Not bad today."

He nodded, dripping in sweat and still panting. Fatigue finally hit him. The lessons ended at eight p.m. and since he began, he never had a problem getting to sleep.

"Hey!" Jake called out as I began walking out. "Here next week?"

"I'll be here."

"Awesome," he replied.

A couple of years ago, a man like that would see no reason to interact with me. I was in the upper-class strata, pampered since infancy, who never had want or real uncertainty. My parents and the best teachers money could buy cleared all real adversity from life. He would have smelled my discomfort talking to someone like him, read the fake comradery and the insincere social graces that plagued people who lived my life. He came from the opposite background.

Regardless of the environment, I spotted a person who grew in harder conditions in his mannerisms. He didn't grow up where he had superiors teaching how to talk the refined way, to have the right views. It forced him to see, and act, to attack reality head-on, without a comforting filter.

Instead of class and upbringing, I now only filtered possible expansions of my social circle into three categories: strong men, weak men, and weak men who wanted to be strong. I only made company with strong men or weak men trying to become strong. I had a special sympathy for the latter, since no matter how disciplined, someone out there knew your true capabilities, and one always came short. Strength and weakness weren't so much physical characteristics as much as a man's will to expand his domain, to conquer a sphere, whether it be social influence, productive skills, or literal land. And every type existed in every socio-economic stratum.

The vigorous men who didn't share my views deep inside were slim. The bug-like qualities of the masses of weak men worked to tear the confident and powerful down to their level, to bring them to entropy. They posed more risk than the man of power, even in the rare cases I didn't see eye to eye with him. The weak man's most effective weapon was isolating the strong from one another, to keep the impulse of real greatness contained, to be safe. The morality of the current age condemns ascension as depraved, and unthinking conformity and lowest denominator consumption as virtue. They're a crab bucket taking human form.

We walked out into the parking lot, my head in a swivel for any potential threats. It wasn't a war-zone like the worst parts of Detroit, but it was the sort of area where payday loan stores were ubiquitous, alongside storefronts with only the word "Liquor" highlighted in neon lights. The dojo stood as the lone survivor of the strip mall, the other businesses long gone. Thirty years ago, things were different, where a working-class family could live in this area in safety and community and local shops owned by local people resided in the now bare storefronts. Like the rest of the country, the rich areas sprouted with 3,000 square-foot houses, while areas like this, with 1,200 square-foot houses built in the 1960s, were unfairly seen as a historical eyesore, along with the people who lived in them. At the end of the day though, everyone fell victim to the same malaise. It was just easier to see here, as money could not mask the social rot.

I remembered looking for a good dojo. At the first, and more so at the second, the friendly instructors tried to make sure everyone felt comfortable. As teachers, I had no issue with them though. They knew their stuff. The dojos were clean, well maintained, with a disciplined clientele. My son would have done fine, but I knew something was missing and found it when I parked in this lot and walked in. The instructor here, a brash, bald man with a long, white beard, examined my son up and down, assessing whether the kid was even worth his time.

He simply said, "You ready?"

My son nodded.

"Good, then get in line," he replied, and the day's lesson began. No welcome, no comfort, just business. I liked him.

We got into the car, and I checked my phone to see my wife, Priscilla, called. Originally, she had ambivalence about martial arts, as she came from a similar background to me. As I changed, though, she changed. At peace with the new me, she only asked that I call on our way home to explain how lessons went.

My son buckled up and grabbed his book, opening to where he left off for the twenty-minute ride home. I called my wife back.

"Yup?" She answered.

"We're on our way back," I said, making a slight swerve to avoid a pothole.

"Good session?"

"There was a new kid there Tim sparred against, real killer. Talked to his dad for a bit too and hit it off."

"How'd he do?" she asked.

I looked over to Timothy, who had already absorbed himself in his book. For him, that was always his escape after a hard session, whether it be school, music, or fighting.

"He did fine."

She knew that meant he lost. "Okay, good to hear he's getting some good competition."

Years ago, she would have gotten into an argument that it was unfair for such skill differentials to pit against each other. Now she just accepted it. "By the way, did a workout with Samantha and we just finished. Just FYI, we have company."

I shook my head in irritation. Of all her friends, I couldn't understand what she saw in Samantha. "Okay. How did the workout go?"

"Definitely pregnant," she replied. "Got through it. We're going dancing this Saturday, right? Sam wants to come with her husband."

I bit my lip. "Let's discuss this when we get home."

She chuckled. "Okay, fine. See you soon."

I still had a hard time processing her assertiveness. For most of our marriage, I could hardly convince her to make her wants explicit, instead passively expecting me to pick up clues and read her mind. Then she went from ashy wallflower to matriarch of the neighborhood. Barely a day went by when either of her friends weren't over our house or herself over a neighbor's place, always finding time to bring homemade goods. The woman who once needed two days to prepare for even the most innocuous visit now had impromptu gatherings with fifteen minute's notice. It shouldn't have been a surprise. I became a completely different man in the last five years, and she followed suit. A more difficult woman, true, but in a good way.

My transformation started with as simple a catalyst as walking in a sporting goods store, originally intending to buy some running shoes, only to see a hundred-pound punching bag hanging near the middle of the aisle, begging someone to beat the shit out of it.

Half-jokingly, I did. The impact felt good, so I hit it again, and the same exhilaration entered me. Something unseen, primal, connected my fists to the bag's leather. I tried on some boxing gloves and embraced the rush of energy and adrenaline that emanated out to my body, ancient forces seeming to direct my energies in avenues once unknown. Satisfied, I bought the bag and gloves and set it up in the garage that night.

Originally, Priscilla reacted with a mix of annoyance and dismissal. Boxing was nearly profane for a music professor to indulge in. She could only describe such exercises as uncouth for a man of my class. She assumed I would use the bag once or twice and then forget the whole matter, and she would hint she wanted it taken down. Then I would oblige and we would revert to our normal life. After two months of getting up at five thirty to hit the bags, she realized something had changed in me, and I'd just gotten started. My son, six then, began hitting the bag with me too, much to her chagrin.

We used to sit in the living room every night, and I watched TV while she stared blankly at her phone. Then she sat with her phone by herself while I chatted with old friends, read in my study, or practiced my cello in the music studio. Though a musician herself, she stopped practicing with any sort of regularity years ago, and I only did the bare minimum for years. I could sense her frustration at my sudden increase in personal standards.

With time, she overcame her initial inertia. How much credit I deserve, I don't know, as maybe I was just dragging her down to my level our entire marriage, giving a boring comfort and familiarity. All I know is she dropped her phone and a new vibrancy entered her eyes, where for the longest time there only existed the dull stare of pointlessly scrolling social media. As I taught my son boxing, she taught him the violin. As I talked with friends, she got to know the parents in the neighborhood. Soon she knew every birthday, every interest, and every important event in the community. We became the home where everything happened, and I joked she conquered the entire neighborhood with apple pies and book clubs.

Still, Samantha was a lost cause. She laughed at me, saying I just didn't understand women, and she would pull her into our orbit too, just like how she did to the other milquetoast neighbors. I highly doubted success with Sam. Regime propaganda was the air that woman breathed.

I kept the music off and looked around as I drove, the streets becoming newer and better maintained, along with the buildings. The neighborhood became richer and cleaner, but still plagued with the same lack of character as the older neighborhood. Wherever you drove, you had the idea you could plop these places down anywhere in the country and they wouldn't feel out of place. While nicer and with less crime, it remained only a place to drive past, maybe stopping at a generic store on the way home to the same cookie-cutter, suburban landscape. Every bit of architecture and building seemed transactional, something to move past. When overcome with such blandness in my day-to-day life, I knew I had to double my effort to create the right aesthetics in my home and relationships to avoid getting pulled into the same rootlessness. The structure of the outside world of markets and independence could only create simulacra of roots based on fake identities, whether they be passing styles, sensibilities, or diversions. It gave the idea one had roots when nothing even dug into the ground below. The masses floated in empty space, begging for an outside power to guide them on the right path.

I thought back to the lesson, and the last match still bothered me. I had important ideas to impart to him and debated whether to tell him. I originally wanted to wait, let him grow a little more before I told him about the harsh realities of our age. He still sat absorbed in his book, not budging an inch since we left. He had incredible focus, and I could probably drive across the state before he would start wondering why we weren't home yet.

"Hey, Tim."

He looked up. Usually, I just let the car be quiet for the ride home to give him a mental break.

"I know it's late but I want to do a quick sparring session when we get home."

He sighed. "I'm tired, dad."

"It's important. I'll make it quick."

I pulled into our neighborhood, the gates to the suburb not yet closed for the night. I drove by pristine, green lawns and shrubs, with carefully laid rows of trees shading the road. Most hired the same contractor to do their lawn work. They did a fine job, and I had the same one for a while before delegating yard work to my son and myself. It took us three times longer than the pros, but there's a pride in mowing, raking, and planting that gave a grounding reality to one's life. Sweat and labor makes home a home.

The setting sun put long shadows over the neighborhood, a last gasp of light before nightfall. I turned onto our street and looked at the home of Samantha and her husband. Their grotesque LGBT rainbow lawn sign was missing.

"Huh," I muttered.

"What?" Tim asked.

"Don't worry about it."

I drove up the gently sloping hill and pulled into our driveway. I parked next to the colonial-style, red-brick house, one of three in the neighborhood with only slightly divergent designs. We celebrated the coming Fourth of July Weekend by hoisting the simple black tree with a white background, the words "An Appeal to Heaven" across the top, the flag of the Pine Tree Riots. We always tried to subtly galvanize our allies and confuse others, who knew that we were making a statement, something outside the appropriate political bounds, but could not understand. We converted no one by explicitly talking politics, but gained a multitude by working the edges as they slowly dismissed the air of the old culture they breathed and entered ours.

I turned off the ignition and tapped my son. "I'll get the gloves. Get in the front yard."

He sighed in fatigue but knew disobeying his father was a losing battle. I would just make everything harder and still get my way.

I glanced at my phone, noticing I received a message from a number I didn't recognize. It read, "Hey, Gary, is that offer still open? Let me know." In recent memory, I didn't remember making any offers, so what could this unknown person be referring to? He knew my name, so I must have said something to somebody. Asking his name would just make me look like I said something flippant when I was dead serious. Now I said nothing I didn't mean. Sighing, I put the phone in my pocket and made a mental note to unearth some clue as to who this person might be instead of putting his information in my phone. Priscilla wouldn't have made such a stupid error. She was queen of her domain, and I had yet to be king of mine.

I grabbed the gloves. On the front lawn I could see inside the studio through the window, two violins and a cello sitting against the wood-paneled walls. We never missed a day, and he hadn't practiced yet, but this was more important.

I tossed the gloves to my son as I put my mouth guard in. He resigned himself to the session, any sort of frustration or fatigue leaving his face.

"Alright, I said this would be quick. You listening?"

He nodded.

"What I want you to do is simple. I want you to come after me with every intent of annihilating me."

He looked at me confused, not so much because he had fears of doing actual damage, but because he didn't want to contradict what I told him at other times about always keeping his cool. He furrowed his breath, took a few hard breaths, and took two wild swings. I blocked them and hit his forehead hard enough to force him back.

"I didn't say flail in rage," I calmly replied. "I want every thought in your mind intent on winning, on beating me down like I had the intent to send you to the hospital. Like I was going to hurt someone you loved."

He nodded, and I stepped in with a jab, which he deflected, getting under my glove and nearly laying me out with a well-placed uppercut.

"Good," I said.

We went back and forth for a couple of minutes before I called it off and we tapped gloves. I crouched down to his level and began: "That kid was pretty tough today, wasn't he?"

"Yeah." He nodded.

“But you almost got him. Do you know why?”

“Yeah, he threw himself off balance.”

“He was arrogant, and didn’t respect you, trying for an easy win, and it allowed you to use your leverage. And you could have finished him if you went all in.”

“I—” he started.

“You did fine. Overall, he’s a good kid and has a solid father. I’m not denigrating anyone. I’m saying you’re going to need people like that in your life. You need people like that to respect you, and the only way they’ll respect you is to be a killer yourself, going in every time with the sole intention of destroying him, and then afterwards shaking and being pals, or at least equals. It tells him you’re made of the right stuff and he can trust you not to run when things get hot.

“I grew up and never got a punch in the face. There was never a time in my childhood I knew what real danger really was. I thought combat was a preoccupation of uncivilized, unenlightened people. I grew up in soft times where I could think like that. When you get older, you won’t have that luxury. You’re going to need an iron will, you’ll need firm allies, and you’ll be starting from only what I and some others create. You need to have a personality and will that pulls people to you, and a character that forms unbreakable bonds.

“Small, petty people are going to come after you for wanting to live in a way every previous generation took for granted. They are going to say you are in the wrong for just existing. They will use every psychological trick to break you down and every bit of propaganda to anathemize you and make it impossible to form your männerbund. You need to break through. Your mother and I are starting here, and there are others scattered around the country. We need to take our ranks right now, find them, grow them, and eventually create an army. Everyone has a role, whether an artist, craftsman, or warrior.”

The front door opened behind me, and I looked back to see Priscilla, in workout shorts and sport top, her four-month pregnant belly protruding slightly, finishing up chit-chat with Samantha. I shook my head and chuckled. Samantha dyed her hair a natural brown, eschewing the odd, blue-dyed hair she used to have. Priscilla put her hands through her jet-black hair and gave a coy grin in my direction, inferring she told me so. I couldn’t be happier to be more wrong.

“Anyway,” I finished, “I don’t have the answers to what’s coming, but I love you and will do everything to make sure you’re ready. And when the time comes, you will lead others in the same way. Understand?”

“Yeah, okay,” he replied, unsure of what to make of anything I said.

As he entered the house, I wondered if I talked to him too soon. I reassured myself that he needed to hear it eventually, and though I could have been far franker, at least he would know the reason for why I did what I did.

I sat on the front porch, soon accompanied by my wife. I listened as the neighborhood turn quieter, the number of cars going by dwindling, the birds becoming silent. The sun made its descent and some of the first distant stars appeared in the sky. Many of these brilliant spheres of energy had a multitude of planets they drew into their domain, invisible to our eyes, directing their destiny through the cosmos. Those cosmic balls of energy destroyed as well as created new life, their primordial power rebelling against the stale entropy of most of the cosmos, against the void. Nature is, at its core, a force of will that no one can escape, but only harness. After a long slumber, my people were awakening from their comfortable but banal sleep. I could sense it. Now was the time for Western Man to forge his destiny again, bring about the second renaissance to reconquer and shape his destiny. I only hoped to be part of the great power that pulled our people together to prominence once again.

Cemeteries

Anthony Schneider

How long has it been? Six? No. Eight years. I'm trying to do the mental math as I park by the old library. I exit my truck and look around the massive parking lot. Still one of the biggest in the county I figure. Next to the library is a small strip mall with a pizza place, a convenience store, and a post office. The storefronts appear unchanged since my childhood, as if it were some sort of commercial mausoleum. It makes me wonder if the workers I remember have been similarly preserved. I glance over at the front of the old pizza place, but the sun's glare only reveals my own reflection in the dusty glass. I check my watch and face back towards the lot. The county festival began an hour ago, but there's still plenty of open spots.

This was the time and place we agreed upon last night. A single online message breaking an almost decade-long silence. I squint in the sunlight as I await his arrival. My new job has accustomed my eyes more to the cold glow of the computer monitor than that of the bright sun, the same job that's kept me from this town for so long. Spring and its welcome warmth have finally arrived, yet a strong wind blows. I'm grabbing my old field jacket out the truck when I hear the whine of brakes in the parking space beside me. A different, yet equally rugged truck is now beside mine. I already know who it is.

As we walk towards each other, I want to say something meaningful, but like a train car switching over to an old yet still existing piece of track, my throat and tongue works before my mind does. "What's up, bub!" I blurt out, a stupid grin reflexively spreading across my face. We begin to shake hands but hug instead. Then we interrogate each other for a few minutes:

"How long's it been?"

"What're ya doing nowadays?"

"Where ya living now?"

"How ya like your truck?"

We turn towards the main street, and the conversation continues. My legs move under me, although I do not order them. My mouth opens and shuts at the whims of an unbridled tongue. My eyes view scenes so familiar that they are as good as blind. Some would call this a "flow state." Perhaps more accurately, I'm a reanimated corpse.

Making our way up the street, we reach the edge of the festival itself. The mixed scent of barbecue and funnel cake fills our nostrils. A crowd gradually grows the farther we go up the street. Suddenly we are wading through a sea of old couples, families with legions of face-painted children, and enough twenty-somethings with dogs to make a Chinaman's mouth water.

Entering a bazaar of pop-up tents, we are surrounded by vendors selling all sorts of handmade kitsch, items undoubtedly destined for the walls of suburban homes. The market's presence is comforting, although we're not interested in the wares. We lament that the beloved rubber band gun salesman of our childhood is nowhere to be found. It's a memory tied to a time and place with the strength of a marble tombstone, one of many that spring up as we continue our walk up the street, soon finding ourselves in a veritable graveyard.

The houses that flank the pavement where we spent innumerable Halloweens filling pillow cases with candy. The unchanging storefronts that house ageless breakfast restaurants. The street itself where we once marched in parades, khaki clad in Boy Scout uniforms. Rows upon rows of graves that put Arlington to shame. We point out to one another old classmates as they pass by us in the crowd. They either don't notice or don't recognize us. Like gargoyles and statuary, they dutifully guard the hallowed ground whose limits they've never dared escape.

Eventually, we reach the epicenter of the festival in the old courthouse circle. Inside the original county seat delineated by a low brick wall, a couple more vendor tents are squeezed in. Festival goers mill about here like guests at a wake. Jubilatory, but unwilling to acknowledge the body in the room with them. For at the circle's center lies a true monument to the dead, one that overshadows the innumerable imagined gravestones of childhood memories. It is a roughly hewn granite obelisk, adorned with names listed in descending rows upon its four sides. They are the names of fallen soldiers, organized by the company in which they served. A simple epitaph is etched at its base:

TO OUR CONFEDERATE DEAD

"It's still here. . . ." my friend mutters.

We approach it in an awkward and unplanned reverence, both of us astonished to find the memorial still standing.

I scour my mind for some suitable quote from the Southern canon but draw nothing. Faulkner weeps. Instead, I reach out to touch the granite rock, as if the tangibility of the monument itself will inspire my tongue to profundity. "I'd die to keep this thing standing," I say with a sigh. My old friend nods in silent agreement. An older man, who has to be in his sixties, walks by as I speak. He shoots us a glare of thinly veiled confusion, yet walks on. I look back at him and chuckle.

Would he stare the same at a Jew at the Western Wall? A Muslim circling the Kaaba? A Christian on the Via Dolorosa? I shake my head. The pilgrim never gets the luxury of choosing where he is compelled by tradition to journey. I gaze back up at the names on the monument's face. As I ponder the lives of the listed dead, it occurs to me that they also would find my apparent pilgrimage quite curious. How blessed were they to have no need for a memorial, the likes of which they themselves are immortalized on. For humanity only builds monuments to things they fear will be forgotten.

For those long dead men, the hills, streams, forests, and fields of the county were their eternal cemetery. Every inch of the soil cried out in ghostly review with the names of their forefathers. No need for monuments. No necessity of memorials. Nation, country, family, people, race, destiny: all synonymous, self-evident, and unchanging as the blue of the sky. A reality now utterly foreign to most all their own descendants a few generations later.

I release my hand from the stone and quickly turn away. I can't stand to look at it any longer, downtrodden in realizing the dead have already buried their dead. I walk out of the circle, beckoning my old friend to follow. We passed a brewery on that old main street, and I owe him a long overdue beer. The last time we shared in each other's company found us both well below drinking age. We do the rest of the catching up there, and a thousand more utterances of "remember when" follow.

Very slowly and almost unwillingly, our conversation begins to shift from the past to the future. He's got some land out in the hills the state over, my friend tells me. Bought himself a trailer and planted it on the unimproved plot. He needs other guys to help him turn the wilderness from nothing into something. He wants me to tag along.

I raise the pint glass to my lips as I consider his offer. With sadness that borders on regret I recall my earlier oath to the monument. I place my beer down. Such a declaration would ring rather hollow if I were to entirely abscond from my ties here.

I stare down into my glass as if trying to divine an answer from it. My own reflection is all that stares back at me from the dark brown surface of the beer. I raise my head to face my old friend as I clasp his hand in agreement, finally realizing what the men on that monument went their whole lives knowing:

Without lives worth remembering, the cemeteries aren't worth visiting.

The Eldorado Effect

Rune Stenbock

Reality is that which, when you stop believing in it, doesn't go away.

–Philip K. Dick

She entered the diner with an empty water jug and her bangs plastered to her forehead, dragging her scrawny body behind her like someone fresh out of the sauna. Coming to the counter she put the jug down on the countertop, wiped her bangs out of her eyes and said, "Do you mind if I use your tap out back?"

The waitress was at the far end of the counter serving beer to a bunch of weather-beaten customers. Without turning her head, she said, "All you're likely to get from the tap out back is a mouthful of rust. Just give me a second, honey, and I'll fill your jug right up for you."

"It's not for me, it's for my car."

"Well in that case, you just help yourself. I'd still let the water run a while though. God only knows what's in them old pipes."

"Thanks. By the way, are you still serving breakfast?"

The waitress wobbled to the register and with a professional smile she said, "What would you like?"

"Bacon and eggs. Pancakes. Coffee and . . . do you have iced tea?"

"We have lemonade."

"Is it cold?"

"Ice cold."

"A large glass then, please."

"Anything else?"

"Yeah, you wouldn't happen to know the way to Schrodinger, would you?"

"Going down to see the rock formations?"

"Yeah, that's right. You know them?"

"Everyone around here does, honey. Just keep south on the highway and take a right by the old gas station and you should be able to find it."

"You know how far it is? Roughly?"

"I'm afraid I don't. Shouldn't be too far though. You'll be there in no time."

She thanked the waitress and exited the diner.

The water gushed out brown and odious from the tap. She took in her surroundings while she let the water run.

The diner was an oasis in a flat and monotonous desert landscape dotted with creosote bushes and ocotillo. A range of mountains stood in the distance, shimmering and mirage-like. Above her hung a perfectly blue sky untouched by clouds. The sun blazed like a torch, and its heat pressed down on her as if the heat had gained mass.

The tap water cleared. She splashed it in her face and poured it on her neck before she filled the jug.

Steam rose and hissed like an agitated serpent as she poured water into the water tank. Having filled the water tank, she entered the car, turned the ignition, and checked the water gauge. The needle still lingered in the red zone. Maybe the car just needed more time to cool down? She walked back towards the diner with her stomach rumbling and a savage thirst burning in her throat.

She grabbed a booth in a dark corner and gorged herself on the food. She ate too fast and soon had the hiccups. She washed them down with coffee and lemonade for chasers and picked up her phone and checked the GPS.

Twenty-three miles lay between her and Schrodinger. It seemed to her that she had gone at least twenty-five down the highway without finding neither gas station nor exit. Maybe she had gauged the distance wrong?

She re-read the travel review that had motivated her trip to Schrodinger and compared the location of the town on the travel review map to the GPS. The locations corresponded with each other. Had she been too distracted by the car overheating to notice the exit? Had someone taken down the sign that marked the exit? She would make a new pass along the highway as soon as the food had settled in her stomach. She put her phone down, enjoyed the post-meal sluggishness and gazed at the weather-beaten bunch by the counter.

They seemed to be a part of the diner's interior just as much as the checkered floor, the red vinyl booths, and the faded Americana on the walls, as if they had been installed by the counter to lend the place a sense of rustic authenticity. One of them was a pockmarked man in a baseball cap and a denim jacket. The other two were women: one a gaunt scarecrow with old cowboy boots on her feet; the other one a bitter-looking type with her hair up in a greasy ponytail.

"Can I get you anything else, honey?"

She looked up at the waitress who was busy clearing her table and said, "You said follow the highway south and take a right at the gas station, right? Because I've been down that way and . . . I don't know. I couldn't find the exit."

"I suppose you've must've missed it."

"Yeah but . . . twice?"

"Twice?"

"Yeah, when I didn't find the exit the first time I doubled back. I was just about to turn around again when smoke started coming from my car and, well. . . . Here I am.

"You didn't go driving without your glasses, did you?"

"I wear contacts."

The waitress thought it over, turned to the counter and said, "Hey, Carl? This young lady here's looking for Schrodinger but can't seem to find the exit?"

The pockmarked man by the counter nodded like that was perfectly alright and said, "Goin' down to see the rock formations?"

"Yeah."

"Thought as much. Only reason people ever ask for Schrodinger."

"Wow, guess they must really be something, huh?"

"So I've heard."

"So have I. I mean, so I've read."

"What you wanna do is take the highway south until you come to the old gas station. When you see it, just take a right and you should be able to find Schrodinger."

"She says she's been down that way," the waitress said. "Says she can't find the exit."

Carl pointed towards her phone and said, "It didn't come with a GPS?"

"Yeah, it did. It's showing the right location and all but—"

"Sure it's working right?"

"Yeah. I mean, it's been working fine since I left home."

Carl hopped down from his barstool and shuffled towards her with hunched shoulders and his hands in his pockets. Reaching the table, Carl picked up his own phone, opened the GPS and entered Schrodinger in the search field. When the result appeared on the screen, he compared it to her phone.

"Seems to work alright to me."

He held his and her phone up next to each other. The location was the same on both phones.

"Well, I guess I just missed the exit then."

"Guess so," Carl said and gave her her phone back. "How come you wanna see them rock formations anyway?"

"I don't know. I just read about them and thought they looked kind of cool so I thought, hey, why not go down and see them over the weekend?"

"I suppose there's worse ways to spend a weekend."

"Yeah. Now I'm just kind of hoping they're worth the drive."

"I couldn't tell ya. Never visited them myself but . . . hey, Moon Pie? You ever been to Schrodinger?"

The gaunt woman with the cowboy boots said, "No."

"You know if the rock formations are worth the visit?"

"No."

"But it's down the highway, right? By the old gas station?"

"Yep."

"Well, see, this young lady here says she's been down that way but she can't find the exit."

"What you want me to do about it?"

"I dunno. Thought you might have an idea."

"You got a roadmap lying around back there, Inez?"

"I'll check," the waitress said.

She thanked Carl who tipped his cap and went back to his seat by the counter, and while Inez rummaged through the shelfs and cabinets behind the counter, she finished her lemonade and wiped her face with a paper napkin.

The day was growing hotter by the hour. The ceiling fan didn't seem to do much except shuffle the hot air around. Sweat trickled down her back and sides, making her clothes stick to her moist skin. She shifted in her seat, scratched her itching scalp, put the ice cubes in a fresh napkin, and pressed the napkin against the base of her neck. Finally, Inez emerged from behind the counter and came over to her table with a Rand McNally Road Atlas from the eighties. She thanked Inez and ordered another lemonade.

She studied the road map, compared it to the GPS, double-checked and triple-checked, and finally put the phone and map down. When Inez came with her lemonade she said, "You wouldn't happen to have another map would you? Something, uhm, more up to date maybe?"

"I'm sorry, honey," Inez replied. "That was all I could find. Why?"

"Well, I—I can't seem to find Schrodinger."

"Mind if I take a look?"

Inez put on a pair of reading glasses that hung from the collar of her blouse and studied the map. She closed it, inspected the front and back of the cover and said, "Well, that's peculiar. I can't seem to find it either. Carl? Come here a second, will you?"

Once again, Carl shuffled towards them. When he arrived at the table, Inez thrust the map into his hands and said, "See if you can find Schrodinger for me."

Carl studied the map, took off his cap, and ruffled through his hair and said, "You're sure this map's correct?"

"You can't find it either?" she said.

"No. Maybe Schrodinger wasn't built in the eighties?"

"It was. They built it during the early years of the oil boom."

"Hmm. Well, I . . . hey, Moon Pie? Come here and take a look at this."

Moon Pie sighed, slid down from her barstool, and walked towards them in a bandy-legged stride.

"We can't find Schrodinger," Carl said.

Moon Pie took the map from Carl, sat down in the booth, put the map down on the table, and studied it. After a while she said, "No Schrodinger in here that I can find."

"But—but how can that be?" she said.

"Well, how many towns and villages you reckon' are in a map like this?"

"Must be hundreds of thousands," Carl said. "Millions even."

"A lot of towns to keep track of. Suppose they missed one and didn't notice? Or didn't care to rectify it."

"A misprint," she said. "Yeah, that must be it."

"Yep. I wouldn't fret if I was you. You just follow the highway south and you'll find the exit sooner or later."

"That's right," Carl said. "Just keep a lookout for the old gas station and take a turn there and you'll be in Schrodinger in no time."

She thanked Moon Pie and Carl for their help and asked if she could get them anything for their trouble. Moon Pie said she wouldn't mind a beer, and Carl seconded that request, and a third gravelly voice said, "I would like to know your name, if you wouldn't mind."

She turned to the voice. It belonged to the bitter-looking woman with the ponytail.

"Me?" she said. "My name is Kate."

"How familiar are you with the Bible, Kate?"

"Uhm, not very."

The bitter-faced woman spoke without turning her head, sat staring right in front of her as if the other side of the counter was Kate's proper physical location, somewhere she ought to be instead of the booth where she actually sat.

"In Matthew 15:14 it is written that if the blind lead the blind, both shall fall into the ditch. Is that where you want to go Kate? The ditch?"

"Uhm, no," Kate said. "I want to go to Schrodinger."

"Then I would advise you to stop following the blind."

Carl and Moon Pie traded looks, and Carl said, "You're referring to us?"

"I am."

"We're not blind," Carl said. "At least, I'm not. I might not have twenty-twenty vision, but I sure ain't blind."

"It's not your vision I'm doubting, Carl, it's the validity of your directions."

"Well, you can stop your doubting 'cuz it was Moon Pie who gave them to me and I know Moon Pie wouldn't lie to me, would you, Moon Pie?"

"Sure wouldn't," said Moon Pie.

“And from what inviolate source did you receive your knowledge of the way to Schrodinger, Moon Pie?”

“From Inez,” Moon Pie replied.

“Inez,” the bitter-looking woman said, “when was the last time you visited Schrodinger?”

Inez thought for a moment and said, “I can’t recollect ever being there.”

“Yet you feel confident to give directions.”

“Of course, I do. Everyone around here knows the way to Schrodinger, honey.”

“Which is all the more intriguing since no one has been there in person.”

“Oh, stop your fussin’, Frances. It was Jenny who told me and. . . . You know Jenny who used to work here? She used to tell them tourists who came looking for the rock formations the way, and when she quit, I took over the direction-giving.”

“Did Jenny ever visit Schrodinger?”

“Jenny never traveled more than ten miles from her home. Said all she needed to see was on her computer or on the TV.”

Frances nodded slowly, slapped her hand on the counter, and said, “Inez, I will have a root beer. I have the feeling it will be much needed.”

Frances got down from her barstool and walked toward Kate’s table with slow and measured steps, one hand stretched out before her as if the diner was submerged in complete darkness.

When she reached the table, she felt around the edges of the table, grabbed the edge, and carefully sat down next to Kate. It was when she turned toward Kate that she understood why Frances walked in such a strange way.

Her eyes looked like someone had poured milk into them. They were veiled with an opaque film behind which two murky pupils swam in pools of palest blue. Most people would have worn sunglasses to cover eyes such as those, but Frances wore them like badges of merit, as if they were a Gucci handbag or a WBC heavy weight belt. She stared at Kate unblinkingly and said, “You’re being sold a falsification, Kate. A copy of a copy of a copy.”

“I—I don’t think they’re trying to sell me anything. They’re just trying to help.”

“I know they are. But are they, their directions being based on nothing but hearsay?”

“Well, I—I didn’t know that. I mean, how could I, right?”

“I suppose you couldn’t. Still, help seems superfluous with a GPS on your phone?”

“Yeah, well . . . it’s not working right or something.”

"I thought you and Carl established it did work?"

"Yeah but . . . I don't know. Must be something with the reception."

"And the road map?"

"It's . . . there's a misprint."

"That would seem to be the likeliest explanation. And as a general rule, I'm always in favor of the likeliest explanations. But did you ever consider something more esoteric?"

"Such as . . . ?"

"Well, let us summarize, shall we? You have driven up and down the highway without finding the exit. Schrodinger doesn't appear in the road atlas, even though it should, but it does appear on at least two GPSes, even though it hasn't led you to Schrodinger, and the directions provided to you are based on nothing but hearsay. What conclusion might one draw from this?"

"That Schrodinger is very hard to find."

"A very sound assumption. But have you ever contemplated the possibility that Schrodinger, bizarre as the idea might seem, simply does not exist at all?"

Inez came with the drinks. She gave each one what they had ordered and said, "Oh, stop putting ideas in her head, Frances. Of course, Schrodinger exists. Everyone knows it does."

"Ah yes, general knowledge. It's a fine substitute for the truth, isn't it?"

"Look," Kate said and held up her phone. "There's a very easy way to find out."

"That's right," Carl said. "There must be official websites, government websites."

"Yes, the government, the bastion of unmuddied truth and unblemished virtue. Surely, they would never lie?

"Why the hell would the government lie about Schrodinger?" Moon Pie said.

"Who among us can claim to know the insidious machinations of the state?"

"Well, I sure can't," Carl said. "I can't even figure out the insidious machinations of my wife."

"Very few can, Carl. And I'm not saying the government would lie about a topic such as this; I'm saying it isn't outside the realm of possibility. Improbable but not impossible. I'm certain we can all agree on that?"

They all nodded and took a swig of their drinks, as if agreeing with Frances left a bad taste in their mouths they desperately wanted to wash away. Frances downed half the bottle of root beer in one mighty gulp, wiped her mouth, and after burping said, "Let's rule that out as a legitimate source then. Kate, where did you first become aware of Schrodinger?"

"I read about it."

"Where?"

“In a travel review on a message board.”

“And what made you trust this review to such an extent that you decided to make the trip?”

“There were pictures, maps, comments and . . . I mean I—I just don’t see why anyone would lie about something like this.”

“Some people don’t need reasons, Kate. Some people lie simply because they know they can get away with it. Or because it amuses them.”

“I guess I just don’t see what would be so amusing about it.”

“Me neither,” Carl said. “And I also don’t understand why, well . . . let’s say Schrodinger doesn’t exist, right? Why then have all them tourists been coming here for years asking about it?”

“Because it does exist,” Moon Pie said. “People’ve been coming here for years askin’ for Schrodinger and those damn rock formations, and not once have any of them come back and said anythin’ about neither town nor rocks not bein’ real. We would’ve heard. Schrodinger might be off the beaten track and hard to find, but it’s as real as this diner, which makes this discussion straight up, straight jacket insane.”

Insane. . . . That was an understatement if there ever was one. Who had ever heard of such a thing: a town that people had come looking for for years being made-up? A town that, according to the GPS, had a liquor store, a souvenir shop, and a supermarket. Not to mention rock formations. And suppose Schrodinger didn’t exist, how come everyone in the diner, except Frances, was so sure of its existence? Was she being played? Was she being ensnared in some cruel mind game, the result of which might cost her more than she was willing to pay? After all, what did she really know about these people?

Kate felt a cold sensation travel up her spine, though it didn’t do nothing to cool her down. She swirled her glass and stared down into it, as if the answer to her questions were to be found among the ice cubes clinking against the cracked glass. They did not turn out to be oracular in nature, neither did the lemonade quench her thirst as it had done before. Had the diner suddenly gotten warmer? Or was it the onset of paranoia that increased her thirst and made her mouth dry? She felt hot and dank and longed for nothing more than the cool and concrete reality of an ice-cold shower.

“Inez? Could I get another lemonade? To go, please.”

“Sure thing, honey. Leaving already?”

“Yeah, I’m going to find a motel and call it a day.”

“But what about Schrodinger?” Carl said. “And the rock formations?”

“I’ve had enough of both for one day. Thanks for all the help and . . . well, thanks.”

She paid her bill, left plenty of tips, squeezed past Frances, and made her way toward the exit.

"Safe travels, Kate," Frances said. "I hope you ponder the nature of our discussion here today. It might save you a trip or two in the future. And Moon Pie, as to why all those tourists have never come back to complain about your directions, did you ever hear of Eldorado?"

Outside the sun was sinking. The sky was all the colors of a mescaline trip, and the shadows cast by the yucca trees were grotesquely elongated, as if they'd been stretched out on a rack. The temperature had gone down somewhat, but the heat still lingered stubbornly, like a child who refused to go to bed.

"Eldorado was the most intricate game of Chinese whispers mankind ever played," Frances said. "What started out as a mistranslation became a rumor that spread among the conquistadors quicker than smallpox spread among the Aztecs. Didn't take long before it was the object of one of the most desperate treasure hunts ever embarked upon. Thousands of people lost their lives in search of the fabled city; in swamps, by jungle animals, out of dehydration or disease or territorial natives. Yet no matter how many of those brave adventurers lost their lives, they refused to give up on their dream."

Kate got inside her car, turned the ignition, ran the AC on maximum capacity, and checked where the nearest motel was located. She then checked if regular water could be used as a coolant. It turned out it couldn't.

"Why did they refuse?" Carl said.

She glanced at the water gauge. Slowly but steadily, the needle climbed toward the red zone. Luckily, the nearest motel wasn't far off. At least if the GPS was to be believed. She shifted the car into gear.

"They refused to give up the quest to find Eldorado," Frances said, "because to most of us, death by poisonous snakes or Aztec knives are to be preferred before admitting that we have been duped, that all this time we thought we were right, we were in fact wrong."

She shifted the gear back into neutral and turned off the ignition. The car popped and whizzed. On the horizon, the far-off mountains devoured the sun, and in the distance a coyote heralded the coming of night with its squealing howls. She exited the car and walked back toward the diner.

Inez was wiping down the counter when Kate entered. The waitress whisked away a fly that buzzed around her head and said, "You forget something, honey?"

Kate shook her head and walked toward the table where Frances, Moon Pie, and Carl still sat. When she reached them, she said, "Uhm, does anyone have a car that isn't overheated?"

"I've got a truck," Carl said. "Need a lift?"

"If you wouldn't mind?"

"Nah, nearest motel's on the way home anyway."

"How about driving me down the highway? Say, twenty-five miles?"

"Well sure, but the motel's up north."

"What if I changed my mind about the motel?"

"What do you mean?"

"What if I said there's a surefire way to find out if Schrodinger's really real or not?"

"You mean drive down there?"

Kate nodded. Carl took off his cap and ruffled his hair while he thought it over.

Finally, he said, "Well, I sure would like to know if the directions I've been giving people all these years have been wrong."

"I'm going too," Moon Pie said. "I wanna see Frances' face when we enter Schrodinger."

Frances finished her root beer and shook her head in bitter resignation. "You didn't listen to a single word I said, did you?"

"Sure, we did," Carl said. "But what else are we gonna do? Sit here all night?"

"Yeah, tag along, Frances," Kate said. "If nothing else, we'll get a road trip out of it."

"I lost my excitement for road trips with the loss of my sight, Kate. But thank you for the invitation nonetheless."

"She's just scared we might be right," Moon Pie said.

"Me being scared would require me having a personal stake in this, which I don't. No, I'm not going because I simply don't see the point in it."

"How about you come along for the company?" Kate said.

Frances turned her blind stare to Kate, scratched the bitter folds of her face, and said after some length, "Well, I suppose that's as good a reason as any. Also, I've always liked the smell of the desert at night. It smells of emptiness and unbridled darkness."

"Inez?" Carl said. "We're gonna need a couple of beers to go."

"And a lemonade," Kate said.

They headed towards the counter. When Kate asked if Frances needed help, she replied that she was the last among them that needed it and proceeded toward the exit on her own with measured steps, one hand held out in front of her as if her arm was a dowsing rod that would twitch and buckle upon nearing Schrodinger.

"Onwards to Eldorado," she mumbled to herself. "And Godspeed."

The End Times

Mark Time

"The end times," Paul muttered while watching his late-night news program.

The TV sat at the end of a long, dark living room. Paul sat in a tattered recliner next to a coffee table with the ashes of last week's cigar. The stale smell made little impression on the man as he leaned forward and gripped the arms of the chair. On the wall to his right was a photo from when he went on "that shooting trip" with his "prepper group." To his left was a plastic cross hung on the wall. He purchased it many years back at a big-box store. Paul couldn't bear to look at the label on the back. He knew where it was made.

"It's gotta be." Paul shook his head as the news anchor detailed the new round of geopolitical turmoil. "Gog and Magog, the seventy weeks, the tribulation."

On the shelf beside the TV was a stack of Bibles in various states of neglect. At the bottom of the stack was the ancestral King James copy passed down from his grandfather. As Paul progressed in life, he graduated from its stodgy and cumbersome language to the modern translations. Sharing the shelf with the Bibles was a slew of books about prophecy. A man of middle age now, Paul was a product of his time. He came to the faith in the late eighties and was immediately swept up in a tidal wave of dread.

"The end times," Pastor Bill warned. "I have it on good authority that the Soviet Union will kick off the war of Gog and Magog and make their move against Israel by 1995."

A much younger Paul would listen, wide-eyed. "Is it really happening in my day?" He would shrink in terror. "I guess I should hold off on that proposal."

As 1995, the Soviet Union, Pastor Bill, and his last chance at love left Paul's life, he still remained convinced.

"It's the rapture any minute now. Prophecy must be fulfilled!" Paul would entreat himself.

Locked away in his home, the millennium loomed over the horizon. The man on the TV said that the computers would fail, the sky would fall, and society was on the verge of collapse.

"The end times," Paul would repeat this phrase as a lullaby. As his own life crashed around him, a small part of his innermost soul longed to drag the world down with him. New Years Eve, 1999 was spent hunkered down with the lights off. He clutched a member of his increasingly numerous gun collection. A sizable stock of ammunition sat dormant in the dark recesses of Paul's house along with Meals-Ready-to-Eat and cans of non-perishables.

"When the pre-tribulation times come, I'll be ready," he whispered to reassure himself as the seconds and minutes edged toward midnight.

As the year 2000 blundered into the pages of history, Paul stayed up all night. The sun cracked the horizon's ramparts as much as it shook his foundation. Creeping his way over to the light switch, Paul took a deep breath and closed his eyes. The lights came on in an instant, but his mind remained in a dark despair.

I was sure it was this time, he thought to himself.

The cascading visions he had of total collapse and ensuing violent chaos drifted further out of reach. Paul shut the curtains and turned off the lights for the rest of New Year's Day. He spent the day in reflection of the times he had when he was young, from the motorcycle trip out west to the hangouts by the lake—his life was different now.

He would muse, "I was really wasting my time with that stuff. You can't live like that in the end times."

After the passing of the millennium, a new vanguard of prophecy broke into Paul's mind.

"Islamic terrorism! How did I not see it?" he marveled in wonder as the speaker at his church's prophecy conference warned of the new threat.

"Mark my words"—the speaker pounded the podium—"the Antichrist will be Islamic. Just look at who Israel's enemies are. Who else fits the bill?" He lowered his voice and leaned into the microphone: "And it's sooner than you think."

The planes hit the World Trade Center only a few months later.

"The end times!" Paul wrung his hands with a mix of emotions while watching the live coverage from a house that increasingly resembled a bunker. As the dust settled and the passports were found, he felt vindicated in his newfound beliefs.

"He was right!" Paul was almost excited.

The loss of life was tragic to him, but the adrenaline of knowing that he was selected to experience the rapture brought a wave of euphoria. Paul began to ignore calls from his aging parents as their health declined.

"The rapture's coming soon enough. I don't know why they worry about these things."

His father passed on the day the US invaded Afghanistan, with his mother following only a few months later.

"If only they had held out a little longer." Paul wiped away the tears as they lowered his mother into the ground next to his dad.

His phone rang a few days after the funeral. It was Louie, a friend he had made at the last prophecy conference.

"Hey, patriot." The Vietnam veteran always started his phone calls with a low, suspicious voice.

"Louie, I can't really talk right now. I just lost my mom." Paul fiddled with the growing collection of apocalyptic literature on his bookshelf as he held the phone against his head like a gun.

"I'm sorry to hear that, buddy," Louie consoled. "If only they had held out a little longer."

His friend took a deep breath. "I know, I know."

"Did you see what Saddam is doing? I think he's gonna make his move against Israel. The attack on the Twin Towers was just a distraction."

Paul's mind began to race. "No, I didn't. What's he up to?"

Once again, his nation went to war. He always skipped past the news stories about immigration, the drug epidemic, and domestic crime to get to what Louie called "the good stuff." Every development of the news brought more confirmation of what Paul already knew.

"The rapture is coming at any time. Things are getting too crazy out there," he reassured himself as events got worse in tandem with his vanishing ability to adapt.

"Hey, Paul," Louie called again, "I hope you're prepping for the big one."

It would be months, sometimes years, between Louie's calls. Paul anxiously awaited them like a farmer straining his eyes to the horizon in anticipation of rain. It was not growth he craved—it was shrinkage. Paul yearned for the "big one" and its redeeming fire that would wash away his inadequacies.

"Iran is gonna get the bomb soon. Bush's term is about up and this Obama guy is real friendly with the Islamics. With the economy being how it is. . . ." Louie droned on with an eschatological hush.

"So how does this fit into prophecy?" Paul would inquire without wondering how it fit into the bigger picture.

"It's the end times," Louie would reply. "The rapture is right around the corner."

When the financial crisis heaved into view, Paul was certain it was happening this time. "When I'm taken up to heaven and everyone's left here for the tribulation, then they'll really be up a creek!" He gripped the steering wheel as he drove past a cemetery.

Paul stopped attending church about the same time he got what Louie called a "real computer." With home internet and the host of human knowledge at his fingertips, Paul's withered faith in the rapture gained new life with a thousand new perspectives.

"Ah, there it is." He sat back from the screen after browsing various forums and prophecy news sites. "I knew this all fit in somehow. It's the end times."

Paul emailed the article to Louie. His last phone call was a few weeks back. His friend's voice sounded weak and haggard as he decried the backsliding of the culture into "the times of Noah." This postulation was always devoid of any plan to oppose it.

"Why would you want to stop the end times? Things have to get worse before Christ returns," Louie wheezed into the phone.

Paul was vaguely aware of the veteran's health struggles, but they both blithely brushed it off. He just needed to hold out a bit longer. A few more weeks passed until another phone call interrupted Paul's hand wringing over Obama's second term and the Islamo-fascism he was sure to bring in.

"Hello? Is this Paul?" a female voice greeted.

"Yes, who is this?"

"Hi, my name is Sarah. I'm Louie's daughter." Her voice buckled under thinly concealed grief. "I was looking through my dad's phone to find people to come to the funeral." She let out a few more sobs. "He was so private about who his friends were."

Paul nearly dropped the phone. "What? What happened?"

"All that smoking caught up to him," Sarah sighed. "I told him it would."

His friend recalled how certain Louie was of his convictions. He thought that if anyone knew they were in the end times, it was him.

"When did this happen?" Paul shook his head.

"It's been a months-long process." The daughter took a deep breath. "He refused treatment for lung cancer. I thought you knew. I noticed there were a lot of outgoing calls to your number"—she paused—"more than he called me."

Sarah continued to lament the fact Louie sold his life insurance policy and reversed the mortgage on his home. Paul heard none of these things. Her voice trailed off in his mind. *None of that matters*, he thought to himself.

"And all we have left to sort through are a dozen cans of rice and a bunch of these old books. I don't know how we're going to pay off this debt!" Sarah began babbling.

Paul callously interrupted, "When's the funeral?"

"Next Saturday," she stumbled on her words.

He hung up the phone shortly after getting the time and location. Paul held the phone weakly in his hand, clasping it like a talisman. Pressing his balled fist to his chin, he took a forlorn glance out the window. In an otherwise clear sky, a solitary cloud sojourned eastward.

"Was he wrong?" Paul gripped the phone until the plastic creaked.

His gaze drifted to the stack of prophecy books. Brushing them aside, he took up his old appointment book. Somewhere along the line, he stopped writing things down. The utility of such things waned in the face of an apocalyptic showdown. Social functions, family reunions, dinner dates, and church potlucks faded from his appointment book inversely with his anxiety. The range of the book only spanned through 2009. Even still, Paul felt compelled to write down the date of Louie's funeral.

Ill-attended, poorly organized, and underfunded, the funeral was a dour affair. A few old war buddies filed in the row behind Sarah and a few of her other siblings. Paul took up his seat in the back. When it came time to pay respects at the casket, he slipped out.

"He couldn't have been wrong. I just know we're so close!" Paul yanked at his car door. "He just had to hold out a little while longer!"

Squealing the tires out of the church parking lot, the aging man set his course back to the comfort of his own home about an hour away. On the country roads stringing the various hollowed out small towns together, he came across a sedan on the shoulder. Paul slowed down to peer inside. The car was totally abandoned.

"There's no one there," he remarked to himself aloud.

Driving on, his pulse began to skyrocket. The next town showed no signs of life either. A United Auto Worker post laid dormant next to a shuttered mom-and-pop hardware store. All the markers and trappings of a bustling little community were absent. The rotted carcass of town after town buffeted Paul's psyche like the incessant beating of the tide.

"Did I miss it?" Paul checked the mirror for no particular reason. "No! Did I miss it? Was I left behind? Where is everybody?!"

His anxiety rose as mile after mile of country roads heralded no contact save for a few birds. Even the various farm houses seemed to show no signs of life.

"Lord, please no!" Paul cried out.

Craning his head to see in the window of a house marked with a little cross in the yard, he spotted a family praying before dinner. Relief washed into his mind just as he blew through a stop sign.

The impact was unlike anything he had experienced. His car took a roll after a savage T-bone hit from a semi-truck. After his momentum dissipated, Paul took a gasp for air as the smell of the airbag's explosive charge filled his airways. Looking down, he observed a large piece of metal debris sticking in his chest.

"Not yet!" Paul writhed. "I'm so close!"

By the time emergency responders cut his seat belt, Paul was already gone. They found him clutching *The Late Great Planet Earth* to his breast. He was declared dead on the scene.

“If only he had held out a little longer,” one of the responders remarked grimly as he surveyed the inside of the vehicle.

“What’s that book he’s holding?” one of the other responders asked.

The man shook his head. “No idea. I would’ve grabbed that Bible in the glovebox.”

His co-worker sighed, “Must’ve been a pretty important book to him.”

Paul left his earthly bounds with little to mark his passing other than a few life-altering injuries to the truck driver who hit him. The family he had craned his neck to see in his last moments witnessed the accident. After rushing out to the road, the father called the ambulance. The dust settled, and the mangled vehicles were cleared away. Traffic resumed on that lonely country road as if nothing had happened.

“Daddy?” The father’s youngest daughter tugged at his pant leg. “What happened out there?”

The man struggled to find the right words. “There was a car crash.”

“Did he die?” the little girl asked with a trembling voice.

“Yes . . . yes he did.” The words came slowly.

His daughter’s face dropped. “Why?”

“I suppose God just decided”—the father nodded somberly—“it was just the end of his time.”

If Only. . .

Rémi Tremblay

I was there. It was after all inevitable, as I had said a hundred times on 4chan. But a hundred times I had only half believed it. Enough to interest people, not enough to prepare myself with the utmost seriousness.

The sun was finally rising, its icy rays sweeping across the horizon of icy steppes bounded by tall coniferous hedges. Incredible all this whiteness, this biting cold. Only people from the north understand that these sunny days are always the harshest, while the torments of storms are usually tolerable. At this time of year, it's as if the sun is throwing out gaseous ice instead of the heat it should have.

I sank a little deeper in search of relative comfort. Yes, this is where we were.

How ironic. How many times in my posts and my fiery speeches I had complained about being a Cassandra. I was listened to, but never taken seriously, even by myself, my own most faithful reader who had never missed one of my posts, intended for people who would do what I lazily refused to do: act.

I warned you. I warned myself. But no one saw fit to take action, not even me, intoxicated by the idea that what I was saying had a purpose in itself.

Then the smell of urine invaded my nostrils and brought me back to reality. I had done it; I had managed to empty myself without moving, especially not moving, not getting up. The warmth that spread through my pants quickly turned to freezing cold, nature taking over. What a shame, but after all, hadn't Edmond de Valera escaped from prison by disguising himself as a prostitute? At least that's what Liam Neeson's epic movie claimed. I promised myself that I would check this information one day, but never took the time to do so.

What an unappetizing sight I was. What would all my former friends say? If they saw me, they would deny having known me more than three times before the first crow of the cock. Cowardice had made progress. It was probably the only area that had.

Finally, all that was behind, a bygone era. That of the web as well. Those great rants, those drinking parties where we remade the world, but also those days spent under the dim light of the library studying Hillard, Drumont, and the others. Some had tried to dissuade me from these sweet wastes of time. They had chosen to go north, trunks full, hands ready, to join that little corner of paradise; well, it looks like it today, now that they spent years building. A community of like-minded men, now spared by today's madness. "The Cicada and the Ant" was constantly replayed, no matter the place or the time.

But, bitter consolation, they had not had the joy of knowing the prose of Robert Poulet or Lucien Rebatet, nor that of these new talents like Xavier Eman and Julien Langella. Yes, they didn't know them. That was a point for me. The ant was boorish.

I had glimpsed in those dusty or custom printed pages our future. I had said it; I had written it. I was right. I am right. But what's the point?

No more daydreams; I had to go back to the concrete. I stuck the icy metal on myself; to comfort myself or to wake up, that was not clear. The tiredness went up, and I wondered if I stuck my tongue on the icy metal if it would stick as in my youth or if it would resist the attraction at such an important moment. Could the laws of nature be suspended at certain crucial moments?

This was a silly question. This kind of thinking was the result of my mind wandering while my body was grounded, immobile.

Focus, waking up, that's what was needed.

Someone had said "my empire for a horse;" I would be willing to trade anything for a coffee, even one of those lattes that had eventually caused our downfall. This vogue of refinement, of deceptively fair overconsumption, was what had got us.

With my eyes fixed on the deserted road, the same one that had led me to so many fantastic places to experience great joys, I began to think about Péguy.

Why him, when I had never opened one of his books?

I promised myself that I would do so when I retired. Ha, *la retraite*! A bourgeois concept for which my people had gone out into the streets and shouted. But these same people had refused to consider the real underlying problems we were facing. When it came to our replacement, they were silent. They saved their strength for the fights related to their wallet, their little person.

Yes, all this could have been avoided. It could have been fixed. If only someone had listened to me.

But Péguy, whom I had not read, spoke to me. His drama appealed to me. The cultivated man with recognized talent mowed down by a bullet perhaps fired by an illiterate. Yes, this unmentionable, snobbish, and contemptuous thought crossed my mind. There are some things you can never really get rid of.

It was my turn to risk my skin. Was it worth the other side's? My fight was somewhat based on this premise. I was better than the people on the other; otherwise, what was the point? Of course, things had gone so fast that it was impossible to ask the question seriously about the why, the what, and the how. Montreal had gone up in flames, and the Francos had been ousted. The process that had been going on for a few decades had suddenly accelerated. The reaction had been more or less rapid everywhere in the *Belle Province*, and the clashes had multiplied. That was all it took for the Marines to intervene. Chaos in their backyard was intolerable, and the White House's world referee had to send his boys in an operation that was too reminiscent of the Seven Years' War. Everything had calmed down, then the repression had increased. These French-speaking bolshevos who wanted to preserve their language, these white American negroes, had to be brought to heel. At first, everyone took it. Three centuries of humiliation and domination; one more, one less, why not? But then they pushed it too far and some remembered that their ancestors were free men, walking the woods with guns in their hands, ready to defend themselves and stand their ground. The sons of the *coureurs des bois* had gone back to where one could survive. Not to live, but to survive, between the state of a beast and that of a human. But the man is only human by the straightness of his column. Bent over, he becomes a simple primate like the others.

This burst of dignity had forced the Yankees to do a little more for the promotion of democracy, equality, fraternity, and freedom. They had raped in the name of good feelings; they had killed in the name of a better world; they had massacred in the name of love of neighbor. Even those who were prepared to keep their noses to the ground could not take it. In spite of themselves, in spite of their nature, they had to join the descendants of Father Le Loutre. . . .

But this time for me, there would be no Evangeline to pursue. She and Gabriel had not known the joys of carnal love, but the happiness of shared and intangible love. I had known passionate love, but my Evangeline was now resting in the coldness of Canadian soil with those who were born of it. Yes, that was it. No more Evangeline. The tears would flow if the tear glands weren't completely frozen. At least the bladder was still emptying.

This could have been avoided, but it was too late. Today all that mattered was shooting the driver of the first truck in the convoy that was going to thrill the democrats in the east. Lying on my bald hillside, overlooking the road, I glued my eye to my scope.

It took some time to adapt to the blazing light of the sun. Icy as they were my eyes could have easily played tricks on me. Were those cold fumes on the road or the smoke of the diesel trucks I had to stop? Yes, that was it. My role was about to unfold. I stretched my fingers to break the spell of cold and make sure they would respond timely when my index would be asked to press the trigger. I focused on the shape of the convoy in the distance. I could not miss. I would not miss.

And then suddenly there was this roar. No, it couldn't be the sound of engines, not at this distance. I turned around and saw it approaching, staring at me. A drone.

With white star on its thin belly. Why not? So this was where it all ended. Without a shot.

All of this could have been avoided. All of this. When it was time.

Is Someone There?

Anonymous

Mark couldn't take it anymore. The city's sound, sight, and motion had reached a boiling point. Even when he closed his eyes, the HUD on his retina was as clear as ever. He lifted his free hand and rubbed his head while his other dangled a briefcase at his leg.

He retreated from the walkway, finding refuge outside the moving people. The surrounding structures towered endlessly above, and though Mark could not see it, they layered endlessly below. Several airplanes, helicopters, and flying vehicles cramped the sky overhead. Still, the rain was the last nail in the coffin, turning all passing light into momentary streaks.

Mark held onto his briefcase, loosening his tie and skirting the building's cover. He looked toward the city block's center. A small, artificial garden huddled between the concrete and electronic monuments. Few pedestrians crossed the pocket forest, for sticking to the buildings' grid was more time efficient. And even though his eye's interface alerted him to return to the street, he refused and walked into the fake trees.

Mark had heard of the manufactured parks but had never seen them. He had also never visited one. As he entered, the rainfall above turned to a soft drizzle under the canopies. The trees were easy to fool a passing eye, but the imitation failed once closer. Mark used the bark for support, revealing that the solid facade was a soft, pliable material. As for the foliage, the leaves were tough and pulled on his black slacks like sandpaper. The man-made nature enclosed him, though the exterior buildings, streets, and people were still visible. Nonetheless, it was quieter, serene, and comforting.

Yet Mark didn't know any better, foolishly believing this was what nature was, how it felt, and what it looked like.

He stepped across the stone steps of a small river. It split at the block's right border and flowed down both sides, reconvening at the other end. The outlet swept into a rushing waterfall with a cityscape view above, and mist clouded the atmosphere. The garden's elevation did wonders for the sight, albeit all an onlooker saw was more city. Buildings stretched on for miles, blocked only by other, taller structures. The spires of screens relayed animations and advertisements. But rainfall made them hard to see, and the water's mist turned the pictures into flashing colors. Below the distant high-rises, the city trekked along as it did around the garden.

Mark's breathing had slowed, and his skin cooled. He looked for somewhere to rest and, in doing so, found an older woman sitting alone. She was equally entranced by the city's view, or so Mark believed, until he noticed her eyes. They were dull, grayed, and lacked attentiveness.

Mark lowered his briefcase, and it sounded against the stone walkway.

With unfocused eyes, the woman's head tilted to the side, turning toward him. "Is someone there?"

Mark's HUD blinked red, and his ears filled with a soft alarm. His fingers feathered the limp briefcase handle, but he did not pick it up.

"Yes," he said.

"Oh!" the woman replied, tapping the stone wall beside her. "Sit, sit."

And so he did, though it was not very close to her.

The woman continued. "What brings you off the grid?"

"I'm . . . I'm a bit anxious," Mark said, clearing his throat.

"You sound more than anxious."

Mark eyed the hermit. "Yeah . . . I think I had a panic attack." She lifted her eyebrow, and Mark corrected himself: "I'm having a panic attack."

The hermit nodded. "Then please, stay as long as you'd like."

Mark nodded back, stopping halfway, for it didn't matter. "Thank you," he returned.

The stone walkway circled the garden's core, and an odd grass patch grew at the center. It was different than the rest, more colorful, almost dewy. The turf blades were imperfect, unlike the flawless nature surrounding him. They bent, split, and some had no tips at all.

Mark's alert rang again. He slapped his ear in frustration, briefly closing his eyes and reminding himself his HUD shone behind the eyelids. The hermit twitched at the pop, and Mark calmed himself. His leg fidgeted, and he asked, "What is it like? To live in darkness? To shut your eyes and see nothing?"

"Well . . . I don't have to shut them. I see nothing all the time," the hermit said, shrugging. "I would ask you what it's like to always see something, to always see the light."

"It's immensely annoying and sometimes sickening. . . . There are brief moments, moments when I forget, moments when my mind has convinced itself these eyes are natural," Mark said, shaking his head. "But it only takes a tiny blimp, a glitch, an unexpected flash, and it all returns. The restriction, the imprisonment, the hopelessness."

The hermit nodded. "And in answering my question, you've answered yours. Of course, besides the flashes of light. I can only imagine what that'd be." Her nostrils flared, and her lungs expanded. "That hopelessness you speak of, that is why I come here. Here I can smell a hint of the natural world and imagine I live in it."

"What do you mean?"

"The grass is real," she said, gesturing ahead. "It is small, but it is real." Mark stared at the grass, and the hermit continued, "So, sit, breathe, and listen to the running water, to it pour, to it fall." He began to move forward. He'd never seen natural grass and wished to touch it. "I said sit," the hermit said. "You don't need to feel it. Be happy you can even see it."

Mark paused, and as he decided what to do, he realized how much the hermit reminded him of his late grandmother. And perhaps that was enough to listen wholly. So, he did. Mark sat back, breathed, and listened.

Soon, his stress lay upon the river's current, on which it swirled, curled, and fled away to someplace different—to someplace not with Mark. His HUD alerted him again, but the anxiety did not catch. Instead, he ignored it like he once had the city's artificial nature.

"You know," the hermit chuckled, "we once believed in things, that gods were born of sound, that we were birthed from noise. Some even thought we came from nature, evolved from plants, from grass." Her smile dimmed. "But now, now we don't believe in much."

Mark heard the truth in her words.

"Introspective," he said. "That's what your eyes have made you."

She agreed. "And yours have made you extrospective."

"Is that a word?"

Disregarding the question, she said, "I know much about myself, who I am, what I like. Though now, I may never change. You, on the other hand, can't stop. That isn't necessarily bad—change is good—but you don't know who you are or what you like."

Mark wanted to speak, but he had no response.

The hermit continued. "We each live like no one should, on far, opposite sides. But think of all those who lived between. The ones that closed their eyes to darkness. . . ."

"And opened them to light," Mark finished.

"We were not made for this world, for these screens, for these sounds," she ranted, pointing near the grass. "We were born with that, that grass there. We were born with nature."

Mark shook his head. "And now we are alone."

"So then, I ask you again. . . . Is someone there? A person in that skin? Or are you what the tailored screens tell you to be? Where your eyes tell you to go?"

"There is someone now," he stated. "I feel you've opened their eyes."

She was quick to reply, "Not their eyes, your eyes."

Mark ignored the HUD's warning lights and the buzzing in his ears. He'd get there, eventually. He readjusted his tie and straightened his suit. His clothing was wet, but it was what it was.

"I have to go."

The hermit nodded.

"But I can't thank you enough," he said, lifting his free hand and sliding his thumb across his fingers. "Though maybe this will help."

"What?" she asked.

"I've transferred funds to you."

She went to speak, but he cut her off.

"I challenge you to live a little . . . extrospectively," he declared with a laugh. "Buy yourself something. Live with something besides your thoughts."

She smiled. "And you try having a few more."

He smiled too and bowed though the hermit could not see it. "Take care."

Mark turned and left the garden the way he came. All the while, the hermit watched in his direction.

Even when Mark fell out of sight, she continued to stare. Then, her body glitched, skipping back to a forward-facing position. The swaying grass patch stuttered, rewinding to the beginning of an ambient loop track. Flickering, the hologram's facial features changed and solidified with the sounds of someone nearing.

A businesswoman broke from the garden's artificial trees. Overwhelmed, she sat next to the hermit, an older man that looked much like her late uncle. She glanced toward him.

With unfocused eyes, the man's head tilted to the side, turning toward her. "Is someone there?"

Honorable Mention in Short Stories

Streitkos

Folkene Mine

It was before them, sliding through the tall grass. Golden stalks folded before them in the wind, caressing their mounts as they listened for the warning from the viper. The bells tinkled whenever the horses moved their heads, and Hala stilled Zosimos with a strum and gentle pat of her long fingers on his red, velvety neck. He was four years old, and she had trained him herself since he had been two. *Even Father would not fault him.*

The Ar-pada had shown Hala again and again how to groom horses, as though she did not know how to groom horses. *Always remember, those who would ride must begin with the whip.*

"You cannot civilize the horse," her father would say brusquely. "You must begin with might. You must begin with the muscle."

When she groomed Zosimos, she began with the horse's biggest muscle. She began at the base of his neck and brushed over the long muscle of his back, and she felt like maybe she did not, after all, know how to groom horses. *He is not like other horses*. His eye saw through to the heart of her, almost like it was the eye of the Stag. His mane was black as night, as black as the stallion that had sired him. His neck, his body, and powerful legs, they were all the color of his mother, chestnut and gleaming. Zosimos had been shy and skittish and on his feet within seconds of being foaled. The merr, his mother, imprinted on him immediately. She had licked at his head, whinnied softly to him, and he to her, before nestling up to nurse. But the merr's muscles had seized up. She had taken ill with high fever and died. The little foal might have been lost then, only Hala's father took tribute from the largest herds over a thousand mailia as the horse runs, and he had charged her with the little foal's life. So, Hala had found a way, and she had saved him.

During foaling time, in the late winter darkness, the tribe stood still, waiting patiently for the greater balance of merrs and little foals to be strong enough to move the vast distances over the Steppes. Hala had milked one of the gentlest merrs in her father's own vast herd, a nineteen-year-old that had just foaled her ninth foal. Hala milked her painstakingly, the merr sometimes dancing around Hala from time to time and setting the cedar bucket rolling. Hala persisted. She squeezed with calloused hands until the last milk, the white gold, dripped into the bucket. Then she waited for the rich hind milk to rise to the top. She fed this to Zosimos first, with long strips of silk. The strands of silk were dipped into the bucket, and as she held the foal's head, she stroked him and murmured soothing words while he sucked.

Behar had laughed at her at first. Milking was slaves' work. Even little boys like him knew that much. The slaves would insert hollow bones into the merrs. The bones were much like her father's pipes, the wind whistling through them if she carried them to him by the fire in her hands, instead of in her pockets. But she didn't put hollow bone into the merr's vul-va the way the slaves were taught—this, to force the udder down. Zosimos's milk merr had had lots of practice, Hala decided, and needed no help from slaves or bones.

The slaves were all blind, of course, taken in pillaging and taken in war from the northern lands and out of the raids into the far-off tribal lands of the northwestern Steppe, twenty days of hard riding from the Danu Apara, the upper Danu River. These were the tribes that refused her father homage. In short, they were other Skyte. It was said their lands were made impassable by feathers, which were shed so abundantly the earth and air alike were full of them. It is this which prevented the eye from obtaining any view of the region. Hala knew this could not be true. Those northerners with the pale skin like her own, though with the strange, slanted eyes, as well as the proud northwestern Skyte, had been milking merrs and goats and driving her mother's large wain box forever. Her father's men found a way through and came back every year or so with their due, regardless of whether the folk there had claimed they would pay homage or not.

Her horse's name had been a joke of her father's. *Zosimos. A Greek name.* The Greeks had come to their lands as a beggar comes, presumptuous and assuming but "with an empty bowl," their father said. As Hala grew, she came to know the Greeks through their craftsmanship, coveted assiduously by the Skyte, and by the wine her father drank so prodigiously. They brought the pottery and metalwork, and oil of the olive. Her father did not talk of empty bowls anymore with his children. Everyone knew the truth of the importance of the Greeks. Instead, her father had undergone an attempt to cultivate southern friends colonizing the shores of the sea. The Greek colonists had named the land there inhospitable for hundreds of years and then settled themselves anyway. Chele, Sinope, and Trapezus were the older settlements, and on the southern shore.

Berezan was the first colony settled in the land of the Skyte, near the northern shores of the sea, and connected to the mainland by a narrow strip of land where the Dnepr River yawned. *Even the Greeks' names are wrong.* They called the river *Borysthenes*. Zosimos' mother must have been a young foal when the first Greeks arrived on the northern shores in their long, flat, and pointed ships. The Greeks had struggled there for a little while, encircling themselves with stone and mud bricks and then again by the waters of the sea at the entrance to the great Dnepr River. But then they began to grow too big and fat for the island. Her father's lieutenants and captains did not mutter or complain while the Greeks of Berezan grew in number and strength there—others did. The Greeks called their settlement an island, and it nearly could be, hanging by a thread as it was. The island that was not an island was long and flat like their ships, and they called it *Berezan.* Their settlement there was *Borysthenes. For the river.*

Then, when Hala was nearly grown, whispers came of a new colony. The whispers grew heavier, becoming stones. Soon buildings took shape, prostrating themselves before a large area of earth where nothing was yet built and nothing yet stood, until Sco Adal-a-da, Ar-pada of all the great Scoloti chiefs was consulted. These new Greeks brought the power of the fire of Messenia, the Greek city which had grown so powerful on the southern shores of the Peloponnese beneath Mount Ithome. There had been a great war there, in the time of Hala's grandfather's grandfather, when Euphaes was King in Messenia, far away. The heart fires of Messenia were put out, her people scattered and enslaved, and creeping and crawling they made their way across Greece, some going as far away as Italia, waiting, and growing strong. When Hala's father rose to Ar-pada, some of them came to the land of the Skyte. Zosimos was still suckling at silk when the Greeks came there, and Hala's father had told her and Behar what his southern friends had told him and the stories the Phoenician ships had brought.

From Sicilia came these Greeks. The new Greek colony in the lands of the Skyte was born of a mother city on the northern coast of Sicilia, across from the mainland of Italia. They were children suckled of Messenia, and they came now to the northern shores of the Vel'kavahsi Vannkis, the great sea. Sco Adal had said there might be trouble. Before they were destroyed and dispersed, the Messenians had been at war for many years with Sparta, another great city of the Peloponnese. Now Messenia was dust, but it was whispered that her fire had come with the new colonists and that they had brought it to the lands of the Skyte. The other Greeks who had come had been on the island a generation already. Their mother was Miletus, a great and wealthy city on the coast of Ionia. It was a city that had coveted the fire of old Messenia. A city that had given Sparta gold.

The new colonists rode back and forth in their boats and sometimes walked the long strip to Berezan Island. *To Borysthenes,* Hala reminded herself. The new colonists would trade, they said, and had settled themselves in a cove on the Dnepr River, east and north of Borysthenes. The new settlement on the mainland was surrounded by rock and cedar and wildflowers. There, the colonists set to building the great oven hearts to channel and harness their fire. They began to raise up a temple. The Ar-pada let them. He always slept with one eye open.

"The Skyte must go canny and careful," he said, but Behar and Hala thought him overbold.

"The stallion will always return to the pasture of its birth," was the oft-repeated old adage. So, he and his men waited and watched. Sco Adal had told Hala and Behar there might be trouble, and they waited for it along with everyone else, but there never was. Not yet. The Greeks were farming now, and their father's captains noted this and more at the night fires. Their father told Hala and Behar the crops would sustain the power growing in the land and more people would come. They did. The stone masons, the workers of metal, the builders, they came first, following the farmers. Then the women came. Women came with children, and the weavers arrived, the artists, cart makers, and then colonists who did no work but traded with all, meeting the ships on the coast that began to also arrive in larger numbers.

Behind their backs the Skyte called them *sud cilt menn*, milk-skinned men, and even more honestly, *yalang'och-a manniskor-a*, a naked people. The phrase *milk-skinned* had nothing to do with the color of milk, for they were much the same color as the Skyte, if not always quite as pale, and everything to do with their value, including assumptions of their innate constitutions. Milk was ever a valuable commodity in the world of the Skyte, but unpredictable in output; at times thin and watery, and ever having to be minded. But in the slave markets of Borysthenes the Greeks were called welcome and mostly left alone. The land itself was, however, indeed, unfriendly. The Skyte had come to the region to conquer, but the Greeks came and endured.

Behar did not laugh at Zosimos now. Nor at Hala. Zosimos was wild as the Steppes, soft only under Hala's touch, and a powerful breath of the grasses. She stroked his neck to calm him. *Too excited. Snakes always make you dance*. She whispered into his ear, "Lipiš-gi, du haus vad hu asha. Haus-a li. Haus-a li." *Dear heart, you are wild. Be still.*

Her father had tried to recall the name, but Hala had laughed and told him, "Only dead fish follow the stream." He was strange somehow, her horse. Strange and alien like the Greeks, but for his shyness. When she sat astride his back and felt his powerful leg muscles churn at the hills rolling beneath him, she felt a centaur, one of those guardians of the hero called Heracles. He was a man born of gods whom the Greeks revered. She gave Zosimos his head, but he never did anything other than what she wanted. Or perhaps she never wanted anything so much as what he did.

Hala smiled at Behar from atop her horse. He was five years younger than she, and his cheeks were still rounded and full. "A nestling's cheeks," she teased. He sat straight-backed and tall on his own gray pony while Hala stroked Zosimos again, wondering at her brother. *He is like Mother*.

Her brother pushed back his thick hair, brown, like a deer's. *He is quiet, like a deer. Watchful*. He looked at Hala, his heart in his face. He loved her, she knew. She was fiercely protective of him and he, in his own way, of her. Behar was a quiet boy, but behind Hala's every footfall, she heard the shadow after her. Her brother, the echo. He followed her every move. Idolizing of their father, and reverent of their mother, he loved with his whole being. Vicious when cornered, *like the viper*.

Then the brown and black mottled snake appeared, hissing not far away. Hala waited. Behar's arrow missed its long throat, so she aimed one of her own. The twang from her double-curved bow might have been a sigh. The viper could kill someone such as she, a child still, but it was for the white flaky meat that they did not give this viper a wide berth, not the danger.

She had not taken the bells off her horse. Nor had the others. It was her first trip west without her father, and their coming was meant to be heard. The *dan* out of the Kahazkh lands had come to them this season in shaggy leukcila cat pelts, a cart of ram and ibex horns, tanned hjort hoosay hides, and a caged gribb. Its head was colossal. The scavenger was female and as tall as Xhelal-a-da, son of her father's most trusted captain. The thirteen-year-old had already grown taller even than his father and was almost a man grown. His blond, shaggy mane was shaggier than this gribb's. Its wings were folded in the confines of the cage, but before it had been imprisoned, the captors had stretched its wings, unclipped, across the length of nearly two horses, nose to tail. It was dark, with a pale crown and a ruff of feathers around its neck.

Xhelal turned to Hala, his grin wide. He whooped and dropped to the ground next to his father's horse, tossing his reins to a slave. The strongest and most trusted riders rode behind their masters, the people of the horse, the children of the sky and earth. The Greeks had named them Scyths, but they were the Scoloti, the Skyte.

They had come from the east and the wild north. *Their coming had been a tempest*, their mother said. When she whispered the story of their people, as small children they had nestled deeper under the felted robes and piles of thick furs, chills running through them. Enclosed in the hemp curtains of their mother's wainbox, Hala would see the horse and rider bearing down. Perhaps the rider would be drawing a bow. Other times, the rider would throw a short stabbing dagger and pull out his sword. She saw the rider turn into hundreds and thousands of riders, riding the wave over the land. The sound of them, *like the roaring of the sea*.

It was bad luck to put a dead snake on a horse, so Xhelal put the viper into a sack before he threw it up to Hala. She tied it onto the back of her saddle. Zosimos did not like that, but Hala squeezed at his sides with her thighs and, with Behar, Xhelal and his father and his father's men, the carts and all the rest, she turned toward the dark in the distance—eastward, toward home.

On warm summer evenings before bed, they would pull back their mother's curtains, and the sky would tell Hala of whatever she would find there to be found. The grass Steppes were wide and open, and the night sky fell around them like the curtains of some great wainbox of the world, the stars singing to Hala. The Great Reindeer, the Stag, was always easiest to find. The imperfect square, three lines going up, up from the square, then down again, marking the Stag's neck, which is hunted as prey by many things. *The Stag brings the light and new life.* Hala always found him first. The Ugrian-ana in the far north called the Great Stag *Sar*. But they were wrong. In the far north, they believed the Stag stole the sun from them. The Stag was no thief, Hala knew. He carried the weight of life and death on top of his head, like a heavy crown to be born. The points on his head were the many branches of childhood, adulthood, and death crisscrossing and rising, twisted and curved. He was not a friend, but he was Hala's dearest antagonist, grounding her in the wide spaces of her world. So, she would also find him last as well, pointing him out to Behar-a-da before closing her eyes to sleep.

The leukcila was high now in the sky, its tail pointing north as they rode in the growing darkness. The cat had two bright eyes and high-pointed ears for listening, just as King Lynkos had two bright eyes and high-pointed ears for listening. Hala knew her mother's story by heart: The king had given a supper, and during the supper he had grown more and more jealous of his guest who knew the secrets of growing food in the earth. The king's animal ears listened for opportunity, and his eyes glittered through the darkness. To gain his guest's magic, the king put a dagger to his heart while he was sleeping. But before he could strike, the Greek Goddess Demeter turned the king into a leukcila cat. This tale's moral was two-fold: Guest-rite is as sacred to Greek gods as it is to the Skyte. The second moral was no less important than the first: do not trust the gods of the Greeks.

And there was the Great Goddess, her path of tears scattered across the heavens. Tears of happiness, Hala had once heard her mother tell the tale. The nights their mother told them of the Great Goddess, she put them each on a knee and smiled with them while Sco Adal sat at the fire, drinking wine with his captains. A formidable man. A fierce man. But a man who would laugh with them. *"Behar-a-da, Hala-ias, come."* And they would come, and they would listen to their father until he was finished speaking.

Their mother told them also of King Skyles. He was the son of a Greek mother who paid for his admiration of Greek civilization and Greek culture with his life. Skyles denied the boundary between the deep blue sky of the Skyte and the enclosed spaces of the Greeks. For this, he lost his head. In the end, his brother became king. This was a sadness for Hala whenever she heard their mother tell it and, also, a provocation. Skyles had wanted something more beautiful for his people, but he had almost destroyed his own people in the taking of what he thought he wanted. Hala's own mother had left her home behind when she had been given to Hala's father and never spoke of it, only once smiling sadly when

Behar asked if her home had been very beautiful. Their mother was a tall and elegant woman with hair of flames. Sometimes she wore it down—let it fan over her shoulders—and the sunlight glinted off it even from afar. She was from Elos, near Sparta. From a world far apart and away. Elos: to Hala it was only a name. Despite the distance Hala imagined separated her mother from the land of the Greeks, her father having taken her at all was forever a warning nod toward the hubris of King Skyles.

Hala folded such thoughts away, finishing the plaiting of her hair with red silk. Tonight, folded beneath the starry curtain of their lands, they would feast on spitted snake crisp from the fires, and the bells would dance to drum. The sky was without a moon tonight, and this meant Hala would be painted. She slipped her toes into soft felt boots and tied the bracelet straps around her wrists and biceps. The aged leather was brown and wrinkled against the smooth shapes and shadows tattooed onto her skin. Each line and circle represented a day, each small flower a week, each creature, a year. The flowers sprang from the animals themselves. Sprang from antler tines, hoosay racks, ram and ibex horns, and other horned creatures, twisting and developing into flowered forms.

She opened the tent into the dark. There were children running to and fro, and there were old ones sucking on dried fish. She pricked up her ears and heard the giant gribb in its giant cage across the encampment, thrashing its head about and screeching. There was a wheel moving, and another wheel, and thousands of horses far out into the night. The Ar-pada's camp was located at the innermost ring of the entire encampment, always. Hala did not have to walk long before reaching her father's fire, and the small boulders marking the outer of the sacred ring. The fires beckoned to her every evening and, like so, this night bade her come on.

She sat near Behar, pulling the heat from the circle, and let it waft over her in waves. The firelight shown off Behar's braids, and his sudden smile glinted white like the surf of the sea. Hala could not see the bottom of the hill where they sat, yet she knew the men of this night's watch were there, in darkness, patrolling the outer rings of the camp. Beyond them, the sea struggled on its path to the shore. The white caps pushed to the side in the wind, glinting off starlight. Hala might have watched that long, but the drums thumped a new pulse, a strong and varied meter. The pipes were passed, and Li Skeud-a-da brought out his tools and unfolded them from their binding, a combed animal hair hide. He readied his inks.

At each moon turn, Hala would sit with her brother on sheepskin. Sometimes they would sit through the night and long into the day following, being painted. They were usually painted in their father's tent, but tonight Behar and Hala had brought tribute, *the dan*, out of the Kahazkh lands. Their triumph would be witnessed underneath the sky, for all to celebrate.

Li Skeud was a celebrated skin marker. It was said that his grandfather had created the deepest black on the Steppes from the burnt offerings of oily kannabis seeds and ash of red deer gi. The bloody heart of the deer was burnt black under the kannabis seeds, all covered and hidden beneath a golden ceremonial bowl while the fire burned. The bowl had two vents at top, and after Hala watched Li Skeud-a-da at his art as a child, she discovered the smell was bitter. The man could make several blacks, all different, and the Ar-pada made sure the celebrated artist used each one on Hala and Behar. When Li Skeud had boasted of a gray made in secret, Inmet-a-da had laughed—he and others. Inmet-a-da laughed easily, like his son. But his hair was dark, where Xhelal's was yellow and bright. Sco Adal-a-da wanted to see the ink, however, and bared his forearm for Li Skeud then sitting astride his grim stallion.

Li Skeud began tonight with Hala. *He will ask for a small thing—too many others waiting.* Hala wondered if he might continue the Great Stag at her shoulder.

"Ah, the Stag needs more of my attention, but not tonight Hala-ias," he said. "Now, close your eyes. Tell me of your journey."

His brown hair was pulled back in a thong, but his graying beard wagged at her as he searched for fresh skin, a new patch to paint. Hala tried not to giggle like a little girl, tried and failed. By then Li Skeud was already humming at his work, carefully wiping her collarbone with a wet cloth.

"You stalked a snake in the grass today." Li Skeud's old smile was missing a few teeth, but his eyes twinkled in the firelight.

Killing snakes was common enough. "It was nothing," lied Hala.

She closed her eyes to see it again, black in the grass, its hood spread open in warning, Behar's arrow flying foul. She did not want a snake anywhere on her body. She opened her eyes to find Li Skeud's on hers. He picked up the antler tine. It was covered with a row running down its length, of needles made from bone. Each needle was razor-thin, and each point dipped in ink.

"Hala doesn't miss when she shoots," said Behar. He grinned. Li Skeud tilted his head, eyes narrowed thoughtfully at Behar a moment, and nodded.

It hurt. Sometimes not so much but was more irritating like the silver-winged flies that plagued the Steppes for hundreds of days every year. Tiny bite after bite, pictures and forms would take shape on Hala's skin and redden in the dark while she sat or lay on a pallet. Li Skeud-a-da moved the tine like it was a seat on wide bows, rocking back and forth in constant motion, like one of the chairs rocking beneath the old readers in their wainboxes. His rhythm was even and smooth, and her skin was painted under it.

Li Skeud had been a fixture as sure in Hala's memory as Zosimos, and earlier. A constant to be expected with the turning of the moon, their mother often waiting nearby with salve of dried flowers for the skin. Tonight, their mother joined them by the fire, sitting quietly. She did not coddle them. Their father forbade that. While Li Skeud worked, her mother touched Hala only to move a braid out of range of his deft hands. Sometimes she would comb their hair while ink worked its way into Hala's and Behar's skin. She would smile when a picture pleased her.

Hala looked up to see her mother's face lit by firelight. Her eyes were narrowed, and Hala could not say if she were pleased or not as Li Skeud again brought up the shorter tine, the one he used to detail small flowers, laying out a thin arrow, straight and true across the collarbone. She could feel it. The tail of it didn't quite reach halfway to the center of her throat. The tine carefully pressed a tiny round geometric pattern, just to the side of the indentation at the base of her neck, reaching further down toward the shoulder and the crown of the Stag rising there.

Hala reached up to touch the new markings, and the skin marker slapped her hand away as he finished the sharp arrowhead point reaching, also, for her shoulder. Li Skeud then finished quickly, drawing felt cloth softly and gently once more over the dots of red skin. Finished with Hala, he immediately turned to Behar, wiping off a similar spot on his collarbone as well.

As Hala looked at her bared shoulder now, the Great Stag's unfinished head looked a bit swarmed with some humming line of bees. Her eyes crossed as she found flowers in the detail. Each small flower representing the weeks she had been gone, wound around the Stag's head up into the tree of his twelve-pointed crown. They spilled over her collarbone onto the arrow, its head nearly piercing the eye of the Stag—*Streitkos*—and, she knew, one day these would file down her arm and across her back as well, to tell of her marriage inside of time and outside of time to earth, sky, and Skyte.

Lifting her forearms to her face, she touched her forehead briefly to her brother's. Then, rotating her wrists as her mother's long white fingers applied the soothing salve to her skin, she listened to the bells.

Honorable Mention in Short Stories

A Duck's Ardor

Anonymous

Alone, perched atop a bench, was a duck. Yet, this lovely, orange-beaked creature wasn't ordinary—*he was a mallard.* His green and brown feathers gleamed in the midday sun, and his padded feet scampered proudly on the ground and in the water. The locals, those odd featherless humans, called him Marvin; he thought it suited him since the name Marvin obviously meant "the best mallard duck of all time and space."

The locals were *weird* creatures, always speaking in *weird* tongues; there was that chance that one would bend down, tilt his or her head, and spit out some gibberish in Marvin's language, but their words were just that: nonsense. Even worse, the majority of the humans he saw were *always* staring wide-eyed at black, glowing rectangles; they were simply queer. Alas, he could not communicate with these long-armed and legged beings, but Marvin knew there had to be *something* in common between him and the humans.

Both creatures lived near the pond, both ate of the land, both *tried* to communicate with each other, but to what avail? What was the purpose of quacking at the odd beasts if he didn't even have any common interest or moral to stand upon with them? Marvin *needed* to know what they were and if they were truly sane, likable creatures. After all, he had friends and family living on his pond, and what if one of the tall humans hurt them? That would be on Marvin and Marvin alone.

He shook his head, grumbling as the matter troubled him; somehow, he would find out *who* the humans really were.

Marvin fluttered—well, more like flopped—off the bench and onto the gravel sidewalk. He waddled down the path, past his pond, and towards the neighboring forest. The humans' trail, as Marvin had discovered, led straight to a sweet stream. He had no idea why other ducks didn't join him at the shaded brook, but he was content by himself.

The duck took a detour through the short grass, squeaking in relief from the change of sharp rocks to soft green. He shuffled his way through the forgiving turf, gazing down as sunlight glinted through its blades. A splash of yellow stopped his webbed steps, and he stooped to stare at a golden dandelion. *Marvin loved dandelions*, but what would a human think of his ardor? Would they share it?

He reached down and plucked the flower, rising and striding with his new treasure. He didn't make it five steps before he halted *again*, this time catching a red bling burning on a leaf beside his head. He turned, inspecting the blaze of a caterpillar chowing on the leaf. Marvin nudged the insect, and it must have seen his flower, for it immediately crawled onto his beak and sat contently, still eyeing Marvin's dandelion. He had company!

Marvin shook with glee, his wings flapping. He continued waggling through the forest, wondering if a man would enjoy his flower as much as he did. In fact, he hoped he would encounter one just so he could show off his flower and new friend. No sane being could frown at the sight of them, but if a human did, then it would prove the creatures were bad.

Marvin nodded to himself and kept on trotting.

A few minutes into his journey, he heard a gentle trickle of cold droplets flowing and bouncing through a rocky bed. He quickened his totter, a deep quack rumbling in his throat as he pushed into a small glade.

A breeze ruffled his feathers as he gazed upon a flat nest of grass beside a bubbling rivulet. He hummed with joy, fumbling through the grass with his palmated feet. Light floated through the branches above him and danced through the hopping water and swaying grass.

Marvin took a few steps forward, then stopped, turning his pearlescent, tufted head at the sight of a man! The giant creature was sprawled across the ground, its eyes closed, and a faint smile on its lips. Shaggy hair fell across its face and over its hands, on which its head rested. There was a backpack a few feet from him, and, to Marvin's approval, there was no black, thin rectangle in sight.

Oh, he had found a human! This could be the moment he discovered the truth, discovered the common ground!

Marvin blinked, waddling closer to the man and burbling a small greeting; the beast did not move. Marvin put his padded foot on the man's arm, yet it did not stir. So, he flapped his wings, sending wind on its face, yet still it didn't wake. Even his continuous quacks of frustration did nothing.

Marvin glared at the man, examining his carefree slumber. It did look *extremely* comfortable sleeping there on the dirt-embedded grass. Taking a leap of faith, Marvin literally *leaped* onto the man's chest, bending down to look over its face; you could tell a lot from one's face. A stubble of a beard was planted on the man's chin, but the majority of its angled face was bare. There was a plane above the creature's eyes and underneath its brown locks; there Marvin deemed it a worthy place to set his dandelion and friend caterpillar. As for himself, Marvin settled down atop the man's strong chest, gazing down at the peaceful beast.

A set of hazel eyes suddenly stared back at him, causing Marvin to quack with surprise. The eyes traced his figure, taking in the no-doubt daunting sight. Marvin waited, shifting as the man's hand rose up to his height. He glanced at it warily, watching the man's expression for any release of emotion; he got none.

The hand inched closer until it landed atop his wing, petting him. Marvin was so shocked by the gesture that he quacked again, bringing a smile over the man's face. The beast closed its eyes again, letting its hand fall back as it basked in the light and wind.

Marvin smiled, dozing off to a pleasant sleep. He had finally found something both a man and a duck had in common: the ardor of soft grass beside a gurgling stream and under a waning sun.

Second Place Winner in Short Stories

Crossing the Threshold

Vingul

It is said that after the creation of the world, yet before its completion, all was rocky wastes and a frozen sea, and nothing. . . .

But that time of unchanging must come to an end, and soon enough cracks appear in stone, and surging fires from the inner earth erupt in cascades of flaming rock; mountains of ice drift and tumble, and the ocean itself turns around like a dragon awoken from its winter sleep.

Whatever once was is blasted to pieces, scorched by searing heat, buried, frozen over, destroyed. Water flows where once was dry land; there are new seas under the sun. The years pass by like leaves in a river, and there is no one there to count them.

A long while followed in which, some say, lesser gods or spirits of several kinds descended upon the earth or otherwise came into being, and they set up their abodes in places from the high mountains to the deep trenches of the sea, and in those ages the land was covered with grass and trees and other of the first wholesome things. Birds were taught to sing, and the world was enchanted.

Moments and eternities intermingled until man stirred at last and found himself in a world of beauty and grief, and through tales he passed down to descendants yet unborn he made order out of seeming chaos. Many are the threads of story, that if woven together would form a splendid and subtle fabric beyond the comprehension of any one man. Yet through each part runs a cord that in some way reflects the totality, and there are moments in a life that may be insignificant enough on their own, that are at first perhaps entirely unnoticed by the world at large, yet echo into the future, shaping what will one day be past events of great weight.

Destiny is a beast which from time to time reveals strange outgrowths. . . .

It was a doubtful season in which our man found himself wandering across the land, though by the counting of days it ought to have been late in the spring. Most of the winter snow was gone, but the landscape was blanketed by a layer of fine gray dust, borne from afar on a foul wind. It had come with the war, and much bloodshed there had been in that country since it started, but as far as his eyes could see the realm lay in a deathly slumber. He had seen no living creature these last days but a scrawny doe. It had evaded his emaciated attempts.

He had traversed some low hills this day, oblong, like bulbous beetles; they were ridges jutting out from a high-lying forest in the west. Facing north and east from his elevated perch, the terrain kept rising in front of him, going from forested hillsides to a high mountain, impressive in its solitude. That was his mark. He would aim for its right flank and go around it on flatter ground; the mountain plateau lined the horizon about halfway up its sides. If there was a trail going this way, he had not found it, but he had become accustomed to taking the untrodden path.

Many regions he had seen; through dells and dales and narrow ravines his travels had taken him, and by dreary lakes under the deep blue of ancient skies he had sat for a while in contemplation of the unspeakable. Rolling hills of yellowed grasslands had followed, and a blackish country of recently petrified rock, where in some places the molten innards of the earth spewed forth in anger and ran in furious streams that consumed whatever petty seeds of life were clinging to dark crevices. Ever he sought for the hallowed places of legend but found them nowhere, and they must be, he thought, consumed by fire or filled in with ashes, or worse: lies and figments of the imagination of his people. But in his mind was a singular goal above all others, and he still believed in its being there.

Whatever power it is that feeds the little birds had withdrawn from the land. They had been born to a spring of dying life, and beneath their nests in barren branches the soil was strewn with pitiful cadavers.

He started for the forested hills, his feet kicking up the dust as he walked. About him lay trees torn from the soil, roots and all, and leaves that had fallen from their boughs before their time. Coming closer to the eaves of the wood, the trees were silhouetted against the sky like frozen black lightning. There was a sinister stillness about the place, as of watchful eyes or some waiting menace in the hills. He took his knife from its sheath before entering.

Dark pines stood like solemn, vaguely threatening guardians all about him, and the air bore a heavy smell of mist. He was only a stone's throw into the thicket when a strong desire to turn back volunteered itself. He ignored it as best he could. Nothing ever happened—or so he told himself, but his senses were tensely surveying his surroundings. A spectre haunted the hallways of his mind, throwing up veils of deception and walling him off from a true perception of what is real, and what is dream or trickery. Mocking faces manifested in twisted roots and knotty trees, leering. He had learned to despise even the remaining living things in the wilderness.

Nothing did happen. He exited the throng of trees soon enough and went through others like it: the landscape was a patchwork of sloping woodland, harsh rock, marshes, and mossy banks by the river that came down from the high places. Where he could, he followed the running water and drank from it where there were backwaters still enough that the gray, ash-like stuff would sink to the bottom. Hunger gnawed.

In a forest clearing he chanced upon the remains of a man, mangled by wolves, probably, and pecked by birds. There were bones with patches of dried flesh and shredded clothes of yellow and green, with the blue clover device of a courier in the service of the king. At ease!—the living man saluted the dead, and went on.

Here and there now was the odd fern that had not quite shriveled, and there were leaves on some of the trees—slender birches, mainly. He shook a stem, and the gray powder fell to the ground, revealing flecks of green on the leaves that fell with it. The presence of small things that grow told him that the defilement of this place was only recent. A silver lining in a world gone wrong: it doesn't take very much to give a man an ounce of hope. But he was too tired to rejoice or put much stock in it. He had seen such signs before, but the wind and its dreaded portage had caught up with him more times than he cared to count.

The flowers of the forest had taken on a deathly hue; rivers that once ran a lively blue were gray. He plucked a wild strawberry from the forest floor, and it turned to ashes in his mouth, the memory of refreshing sweetness rendering its sickening taste the more spiteful.

He looked to the horizon—it stared back at him with indifference. A shadow in the forest grimaced and slunk off to dimmer glades. From the depths of his gloom even the stars in the sky looked like a tangled mayhem. He would ask the north wind for tidings, but it played no more among the tussocks and the trees; a gust reached him from the south, tepid, stale. There arose in his heart a silent cry of longing for lost beauty, and he wilted on into the night.

At last, he decided on a place to rest his bones. Leaning his back against a large rock by the river, he felt safe as could be—but to tell the truth, the mangled remains of that man was on his mind, and he thought of wolves.

A silvery disc appeared from behind the clouds, larger than he had ever seen it, and he imagined that he could actually *hear* the celestial winds that destiny has set to drive the moon into the earth on the day of doom. So they say.

Last night, and the night before, he had pondered the immortal words: *hope springs eternal*. He had always viewed that phrase like an ever-changing image of water on rock, with grasses and ferns springing from the earth around it, and enveloped in the elusive light of hope; ever he could turn that picture in his mind, seeing it at different angles and distances. Sometimes the scene was of floating color as when the eye tries to rest on sunlight in a rushing stream; sometimes there was shade beneath living trees.

But now the water in the scene that was conjured up in his mind had frozen in place, and a dust the hue of dry mud was covering all, and floating in the air were black specks that grew in size and threatened to blot the wellspring from sight. The specks mingled and melded into something that was not merely an absence of light, but an actual darkness. Now this prospect appeared unbidden in his mind again, and he swooned, nauseated.

Hope springs eternal. He had first heard that saying in a story come down from his fathers. Those tales of old, they could encompass a season in a sentence yet leave space for dreaming. Straight to the heart they went, with warmth for the little things and a desire to do great deeds that may live in song for ages to come.

In other parts there must still be many people milling and shuffling about in their various states of unreality, and to what end? God knows. God knows and no one else knows; that's how unknowable it is.

But who knows if God hasn't left this world for greener pastures and new creations, for it to die a death of its own volition, and he taking no heed for the fate of mortal man? Does even God remember this world he once made? Perhaps he has fallen into a forgetful slumber.

Some say that the world is hurtling through the darkness and whirling around itself—yet it is a wonder that so much as a tree is left standing.

His mind spun in many directions, heedless of purpose. All of the hollow inanities of the world came crashing down into one mind, making it implode from sheer vacuity. But next morning he awoke; the implosion had been mere sleep, dreamless. There was no condition more pleasing to him, and he resolved to sleep some more.

By mid-morning an ominous cloud had begun to sweep its way from over the valley toward his sad perch in the foothills. He looked to the mountain, apart from the river his only guide in this forsaken place, but its countenance was forbidding and stern in the darkening morning. Soon the cloud grew awfully large and seemed to draw to it reinforcements from all directions, and there was nothing in it but anger, or at any rate some incomprehensible dark intent. Nearby trees quavered and groaned as the air about him rushed toward the oncoming vortex. Something welled up inside of him as the proverbial hairs of an entire landscape stood on end in nervous anticipation.

He had long prayed for rain, for water to drink and a cleansing of the land, but when he had thought the rain would come and wash everything away, it hadn't, and now that the skies did finally open, the ground turned into a dreary sludge. The world was turning in its grave or raging against death as thunder came roiling across the sky and lightning scorched the treetops to a cinder in the rain. He sought shelter from wind and water under the roots of an overturned tree, the despairing side of him half hoping it would fall back into place and enclose him forever.

With the storm came a toneless music of deep drones and sharp edges, filling the air as with the blaring of trolls and a wailing of crows. A nearby tree cracked at the roots and felled other trees along with it, slamming the ground with an enduring boom of various grim facets. The morning had turned back into night. His cloak, long since torn asunder, soon clung wet to his back. Others less keen on comfort may have sought it in vain, but he had found it: the cruelest kind of weather.

Listening to the outlandish sounds in the wind, it occurred to him that perhaps nothing could be *less* outlandish: he thought of the terrible giants of legend, who in their long slumber had become part of the terrain, with grass, moss, and trees growing on their backs, and who were said to rise in senseless wrath once or twice in an age. He had never before felt so much like a stranger in the land from which he, too, had sprung.

He thought of his home, then, with its gold-rimmed hill-ridge horizon at sundown, the likes of which is not seen elsewhere; of his family, his friends, and a certain someone. When leaving that valley of many memories behind, he had raised his arm skyward and not looked back. Now it was surely a wasteland.

Slow hours passed.

He dreamed of a mighty feast in a hall of stone. Its walls were dimly lit by torches, whose light played on draperies displaying heroic scenes and heraldry, interspersed by paintings that one could wish to wander about in—but their cracked and faded surfaces were a reminder of decay in the realm of the all too real. Well! He found it quite natural that he should be in this place and did not give waking life a second thought: he desired to join with the feasters who made such a jovial din. But as he approached the table of merrymaking, he saw that the knights arrayed there were all eyeless, their teeth falling out of their heads as they feasted on rotting flesh. He ran from that castle and entered other strange dreams.

Morning broke, as it is wont to do; white covered all, and the sloping hills lay pure and peaceful as a daydream memory of winters in childhood. Frost reigned, and our would-be hero was covered from shoulders to boots in a thin sheet of ice. His skin burned, but a coldness pierced his flesh to the bone, and he did not rise but crawled a yard or two from his shabby, tree-root lair into the open. The veins in his temples were throbbing, and he was shivering wildly.

He ascertained that sometime in the night, things had taken a turn from very bad to worse. What a waste it had been, all his suffering throughout the winter, putting all his effort and wits to the task of reaching his lofty goals, only to be bested by a vengeful storm in spring! Very well then, he would die right there, and no one would know. And what would they say of him, who knew him in the time before all this?

That was the unspeakable thing: not death, but to have received more than he had given in life; to die in times of trouble without any worthy deed to his name. But the time for reflection was past—these were all things he had already given much thought, in the case of his untimely demise—and now he was as little more than an animal to the elements, one that must at last forfeit its instincts for survival.

Drat the dastardly weather and its antics!—he would make these his last words, but he had no voice.

Footfalls in the snow; a shadow fell over him. He saw it from behind cold eyelids, closed to the world of light.

"Get to your feet, fool!" said a voice—that of an old man, but at present any voice at all was utterly alien to our despondent man—and there was a violent tug at the neck of his cloak as he was thrust upright.

"Now," said the sudden figure, "do you not know that you are likely to catch a cold lying thus spread-eagled on the ground and covered in hoarfrost?"

The younger man did not even open his eyes to look at this strange apparition; at the moment he was rather annoyed to be interrupted in this way. Can a man not lie undisturbed under the sky? He was quite out of his senses, of course.

"Speak! Or is death all you seek?"

Resigned to his apparent fate of remaining a while longer among the living, the young man would answer in earnest, but all that escaped his lips was a hoarse croak.

"Now, now!" the man with the ancient voice broke in, more mildly. "No need for high speech. What is fitting at one time is merely comical at another. I am no king of men. But you have legs that can walk and eyes to see, if wits you have none." But seeing the low spirits of the young man before him, he added: "On my word of honor, I do not think there is reason for you to be ashamed. I believe you passed the test some time ago, though you have not seen the end of your journey just yet. You may look upon the city in time. But come, have a rest."

The city. . . . This old man had guessed at where he was going: the last great holdout of his kin.

Having been led up a slope until he collapsed at the edge of the woods, he was wrapped in blankets and laid on the ground. Eventually, the warmth of a campfire somewhat alleviated his indignation at being taken in such a rude manner from death's cold embrace. Still, it seemed more than likely that his head would explode from the inside, that his skull would simply crack open. A fever was coming on.

Finally, he ventured to open his eyes slightly to peer up at the black boughs of the canopy, fringed by a white that, touched by a calm wind, spread out into the air and drizzled down where he lay. Turning his aching neck to face the fire, he saw the visage of the man who had appeared as if from nowhere; his nose had a high ridge with notches and grooves like a barky branch, his face worn and lined like oak wood split lengthwise. He wore a woolen cloak of like wooden color, its hood resting on his broad shoulders and revealing surprising hazel hair for one of such advanced age. His eyes were green and brown, and a purposeful flame was in them—but a kindly one.

The old man had set a small cauldron to boil on the fire, and seeing that his young companion was alert, he dipped a ladle into it and brought it to him.

"Do not hesitate," he said, "'tis just a bit of strength. Whatever happens after, it is of your doing, and this is your own night to sweat through. I will not hold your hand, but I will tend the fire in your absence." This last bit he said in a frank manner, even mirthfully, and a glinting-eyed, good-natured grin accompanied it.

The strange taste of the draught and what had been meant by *absence* could not be reflected upon for long before he slipped from the waking world.

He stood by the shores of an ocean of time, a blackness of craggy peaks surrounding it. Unthinking, he waded into the swirling silver of its waters, and, his head going under the shimmering surface, he found his feet were no longer touching solid rock, but he was floating in a darksome void interrupted by visions of color and dread, of beauty and grotesquery and the yawning boredom of silent eons. In an unfinished country, languishing under the pivot of the stars, were unaccountable creatures, real or imagined, sitting around waiting for the dawn of time. . . .

After an unknowable while, he was standing before a marshy tarn in a forest much like ones he had known in earlier life. Wisps of fog floated over the water like a procession of phantoms; following them with his eyes they reached the forest's eave and there dissolved—and he saw a real sight. A white stag was there, muscular and elegant, of lofty grace. The sun breaking through the clouds illumined it; its noble hide gleamed like the morning dew. Upon its head was a great crown of horns reaching upward, and the air between its antlers flickered like precious stones in the sunlight. It turned and disappeared between the trees: he would follow it, but fell forward in the mire and sank once more.

The vision shifting, his gaze raced across verdant grasslands toward high mountains, and espying the white turrets of a far city, yon Tórnarsul of old, he was suddenly there. Its gates were wrought of silver and corundum, as the tales tell, and the banners on the battlements were waving in the wind; the insignia emblazoned upon them made him the more certain of his improbable whereabouts.

Unsmiling scoundrels, wide-eyed, crazed, of an overall grim disposition, stood all in a row on a low ridge overlooking the fields before the city, enshrouded in an indistinct dimness, as if they had brought the desert sands with them from distant lands. Now, the frenzy of battle and the clanging of steel against steel; much blood is shed on each side. Suddenly, a note springs forth from the forests half-circling the battle-plain, from some instrument or from the heart of nature itself, and warriors of grace and wrath are revealed clad in tunics of vivid green and hauberks glinting in the sun; their enemies are crushed on the shield-wall and trodden under hooves. The meadows laugh and the flowering fields rejoice at their coming, and their driving back of the dust.

He watched the scene as if detached from the action and from several vantage points, from the air and the ground, now near, now further away, but the impression of the events upon his faculties were always immediate, earth-shattering.

Other splendid and lesser dwellings of yore he witnessed, too, but he knew not their names. Yet he knew these things to be True, though out of Time.

After sights more numerous than can be accounted for, his vision widened and encompassed each of these things at once, and many more again, until all the war and peace and sunlit days and weary nights of all time seemed stretched beyond all scope. The fringes could no longer hold, and the turmoil of past, present, and future turned in on itself, colliding in a cacophony and melding together to a single point at the end of all things, before exploding outwards again, the light from the cataclysm breaking in colors for which mortal men have no names.

Shadows rise and fall with flames in the ether, until all is void, is nothing anymore. Yet from somewhere must the spark to the inner fire be lit, for up from the abyss rises a new world, of pure flame at first but in time covered with a scorching crust; now it cools, and grass covers the earth born anew, shooting up from the ashes as did that world unspoiled shine forth from a darksome crack in the depths of nothingness.

The dome of night gave way to the dim light of dawn. Morning mists blanketed and drifted down rocky crags and ashy slopes of hillside without sound.

The old man was no longer there, but the faintly smoking remains of the campfire showed that he had not been a mere apparition. He could not say how long he had slept, but the snow was nearly gone. He felt both drained and invigorated; the fever was over, and with a pale smile he staggered off to continue his wanderings at once.

Every hill he climbed this day revealed new distances to traverse, but the mountain ahead *did* slowly loom larger. And here, the ashes lay thinner on the ground than before.

The terrain grew steeper, but though it was hard going, the rocky soil that met his feet practically carried him upwards between increasingly smaller trees and bramble. The great waterfall of the river that he had been stalking these last days came down here on his left, its spray floating on the air for a half mile, refreshing to feel on one's face.

Quite suddenly, he reached the rim of the plateau that had formed his horizon since he began the ascent from the valley. Stretches of flatter ground were revealed, and far snowy peaks, but the solitary mountain kept rising sharply just beyond the frothing cascade, and now he could see its lower sides clad in waving grass brimming verdant in the wind, youthful and ancient. Indeed, he was now walking, to his joy, along the plateau's ridge with grasses up to his knees, free from the ashes.

Looking out on the distances he had roamed, it seemed that he was standing on an island, overlooking petrified waves covered with those spiteful grains of dust, a mockery of all that is fair in the world. He turned again to the new vistas laid out before him, and despite all the wonders he had recently seen, he could hardly believe that he had left the harsh places behind even in the world of forms; his elation seemed to stretch all the way up into the center of the sky. And yet, even these green spots may soon rot and perish beneath that dreadful dust spread by a dry wind. Is then nothing truly lasting?

A vivid, almost-forgotten vision from the long night entered his mind, and he laughed, for it was of a great wave of fresh water released from the glaciers by the undying fire, scouring the land of foul things. Too long his people had, like those masses of ice, shrunk into the mountainous corners of the country and laid dormant and dwindling; a flame must be lit in them anew.

Fire is the enduring thing! Fire it is that burns ever in the inner earth, and in the hearts of valorous men, and is tended in the hearth of the worthy home. A great host of men must be roused in that city of fountains that pour water unending from the mouths of dragons, where the people play instruments of wood and finely-wrought metals, the sound echoing amid the mountains whence they must ride forth and put things to right through just vengeance.

When finally they went to war, it would be by the bellowing and braying of boar-shaped horns, with no lack of willingness to do battle under the banner of the bear.

Ha! Three or four moments without care and soaking up sun in the grass. It was as good as a hearty meal for the lifting of his spirits. Very well, the beast of emptiness in his belly still gnawed at him, but his surroundings had gone from drab and gray to swards of grass full of gleam and spark in the full light of day, and the future did not look quite so grim.

A bluebell stood in the grass, and he stooped to marvel at it. Its lilac blue radiated toward him with a faint inner glow. When he stood up, he saw that there were many more, and each harbored a similar secret, at once familiar and incomprehensible to the gaze of man.

Free and easy sauntering brought him to a small stream, and he stood idly by it for a while, listening to its gentle trickle. Its banks were covered in moss, and the shallow waters lay in a humble splendor of bronze and gold, where the rays of the sun touched on a smattering of birch-leaves and pieces of bark. It seemed likely that at any moment he might hear the bells of grazing cows and the lilting song of a maiden come tinkling and soaring out from behind the nearest hillock.

Walking close past the mountain, a mad impulse shot through him: to climb that peak, to prove that he could do it, but it passed out of his mind as suddenly as it had entered it. He was much too frail to accomplish any such feat: a body cannot live on will alone. All there was for him to do was to find his people, and grow strong in their midst. He bowed one last time before the mountain and whatever power was in it, and the dead who might have perished while attempting its ascent. They must all once have been highly motivated men.

It was getting dark with a quickness, but he did not feel like halting: it looked to be a night for quiet walking. A thousand leaves in the moonlight were fluttering like so many silvery ripples on the surface of water. The moon itself waxed poetic across the deepening starry skies; in three more days it would be at full shine. Already it was lighting his way across purple heather and rocks that time had strewn across the moorland only God knows when, and he pressed on into the night.

He sang as he walked, until one day the setting sun gleamed golden on the roofs of that city in which his people abode, and his story could find its beginning.

First Place Winner in Short Stories

Professor Widley and the Greatest Amateur Excavation Ever

Kyrsten Carlson

Packed mountains of cinnamon sand rose and fell in the hundreds, the thousands. The sticky heat and desert wind swept it up and down and around, here, there, left, right, to create new forms in mere days. And, like cinnamon, it radiated an aroma of promise and intrigue. A real-life journey into the unknown, one that left Professor Christopher Widley salivating for a second taste.

Many hot, whispering summers passed since he'd last found himself in this dusty, wild west. It was hard to tell from the shapeshifting dunes, but he knew it was here alright. It was here. The thing which he sought most. A large, metallic *something*.

His commanders didn't believe him. In him. The crew didn't care for a word he spoke, his friends for a word he pleaded. That metal thing, whatever it was, whatever it is, didn't belong in this world-forsaken desert. It belonged to him.

"Day one, Grid Day," he said into a tape recorder. He began driving stakes into the corners, weaving rope around one, walking the length to connect it to another stake, and another, tying knots as he went until he had a large square of virgin sand. With more rope, he went from the border all the way down until he had five columns, which he crossed with five rows. There, a grid.

Hands on hips, he surveyed his work. Even. With purpose. He was glad to be back. But was he happy? No. He'd always imagined returning with a few good men, a few good machines, a few more days. None of these were his. With just one week to find his metal *something*, he had to work hard before being whisked off to explore some other place.

The rope pattern and brown landscape made him think of a great big cake all cut into squares. Or perhaps he smelled one? His stomach raged. Tomorrow he will begin the excavation. For now, he would fuel up.

* * *

"Day two, section A1." Professor Widley was a man limited in gear, options, and fortune, but not determination. "Experiment one, water." He snaked a hose to the grid and waited for the slumbering water to slither its way to him. And when it did, it was wide awake. The spray went everywhere but remained, thankfully, in section A1. After a short battle with the sea serpent, he managed to toss it away from his excavation site, just not before getting half soaked.

In these conditions, it would be easy to complain, but on the bright side, he was now cooled down from the unbearable heat of that glorious globe in the sky. "Experiment one, water, failed." He pocketed his recorder.

It was a journey in itself to turn off the hose and drag its now lifeless corpse back to the inn. But it was not enough for one day; he'd certainly have to do more if he were to complete his life's work. So, he began again, this time rolling a large fan behind him.

"Experiment two, fan, section A2." A1, now flattened, something he wanted, threatened to swallow him up in man-made quicksand, something he did not want. He flipped the switch and suddenly the storm came alive! The fierce wind shifted the dunes to tilt right instead of left, sending sand swirling in chaos. In a flurry of pressure, he'd turned to the highest setting, which tested his ropes, his stakes, and his faith. Professor Widley managed to turn it off, but only after it threw him to the ground, rolling his sweaty, oily, wet self in the dust turning him into a human churro. "Failure," he sighed.

He attempted to shake the dust from his shoulders and mind. "Experiment three, rake, section A2." At least his fan troubles hadn't compromised the layout, though in some places the dunes rose so high they obscured parts of his rope lines. The rake was large, but it would take several passes before the dunes would flatten. Upon completion, the grooved lines formed together like a zen garden, breathing some calmness into his work. "Partial success, rake eliminates loose dune, can't break harder ground." He smiled. "Section A3."

A sound of splashing and laughter hung loosely in the dry air, tickling his ears. He licked his dry lips, eating sand in the process. Smacking them together to work up some life-giving saliva, he reminded himself what he was working for. Changing the world. A few more sections raked, and it was time to retire for the day.

That night Professor Widley lay in bed thinking, worrying, planning. The bed on the other side of the room creaked. "You just gonna play in that sandbox of yours all day? Looking for your whosawhatsit?" a voice asked in the darkness.

"It's real," he whispered softly so as to not wake the moon.

"Your loss," it answered.

A whosawhatsit? What a demoralizing name for the very object that would alter the course of history in a matter of seconds! The desert had people, had sand, had earth, rocks, manual labor, even had water, but metal? He wasn't searching for some whosawhatsitmajig, a fantasy; he was looking for proof of extraterrestrial life! Sand around for millennia packed tightly by time and weather, its surface surely altered, but the layers of mystery and life remain unchanged. It held secrets that promised to twist history around and around, and he was determined to learn them.

* * *

"Day three, section A5." He raked it. "Section B5." He combed it. "Section B4." He brushed it. "Section B3." He flattened it. B2, B1, C1, C2, they, too, joined the ever-expanding zen garden and peaceful thoughts of their master happy with the progress and the idea that the thing, his *thing*, would be found yet. With head held high and spirit higher, he went to dinner.

"Listen, sonny boy, I know you're working real hard out there, but don't get your hopes up too high. Things are lost to time as sure as time itself ticks and tocks." Professor Widley set down his drink. What did Old Man Harrison know about sand or metal or treasures or history or Professor Christopher Widley for that matter? He didn't see the damn thing. He spent all his time whistling on a harmonica or fishing from the inn's pond. He wasn't out there digging, wasn't out there searching, not now, not then. He wasn't out there enough in his thoughts to believe the damn thing was even possible!

Professor Widley went to bed early, angrily, doubtful—though he wouldn't admit it. The white sheets baked brown with his carelessness of washing up after a day spent cooking in the cinnamon dust. It didn't matter. Only the thing mattered, *the thing*, *his* thing, soon to be the world's massive upset thing. Changing history, changing science, changing hope, and truth. He fell asleep.

* * *

"Day four, section C3." Combed. "Section C4." Down. "Section C5." A woman approached. He kept his back to the distraction.

"Hey, Christopher," she said to his bare back.

"Professor, ma'am."

"Professor Christopher," she said.

"Professor Widley," he corrected.

"Did you put on lotion?" He nodded in the negative. Before he could mount a defense, she was rubbing sunscreen onto his back. He felt like a child. "It's awful hot out here. We're going to town if you'd like to join." She didn't ask, didn't command, merely stated it for his inclusion. "Well, alright then, don't work yourself to death, and drink some water. There's a sandwich just inside the fridge with your name on it for lunch. Everyone should return before dinner. If not, there's leftover chicken and peas." She stood and walked away, becoming a sunlit outlined silhouette.

What a woman, he thought. Her hands wrinkled with time, her smile wrinkled with laughter. A thoughtful encouragement, a gift from the world that said, "Keep going, Christopher, keep going," and said so with a smile.

"Section D5." He heard the inn's people gathering for their journey far off in the otherwise quiet summer afternoon. Off they tramped. "Section D4." He raked some more. He couldn't hear their footsteps anymore. "Section D3." D2. D1. E1, E2, E3, E4, E5. He was done with the preliminary raking. The dunes were flattened, the real earth, the real mystery beckoning for him to unlock.

"Christopher! CHRISTOPHER! What are you doing?" a voice called.

"I told you he wouldn't go inside," came another, calmer.

"He's not normal," a third weighed in.

"Oh, Christopher!" He felt his shivering body warm at the touch of arms carrying him away from the love of his life. How long had he been out? It was dark now.

"Professor. . . ." he mumbled.

"Boys are all the same! All the same!" the first said, hysteria waning.

* * *

Professor Christopher Widley awoke in his bed that following morning. He raised up on an elbow while trying to blink away the crust sealing his droopy eyelids. His arms were sore. His back was raw. But the motivation of completely world-changing finds helped him get up.

Glancing at the bed across and seeing it empty surprised him. Normally he was up long before his roommate. He shrugged and put on a new shirt.

What he found in the dining room was not people eating scrambled eggs or biscuits with jelly or bacon. They were each holding a sandwich at a different stage of consumption.

Sandwiches for breakfast seemed alright with him. Times were changing, and he was going to be at the forefront of that change.

"Is there any bacon?" He still loved bacon though.

The woman from yesterday stared at him, eyes big and round with concern. "Christopher," she said.

"Professor Widley," he sighed.

"Yes, Professor Widley," she said.

"Aw Carol, don't; he's wasting away looking for some damn thing that don't exist, never did, never will. Don't encourage him." Old Man Harrison was a rotten, stuck-in-his-ways good for nothin'. . . .

"It's lunchtime," Carol said.

Professor Widley chewed this news over for a moment. He'd missed some hours then on excavating. Digging was supposed to start today. "I'll take mine wrapped up then, thank you." Old Man Harrison slammed his fists down, which made his remaining sandwich do a little hop on his plate.

“Like hell, he will, Carol.” But she’d already wrapped it up and gave it to Christopher. “Why do you encourage him? He’ll never make something out of himself if he keeps searching for nothing and believing in things that ain’t real.”

“It’s real to him, Harrison, it’s real to him.” Christopher closed the door behind him and heard no more. Back at his site, he surveyed his finely combed grid. It’d be a shame to mess up something so clean, but an even bigger shame to rob the world of the potential within it.

“Day five, section A1, digging.” The question was, how far should he dig? He only had two more days. His heart had told him he saw what he saw, his heart had told him to return, and, so, his heart would tell him when to stop. “A2, dig.” If he thought raking took work, digging was three times that. He took a break. Ate his sandwich. There was bacon on it. “A3, dig.”

He hit something. Professor Widley chucked aside the shovel, fell to his knees, prayed to the archaeological gods, and dug wildly with his hands. Like a sandstorm, dust flew heavy all around. Something ivory caught his eye just before sand trickled back down the hole. He blew with all his might in the storm’s last mighty fling, only to uncover a bone.

“NO!” For all he knew, it was a long-lost mummy, eaten away by the year’s sandstorms. Perhaps it was a dinosaur yet undiscovered. He didn’t care about any of that. Oh, a mummy had the power to change the world decades ago, and a dinosaur had the ability to make men fight each other over who could be number one, but that happened ages ago and could only happen ages ago. Mummies wouldn’t change the world now, and dinosaurs couldn’t alter it either, not now, not ever again!

His eyes were filling up, cleaning the grains of sand from them. He thought his constant sweating would dry him up into a raisin of a nobody, but here he was, able to cry. Looking at the many sections of more disappointment and hopelessness to uncover, he cried harder. Not only would twenty-four out of twenty-five hold nothing but empty promise, he hadn’t accounted for where the sand would go that he dug up. Where could it go, but into another section, creating more work for him?

Eyes wet, he rubbed them to gain a clearer focus, only to seal them with sand, sweat, and heartache. Day five was over. He went swimming, rode a bike into town, grabbed an ice cream, and fell fast asleep.

* * *

Day six. He awoke with new purpose; well, really the purpose remained the same, but it was with renewed hope and passion, which only a night’s rest could procure. He got up, dressed, ate, and marched to his excavation site.

There were piles of sand taller than he, ropes hissing in loops at the bottom of snake pits. The stakes stabbed into sand mounds. He walked among the rubble. Holes small, holes big, shallow, deep, random. Then it hit him. It was sabotage. No! It was jealousy! Both! Here he'd spent his days meticulously measuring, raking, digging in a desperate search for the thing—not out of want for glory, but for the world. The world! For a glimpse of the future, buried deep in the past, and they'd come and ruined it all! Ruined it for him, yes, but also for themselves, for they were part of the world and stood to benefit by knowledge. But they'd wanted more.

"Greedy!" he shouted. "Jealous!" he wailed. "Evil!" he cried.

On his knees, he scooped up handfuls of sand and threw them into the air, little bursting brown fireworks of fury. He then brought down his fists and pounded the ground. After the third round, his hand hit something hard, and he fell back to nurse it.

"It isn't fair. It isn't," he said, quiet now, rubbing his hand. Then like a rod through his spine, he shot up. Something hard! Left hand still throbbing, heartbeat thundering, he brushed back the sand. There! In the sunlight! There! It shined, brighter than the full moon, brighter than, than, hell, brighter than the sun! Quickly now, quickly! Hands flying, dust flinging, laughter bubbling out of him like a song skipping.

There it was! There it is! The metallic purple of its side shining nearly as bright as his eyes. It was easy now. Dig, dig, dig. Yes, yes, his hands were around it now. He heaved, he pulled, he yanked, and bam! It was in his hands.

A small spaceship, the size of a football, the color of dusk, with its little alien pilot seated at the wheel in his plastic dome, was once again his pride, his treasure. Christopher hugged it, kissed it, and ran to the front door.

"Mom! Mom! I found it! I found it!" he screamed and cried as he ran all through the house, arms outstretched, spaceship once again flying high. Suddenly he was weightless and twirling all around, a kiss on his right cheek, a kiss on his left cheek, his mother's arms holding him high with pride. "Mom, did you always know that I could?" he asked, softly now.

She kissed his sweaty, cinnamon-crusted forehead and held him close. "Of course, Professor Widley, of course."

www.ingramcontent.com/pod-product-compliance
Lightning Source LLC
Chambersburg PA
CBHW051256210726
48287CB00002B/527

* 9 7 8 1 9 5 6 8 8 7 8 4 6 *